BROOKINGS-WHARTON

bw

papers *on* URBAN AFFAIRS

2006

Gary Burtless and
Janet Rothenberg Pack
Editors

BROOKINGS INSTITUTION PRESS
Washington, D.C.

Copyright © 2006
THE BROOKINGS INSTITUTION
1775 Massachusetts Avenue, N.W., Washington, DC 20036

ISSN 1528-7084
ISBN 13: 978-0-8157-1370-8
ISBN 0-8157-1370-3

BROOKINGS–WHARTON

papers
on
URBAN
AFFAIRS
2006

Purpose   The *Brookings-Wharton Papers on Urban Affairs* is an annual publication containing articles and formal discussant remarks from a conference held at the Brookings Institution and arranged by the editors. The annual forum and journal are the products of a collaboration between the Brookings Institution's Metropolitan Policy Program and the Zell Lurie Real Estate Center at the Wharton School of the University of Pennsylvania. All of the papers and discussant remarks represent the views of the authors and not necessarily the views of the staff members, officers, or trustees of the Brookings Institution or the Wharton School of the University of Pennsylvania.

Richard J. Murnane   *Harvard University*
John Karl Scholz   *University of Wisconsin–Madison*
Robert M. Schwab   *University of Maryland–College Park*
Kenneth A. Small   *University of California–Irvine*
Kristin Turney   *University of Pennsylvania*
Tara Watson   *Williams College*
John B. Willett   *Harvard University*
Clifford Winston   *Brookings Institution*
Jacob L. Vigdor   *Duke University*
Jia Yan   *Hong Kong Polytechnic University*

Conference   Alan Berube   *Brookings Institution*
Participants   Eugenie Birch   *University of Pennsylvania*
Victor Calanog   *University of Pennsylvania*
William Collins   *Vanderbilt University*
William Dickens   *Brookings Institution*
Anthony Downs   *Brookings Institution*
Fernando Ferreira   *University of Pennsylvania*
Michael Feuer   *National Research Council*
David Garrison   *Brookings Institution*
Joseph Gyourko   *University of Pennsylvania*
Andrew Haughwout   *Federal Reserve Bank of New York*
Rucker Johnson   *University of California–Berkeley*
Helen F. Ladd   *Duke University*
Paul Levy   *Center City District of Philadelphia*
Janice Madden   *University of Pennsylvania*
Robert Margo   *Boston University*
Dick Netzer   *New York University*
Carol O'Cleireacain   *Brookings Institution*
Katherine O'Regan   *New York University*
Robert Puentes   *Brookings Institution*
John Quigley   *University of California–Berkeley*
Andrew Reschovsky   *University of Wisconsin–Madison*
Martha Ross   *Brookings Institution*
Albert Saiz   *University of Pennsylvania*
Raven Saks   *Federal Reserve Board*
Isabel Sawhill   *Brookings Institution*
Amy E. Schwartz   *New York University*
Todd Sinai   *University of Pennsylvania*
Audrey Singer   *Brookings Institution*
Betsey Stevenson   *University of Pennsylvania*
Leanna Stiefel   *New York University*
Michael Stoll   *University of California–Los Angeles*
Jennifer Vey   *Brookings Institution*
Richard Voith   *Econsult Corporation*
William Wheaton   *Massachusetts Institute of Technology*
Howard Wial   *Brookings Institution*
Grace Wong   *University of Pennsylvania*

Preface

Brookings-Wharton Papers on Urban Affairs is devoted to publishing forward-looking research on urban policy issues in an accessible manner. The collaboration between the Wharton School and Brookings Institution in this endeavor represents an effort to draw on resources and personnel in both academia and the policy community. We hope and expect that the journal itself will be of interest and use to an even wider audience that includes policymakers and their staffs, interested parties in the private sector, journalists, students, and others.

This journal's existence owes much to the efforts of key people at both Brookings and Wharton. Brookings President Strobe Talbott continues to support this project. Bruce Katz, director of the Metropolitan Policy Program, has been a loyal supporter of the journal and its goals, and his program provides major financial support.

At Wharton, Peter Linneman and Joseph Gyourko, former and current director, respectively, of the Samuel Zell and Robert Lurie Real Estate Center, have supported this undertaking intellectually and financially from its inception. For the last two years, the Wharton Dean's office has provided support for the conference and volume. We have also received financial support for the past two years from the Urban Institute at the University of Pennsylvania, which is codirected by Professors Eugenie Birch and Susan Wachter. We look forward to the continued support and participation of both institutions. The chair of the Department of Business and Public Policy has made an important contribution by allowing Janet Rothenberg Pack to adjust her workload to organize the conference and edit the volume. Gary Burtless, who holds the John C. and Nancy D. Whitehead Chair in Economic Studies at Brookings, serves as co-convener of the conference and coeditor of this journal.

Several people made vital contributions to the conference, where drafts of this volume's papers were first presented, and to the volume itself. Saundra Honeysett at Brookings organized conference logistics and managed the paper flow with wonderful efficiency and good cheer. Sadly, this will be the last volume where she will serve in that role. Amy Liu and Jamaine Fletcher provided valuable support at many stages. The authors and discussants deserve special thanks for making extra efforts to draft their arguments in a clear and accessible manner. Janet Walker of the Brookings Institution Press has managed the production of the conference volume both creatively and efficiently.

Editors' Summary

Brookings-Wharton Papers on Urban Affairs presents new research on urban economics to a broad audience of interested policy analysts and researchers. The papers and comments contained in this volume, the seventh in the series, were presented at a December 8–9, 2005, conference at the Brookings Institution. The papers treat a range of issues examined by contemporary urban economists, including the effects of population growth and changing income inequality on neighborhood segregation, the economic gains from creating express lanes and charging congestion prices on busy expressways, recent trends in the school achievement gap between white and black youngsters, the impact of neighborhood poverty on barriers to employment, the potential benefits of restructuring local property taxes, and the effects of land use restrictions and jurisdictional fragmentation on sprawl and the price of housing.

U.S. INCOME INEQUALITY rose sharply after 1979, increasing the gap between America's rich and poor. Tara Watson examines some effects of this development on the income segregation of urban and suburban neighborhoods in "Metropolitan Growth, Inequality, and Neighborhood Segregation by Income." Watson begins by observing that neighborhood segregation is particularly malleable when the local housing stock is first built. It is more costly to change the physical characteristics and distribution of amenities after housing has already been constructed. Neighborhoods built when the local income distribution is comparatively equal may reflect this reality. Many neighborhoods in a metropolitan area may have a similar average level of amenities, and the distribution of physical amenities may be similar across a large proportion of neighborhoods. However, an unequal income distribution will give metropolitan residents unequal access to housing amenities. High-income residents can afford dwellings with better amenities, including neighborhood attractions such as safe streets, good schools, and well-maintained parks.

Depending on the connection between residents' incomes and their tastes for housing amenities, it is easy to imagine that higher income inequality will be associated with greater income segregation across neighborhoods. Increased inequality can boost residential segregation in both direct and indirect ways. As incomes grow more unequal, rich and poor households will be less willing or able to spend the same amount of money to live in the same neighborhood. As less-affluent households become more concentrated in selected neighborhoods, there may be feedback effects on neighborhood amenities, further reducing the attractiveness of neighborhoods from which well-to-do households have moved. Watson notes that housing markets can easily accommodate changing preferences induced by changes in the income distribution when the metropolitan population is climbing rapidly. Increased inequality translates into newly built neighborhoods in which there is greater sorting by households' income ranks. On the other hand, in metropolitan areas experiencing population decline, the increased demand for residential segregation may not be large enough to overcome the high cost of retrofitting old homes or building new ones. A big shock in inequality may be needed in stagnant or declining areas to cause a shift in residential segregation patterns.

Watson finds a U-shaped relationship between the rise of residential segregation in metropolitan areas and population growth. The greatest changes in income segregation have occurred in distressed areas with stagnant or declining populations and in areas with rapidly growing populations. There typically has been less change in residential segregation in areas with moderate rates of population growth. Watson also finds support for some of her predictions on the relationship between changing income inequality and residential segregation patterns. As expected, higher income inequality is associated with higher levels of residential segregation by income. Also as predicted, rising inequality has a larger effect on segregation in rapidly growing areas compared with areas with stagnant or declining populations. Large increases in segregation are accommodated with higher-than-expected housing construction in distressed areas, but unexpectedly high rates of new construction are not needed in areas with big population gains. Finally, income segregation tends to be persistent within a metropolitan area, and the persistence is more pronounced in cities with an older housing stock.

FEW URBAN ROADS in the United States impose charges on the motorists who use them. Like many public goods that are provided without charge, urban roads tend to be overused, particularly during rush hour when a large number of drivers want access to a limited number of streets and highways. One by-product of overuse is traffic congestion, which greatly reduces motorists' average speed. Even though drivers do not pay tolls for using most streets and highways, they do suffer inconvenience as a result of longer commutes at peak driving times. Economists have long argued that the traffic congestion and its attendant welfare costs can be slashed by charging drivers for the privilege of using roads, especially during peak commuting hours. This suggestion is widely unpopular among voters as well as policymakers, who are responsible for managing the urban highway network. As an alternative, planners have set aside special limited-access highway lanes for vehicles containing two or more passengers. In some cases, motorists who are willing to pay a toll are also permitted to use these high-speed lanes.

In "Differentiated Road Pricing, Express Lanes, and Carpools: Exploiting Heterogeneous Preferences in Policy Design," Kenneth A. Small, Clifford Winston, and Jia Yan examine the potential welfare gains that can be achieved using sensible pricing of highway access. In order to assess the political acceptability of different kinds of pricing schemes, the analysts also determine the distribution of welfare gains and losses across different classes of motorists. The authors collected information from drivers who use a ten-mile stretch of California State Route 91 to form estimates of motorists' willingness to pay for faster and more reliable travel times to their rush-hour destinations. This busy Orange County highway has four free lanes and two express lanes in each direction. Drivers who use the express lanes need to establish a financial account and carry a special electronic instrument in order to pay the toll, which varies hourly over the day. At the time of the authors' survey, vehicles containing three or more passengers were able to use the express lanes at a substantial discount.

The authors collected information on motorists' actual driving choices (their revealed preference decisions) as well as their stated preferences under a variety of hypothetical pricing arrangements. Using this information in a sophisticated statistical analysis, the authors examined three interrelated decisions: the decision by motorists to obtain the electronic fare collection instrument, the decision to use the express lane for a particular trip, and the decision to carry two or more additional passengers in order to qualify for a trip discount. The authors assume that motorists' choices are affected by their socioeconomic status as well as the characteristics of the planned travel, including the trip's total distance, the toll, and expected travel time as well as the reliability of the expected travel time across the alternative travel options. After estimating the average preference parameters and the distribution of preferences in the sampled population, the authors use statistical simulation to compare motorists' choices and well-being under alternative highway pricing regimes.

Among the policy options that the authors examine are the standard high-occupancy vehicle (HOV) policy, which limits express lane use to vehicles containing three or more passengers, and a high-occupancy toll (HOT) policy, which permits toll-paying vehicles containing two or fewer riders to use the HOV lanes. The authors also evaluate the impacts of a policy that assesses the same express-lane toll on all vehicles, regardless of the number of passengers they carry. Finally, they consider policies where tolls are charged both for the use of the express lane and other lanes, but with a higher toll in the express lanes. They consider a variant of this last policy in which high-occupancy vehicles can travel at no charge in either set of lanes. In all cases, the authors use the results of their statistical analysis to select the tolls that maximize the social welfare of the sampled drivers.

Not surprisingly, the policy that imposes rush-hour tolls on drivers in both express lanes and other lanes is the regime that yields the highest social welfare. Traveling times improve markedly, both in the express lanes and in the more congested lanes, and the reliability of travel times improves. However, this policy also causes many individual drivers, especially those from lower-income groups, to suffer losses in consumer welfare. The congestion effects of busy highways are less costly to these drivers than the tolls they would have to pay if highway prices were set so as to maximize social welfare. If the two-toll policy were modified to allow free use of both sets of lanes by high-occupancy vehicles, the welfare gains would also be quite sizable. Again, however, many motorists would consider themselves worse off, because the improvements in travel time and reliability would not be large enough to off-set the higher weekly cost of paying highway tolls. The authors' results show why HOV and HOT policies are more politically acceptable than the more efficient two-toll pricing policy. Even though the two-toll policy produces considerably bigger reductions in traffic congestion and commuting time, it causes many travelers to suffer high and very unequal losses in consumer welfare. Furthermore, the largest losses are suffered by drivers in the lowest income groups, because they assign the lowest valuation to their own time and to improvements in travel-time reliability.

The authors investigate a compromise two-toll policy that has tolls below the socially optimal level in order to overcome some of the problems of the other policies. Specifically, it provides more benefits overall than the HOV or HOT lane policies, but compared to the optimal two-toll policy it greatly reduces the percentage of drivers who suffer large welfare losses as a result of the policy change. The reason for this is that it takes greater advantage of consumers' varying preferences. It provides a choice between two quite different combinations of price and amount of congestion, while still lowering congestion for everyone compared to the situation with no express lanes.

ONE OF THE toughest challenges facing American schools is the achievement gap between black and white children. Recent tabulations by economists Ronald G. Fryer and Steven D. Levitt cast light on the size and persistence of this gap among students in the early years of schooling. When youngsters enter kindergarten, the average language arts score of black children is already 0.40 standard deviations below the average score obtained by white kindergartners. The test-score gap is even larger (0.60 standard deviations) in tests of mathematical reasoning. Even more distressing is Fryer and Levitt's finding that the test-score gap increases steadily in each of the first four years of primary school, rising by approximately 0.10 standard deviations a year. Virtually none of the initial gap or its year-on-year increases can be explained by traditional measures of school resources. That is, the achievement differences between black and white schoolchildren remain essentially the same even when the researchers take account of the differences in school resources available to black and white youngsters.

In their paper in this volume, Richard J. Murnane, John B. Willett, Kristen L. Bub, and Kathleen McCartney replicate and extend Fryer and Levitt's earlier analysis. Their article, "Understanding Trends in the Black-White Achievement Gaps during the First Years of School," is based on a much richer source of information about the family backgrounds of schoolchildren and the classroom environments in which they are educated. When the authors use the same data file analyzed in the earlier study, they duplicate Fryer and Levitt's findings. However, when they replicate Fryer and Levitt's analytical methods using a different and richer data set, their findings differ in three important ways from the earlier results. First, Murnane and his coauthors show that family background variables, which apparently explain much of the black-white achievement gap in kindergarten in the Fryer and Levitt data set, are less successful in explaining the gap in the alternative, richer data file. As Murnane and his colleagues point out, this finding is consistent with most past research on the influence of family background variables. Even after analysts account for the influence of family income and parental education on kindergartners' achievement, most previous studies find there is an important unexplained difference between the achievement scores of black and white school children. Murnane and his coauthors speculate that Fryer and Levitt obtain a different result because they examine results from achievement tests focusing on a very narrow set of skills. When broader measures of achievement are used, the black-white test score gap cannot be explained using simple measures of family background.

Second, Murnane and his coauthors fail to find any evidence in their alternative data file of a substantial rise in the black-white achievement gap in the first few years of primary school. In fact, the gap actually declines on tests of mathematical reasoning. Although the achievement gap in language arts grows, the increase is much smaller than found in the data set analyzed by Fryer and Levitt. Murnane and his colleagues find little evidence that the resources available to black and white schoolchildren differ noticeably. In one respect, however, there is a difference in the classroom environment. Compared with white schoolchildren, black youngsters are more likely to be taught by a teacher with very little classroom experience, a difference that is apparent in both data sets. It has disquieting implications for student achievement, since most studies find that teachers with little classroom experience are significantly less effective in boosting student achievement than teachers with more experience. This finding suggests one way to improve black youngsters' achievement is to increase the percentage of students who are taught by experienced teachers.

The authors find no evidence for the idea that smaller class size will boost the absolute or relative performance of black schoolchildren. Nor do they find any evidence showing that a master's degree improves the effectiveness of classroom teachers. Based on their analysis of the richer data set, they do find evidence that teachers can improve youngsters' math scores by devoting more time to math instruction, but the authors acknowledge this lesson will be hard for school administrators to put into practice. Legislators and school managers can adopt policies that change average class size or increase the percentage of classroom teachers who have master's degrees, but it is much harder for them to influence teachers' time allocation in the classroom.

HIGH UNEMPLOYMENT AND low rates of labor force participation are common in lower-income urban neighborhoods. A number of theories have been advanced to explain the exceptionally low employment rates of residents in high-poverty neighborhoods. One theory, usually dubbed the *spatial mismatch hypothesis,* explains low employment as a by-product of the physical isolation of high-poverty neighborhoods. According to this theory, residents of low-income neighborhoods are geographically isolated from areas in a metropolitan region where job opportunities are plentiful. Since many residents in these neighborhoods do not own a car, they must rely on public transportation to get to work. If job openings are not easily accessible along public transportation routes, neighborhood residents may find it hard to locate or hold on to a job. Another theory explains low employment rates as a consequence of the social norms that prevail in many low-income communities. People who live in high-poverty neighborhoods may be isolated from norms elsewhere in the metropolitan area—norms that place very high valuation on the importance of holding a steady job. If their social contacts are limited to people in the immediate neighborhood who are also jobless, residents of high-poverty neighborhoods may be deprived of information or job referrals that can be helpful in finding employment.

If these theories were correct, the policy tested in the Moving to Opportunity (MTO) experiments should have lifted the employment rate of the people who were enrolled in the tested program. The MTO experiments, which began in 1994, were conducted in high-poverty neighborhoods of five large American cities. Families enrolled in the treatment group were offered the opportunity to move out of publicly assisted housing in these neighborhoods and into subsidized housing in neighborhoods with moderate or low poverty rates. Families accepting this offer were provided with intensive counseling to help them find housing in better neighborhoods, and families that were successful in finding qualified housing were given subsidies so they could afford to live in better neighborhoods. To remain eligible for the subsidies, relocated families had to continue residing outside of high-poverty neighborhoods for at least one year. To determine this policy's impact, the experimenters also enrolled a randomly and identically selected sample of families from the same neighborhoods into a control group, which was not offered the special vouchers. By following the moving patterns of people enrolled in the MTO voucher program and the control group, analysts found that the program had a major impact on the neighborhood destinations of people enrolled in the treatment group. People provided with MTO vouchers moved to neighborhoods with noticeably lower poverty rates. Surprisingly, however, the MTO treatment had essentially no impact on the average employment rate of people who were offered the special housing vouchers.

In this volume's essay "Neighborhood Effects on Barriers to Employment: Results from a Randomized Housing Mobility Experiment in Baltimore," Kristin Turney, Susan Clampet-Lundquist, Kathryn Edin, Jeffrey R. Kling, and Greg J. Duncan analyze the MTO findings in an attempt to account for MTO's surprisingly weak impact on employment rates. Although they summarize previously published findings on moving patterns and employment impacts in the MTO experiments, their main source of information is a set of intensive and open-ended interviews conducted with sixty-seven treatment- and control-group householders enrolled in the Baltimore MTO experiment. More than 4,600 families were enrolled in the experimental and control groups in the five MTO cities, so the people who received qualitative interviews represent only about 1.5 percent of the total MTO sample. The in-depth interviews permitted the authors to develop and investigate hypotheses about the MTO experimental response that are difficult to assess using standard survey data.

The authors note that working-age people in both the treatment and control groups had essentially identical skills and labor market preparation. Since their skills were limited, respondents would have had trouble finding good jobs regardless of where they lived. People in the experimental group who moved to better neighborhoods may have had an advantage finding employment as a result of living near neighbors who both worked and had greater knowledge about possible job leads. Turney and her colleagues conclude, however, that this advantage may have been offset by the fact that the new neighbors knew little about job market prospects in those industries most likely to hire unskilled workers. Moreover, in Baltimore many of the employers interested in hiring unskilled and semiskilled workers, including those in retail and health services, were probably no farther away from high-poverty neighborhoods than they were from the new neighborhoods to which MTO participants moved. Ironically, the new neighborhoods were not as well served by public transportation as the high-poverty neighborhoods from which the MTO participants moved. The authors do find one tantalizing indicator that the move to better neighborhoods eventually may help participants' job prospects. Unemployed respondents in the MTO treatment group tended to express a stronger commitment to remaining in the labor force than their counterparts in the control group. In contrast, many jobless respondents in the control group reported being out of work for a long time, and an important minority of them seemed permanently detached from the labor force. By moving to better neighborhoods, participants in the MTO treatment may have been exposed to norms toward work that differ significantly from the norms prevailing in urban neighborhoods with concentrated poverty.

THE DISTORTIONS IN the timing and density of land development associated with the current property tax system are well known. While land is inelastically supplied, capital is elastically supplied. Therefore the portion of a property tax that falls on land generates no distortion, while the portion of the property tax that falls on capital discourages capital investment, creating deadweight loss. Even though this distortion is widely understood, no jurisdiction in the United States has decided to implement a pure land tax that would not have any distortionary effects, although some have moved in that direction by implementing a two-rate tax system.

In "Effects of Property Taxation on Development Timing and Density: Policy Perspective," Richard Arnott illustrates these distortionary effects with a model of the decisions of a landowner with and without taxation. He shows that even at relatively low rates, property taxes can cause substantial deadweight loss. Arnott then analyzes two property tax systems that do not have the distortionary impacts on time and density decisions associated with the current property tax system. He also discusses the political difficulties of moving toward a more efficient property tax system and considers how these challenges might be overcome.

For developed land, a two-rate property tax system has one tax rate on the assessed value of the structure and a second, higher tax rate, on the land. This tax system becomes a simple land tax if the tax rate on the structure is reduced to zero. An ideal two-rate tax system could allow a gradual transition from the current distortionary property tax system to a neutral, nondistortionary tax system. The author recognizes that a sudden dramatic shift in the current property tax system is not politically feasible in view of the fierce opposition of property owners who would be made worse off as a result of the new system. As a way of moving toward a less distortionary tax, Arnott considers the implementation of a more gradual transition scheme. Political opposition to a two-part tax system is not the only concern. Many tax administrators may worry about the practicality or accuracy of available methods to decompose a developed property's total value into separate values for the site and structure. Assessment offices currently use well-established and reasonably accurate procedures to calculate a developed property's market value, but new valuation procedures would be needed under a two-rate taxation system.

Arnott describes in detail the difficulties of assessing separately the structure and site value of developed properties. Inaccurate evaluations can undermine the potential benefits of a transition to a two-rate tax system and might increase the distortions produced by a property tax. The key to improvement, as mentioned in the paper, is the ability to assess the raw site value of developed land as "what the land would be worth if there were no structure on the site, even though in fact there is." If instead the value of developed land is found as the residual site value—that is, the value of the entire property minus the value of the structure on the site—then a move to a two-rate tax system can increase distortion.

The author analyzes possible Pareto-improving property tax reforms. He describes a variety of simple reforms that can be made to property taxation depending on where the current system is located on the Laffer curve. If the taxation system is on the wrong side of the Laffer curve, a reduction in property taxes will make landowners better off while simultaneously increasing government tax revenue. This represents a Pareto-improving tax reform. Arnott describes a possible Pareto-improving tax reform for undeveloped property if a simple property tax is currently located at the top of the Laffer curve. Converting this simple property tax into a two-rate tax system can simultaneously reduce the average property tax rate and increase tax revenues. Consider a two-rate tax schedule with the following two tax rates: The tax imposed on the raw site value of the property is the same as the tax rate under the old, one-rate tax, but the rate on the residual structure is slightly lower. The new tax schedule makes land and property owners better off, because it slightly reduces the rate paid on structures. At the same time, the tax cut encourages extra investment, increasing government tax revenues at the lower tax rates.

Arnott's aim is to influence future discussions of property tax reform. His analysis suggests that even with a modest tax rate the deadweight loss caused by a standard property tax system can be high. He identifies two neutral property tax systems that would eliminate or greatly reduce the deadweight loss and discusses in detail the difficulties in implementing such changes both politically and in terms of performing the necessary assessments. Arnott acknowledges that his simple model does not account for difficulties found in the real world such as land controls, and he does not claim his results would be unaffected by the complications. However, the model does provide a framework for thinking about the distortionary effects of property taxation and its impact on the timing and density of urban property development.

SUBURBAN SPRAWL—that is, the decentralization of residential, commercial, and industrial activities from central cities to their suburbs and beyond—has spawned a large and rapidly growing academic literature. This is a literature that generally takes a negative view of the phenomenon, although there is a part of the literature, often by economists, which analyzes the underlying reasons for the decentralization. This analysis usually distinguishes between natural causes of sprawl (such as population growth, income increases, and technological change) and market failures and policy biases. One market failure is the underpricing of automobile use, a problem treated in this volume's paper by Small, Winston, and Yan (described above). An example of a policy bias that encourages sprawl is the tax preference for home ownership, including both the deduction for mortgage interest and the highly favorable treatment of capital gains on a primary residence.

Edwin S. Mills offers a commentary on this literature in "Sprawl and Jurisdictional Fragmentation." As is obvious from his title, Mills's main concern here is the relationship between jurisdictional fragmentation and urban sprawl. Mills views sprawl as a function of density-restricting zoning, which in turn increases commuting distances. As he states in the paper, "If the average commuting distance increases more than would be needed to achieve the same density without controls, controls impair welfare." This is a definition (or conception) of sprawl that relies, as Mills recognizes, on a view of urban areas that is no longer entirely valid. It assumes jobs are located centrally rather than dispersed. However, the author also emphasizes that no coherent model of decentralized population and employment exists, though one is sorely needed.

Mills proposes an analysis of sprawl and fragmentation based on an industrial organization framework. He points out the analogy between local governments in a metropolitan area and competing firms in an industry. In a traditional analysis of industrial organization, firms within an industry are defined by the high cross-elasticity of demand for their products. Within a metropolitan area, the cross-elasticity of demand for location across jurisdictions should be relatively high. Rules governing entry—that is, the establishment of a new jurisdiction—and the relations of jurisdictions to one another will be important determinants of urban form.

An important part of Mills's argument about the relationship between sprawl and fragmentation is related to the objective function of municipalities, the jurisdictions that control zoning rules. Mills argues, on the basis of observation in the Chicago metropolitan area as well as observed outcomes elsewhere, that municipalities seek to promote (maintain) high land values. He argues vigorously that to achieve this goal "they segregate the lower- and middle-class residents, especially minorities." Mills concludes that "the purpose of stringent residential density controls in Chicago and similar metropolitan areas is mainly to segregate moderate income (and especially minority) residents from dwellings in upper-middle-class neighborhoods. The result is excessive housing costs, commuting costs, and sprawl."

Mills's proposed remedy for this policy failure is "a free market land allocation system." As in the case of competitive firms, free entry of new jurisdictions would increase competition and "any jurisdiction that introduced controls resulting in house prices above competitive equilibrium would lose population to competing jurisdictions."

TARA WATSON
Williams College

Metropolitan Growth, Inequality, and Neighborhood Segregation by Income

OVER THE LAST THREE DECADES, residential segregation by income has become an increasingly important feature of the U.S. metropolitan landscape. From 1970 to 2000, income sorting grew in large cities. In the 1980s almost all American metropolitan areas experienced a rise in segregation of the rich from the poor, though these changes were slightly offset by modest declines in segregation during the 1990s. More than 85 percent of the U.S. metropolitan population lived in an area that was more segregated by income in 2000 than in 1970. The time trend in residential segregation by income hints that income inequality may play an explanatory role. Mayer (2001) uses a panel of states to provide evidence that rising income inequality is associated with rising residential segregation by income.[1] Income inequality at the top of the income distribution is associated with residential isolation of the rich, while income inequality at the bottom of the distribution is associated with residential isolation of the poor.

It is perhaps unsurprising that the metropolitan areas with the largest growth in segregation include a number of distressed cities in industrial decline, such as Buffalo, New York, and Flint, Michigan. These metropolitan areas had large

The author is grateful for the insights of participants in the research seminars at Williams College, University of California, Berkeley, and University of Nevada at Las Vegas as well as the Brookings-Wharton Conference on Urban Affairs. Gary Burtless, Jerry Carlino, Ingrid Gould Ellen, and Janet Rothenberg Pack provided excellent comments as discussants and editors. The author is also indebted to Larry Katz, Cliff Winston, and many others for helpful suggestions on earlier related work.

1. In a companion piece to this paper, I obtain similar results using a panel of metropolitan areas and an alternative measure of income sorting. See Watson (2006).

1

Figure 1. Relationship between Changes in Family Centile Gap Index, 1970–2000, and Metropolitan Area Population Growth, 1970–2000, Relative to 1970 Population[a]

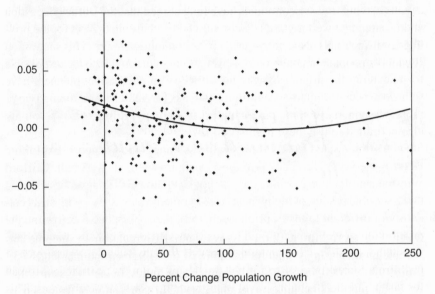

Percentile Change CGI

Percent Change Population Growth

a. Three outliers with more than a 250 percent population growth omitted from graph.

increases in income inequality associated with the demise of their manufacturing sectors. There is a sizable literature examining the flight of white, middle-class residents from the central cities of distressed metropolitan areas and the consequent residential isolation of the minority poor.[2] The implications of this change for housing construction have received less attention. Interestingly, a number of old manufacturing centers, such as Buffalo and Flint, witnessed a fair amount of new housing construction despite population declines.

Income segregation also rose in a subset of booming metropolitan areas. Tucson, Arizona, and Reno, Nevada, for example, saw increases in income segregation over the past three decades that were comparable in magnitude to those in Buffalo and Flint. The relationship between growth in segregation and growth in population is U-shaped, with both rapidly growing and stagnating metropolitan areas experiencing rising income segregation (see figure 1).

2. For example, Wilson (1987).

This paper, which investigates how income inequality and metropolitan growth interact to generate changes in residential segregation by income, proposes a simple model suggesting that rising income inequality creates pressure for income sorting in residential markets. In rapidly growing metropolitan areas, changing preferences are quickly reflected in the housing stock and level of segregation. In slowly growing metropolitan areas, however, the housing stock reflects the preferences of previous generations of residents. If existing housing costs less than the price of new construction or retrofitting, there is little incentive to change the housing stock. Rising segregation occurs in slow growth areas only if the change in market pressure for segregation is sufficient to overcome the costs of new construction or retrofitting. A key feature of the model is that changes to the housing stock are necessary to allow the resorting of income groups.

Why does economic segregation matter? Income sorting affects the distribution of role models, peers, and social networks. Sociologists hypothesize that the lack of neighborhood exposure to mainstream middle-class role models and social networks is a major contributor to urban joblessness and social problems.[3] A number of empirical papers also suggest that the characteristics of one's neighbors and peers in school affect social and economic prospects,[4] though the issue is far from settled.[5] If households sort into different political jurisdictions, economic segregation affects the degree of fiscal redistribution among income groups.[6] Even within political units, neighborhood-level sorting may influence the average level and variance of school quality and other local public goods. Finally, the factors that motivate households to segregate by income also shape the spatial relationship between jobs and homes, in turn affecting commuting patterns and labor-market decisions.

Each of these factors is amplified by the political process because economic segregation itself shapes the context in which policy decisions are made. Bjorvatn and Cappelen (2003) present a model in which income inequality generates residential sorting by income. Residential segregation, they hypothesize, reduces social attachment between groups, and rich children who grow up in segregated neighborhoods are less willing to favor redistribution as adults. In this way, income sorting may have consequences reaching beyond the current generation.

---

3. For example, Wilson (1987).
4. Case and Katz (1991); Cutler and Glaeser (1997); Hoxby (2000).
5. For example, Oreopoulos (2003); Kling, Liebman, and Katz (2007).
6. Glaeser, Kahn, and Rappaport (2000).

Theoretical Background

The simple framework presented in this paper is based on the notion that income inequality creates divergence in willingness to pay for neighborhood attributes, thereby inducing market pressure for segregation by income. Because income groups have different preferences over the physical characteristics of housing, income resorting requires a change in the housing stock. The observed change in segregation resulting from a given change in inequality depends on the cost of adjustment.

Market Pressure for Residential Segregation by Income

One tradition of modeling residential location decisions starts with a classic paper by Tiebout (1956), which suggests that household location decisions can be viewed as choices over bundles of local public goods. Households sort by income at the level of political district because income is correlated with willingness to pay for public goods. Analogously, households might sort across school districts or neighborhoods because income is correlated with willingness to pay for school or neighborhood quality. Sorting by income at the neighborhood level stems from divergence in willingness to pay for neighborhood attributes, including both attributes that vary across political jurisdictions (those emphasized by Tiebout) and attributes that vary within a political jurisdiction. Even within political boundaries, neighborhoods differ in their access to governmentally provided local public goods, such as proximity to public transit or reliability of trash collection, and differ in their nongovernmental local public goods, such as nice neighbors or a good view.

If households of different income levels are willing to pay different amounts to live in a given neighborhood, market forces tend to generate residential segregation by income. Individual households need not prefer segregated neighborhoods *per se*. Rather, differences in the willingness to pay for various neighborhood attributes across income groups attract these groups to different neighborhoods.[7] In a frictionless housing market, market pressure for segregation is observed as actual segregation, that is, rich and poor households living in different neighborhoods.

---

7. If rich neighbors are themselves an amenity for which high-income households are willing to pay more than low-income households, the market pressure for income sorting is further enhanced. For simplicity, I imagine the amenity to be a nongovernmentally provided public good, such as a nice view.

The simplest form of a Tiebout model implies that residential segregation by income should be complete. If all households have the same underlying tastes, the rich always pay more to live in high-quality neighborhoods and complete residential segregation by income occurs.[8] The model has been extended by Epple and Platt (1998) to allow variation in both tastes for neighborhood quality and income. For a given level of tastes, rich households in the model always choose to live in a higher-quality neighborhood than poor households. Similarly, at a given income level, households with stronger preferences for neighborhood quality always live in higher-quality neighborhoods than those with weaker preferences. Because both income and tastes vary across households, the willingness to pay for neighborhood quality is imperfectly correlated with income. In equilibrium, neighborhoods are partially, but incompletely, sorted by income. The prediction of Epple and Platt's model accords well with the observed patterns of residential location in American metropolitan areas.

Epple and Platt's framework suggests that observed economic segregation in American metropolitan areas depends on household preferences and the income distribution. Income inequality affects the relative willingness to pay of households at different income levels. There are two distinct ways in which the income sorting predicted by a Tiebout-style model could be affected by inequality. First, there is a direct effect of income inequality on willingness to pay. As inequality increases, it becomes less likely that rich and poor households are willing to pay similar amounts to live in a given neighborhood. In this sense, income inequality is a primary determinant of the market pressure for segregation.

In addition, the income distribution may affect residential sorting by differentially changing neighborhood quality and thereby changing the relative price of a high-quality neighborhood. For example, if less-skilled men disproportionately reside in low-quality neighborhoods and idle men are undesirable neighbors, then the attractiveness of low-quality neighborhoods is likely to fall as the labor market for less-skilled men weakens.[9] High-income families might be willing to pay more than low-income families to avoid these very low-quality neighborhoods. This change may also push the market toward a segregated equilibrium.

A thought experiment helps to clarify the meaning of market pressure for segregation as it is used in this paper. Consider two identical metropolitan

---

8. Ellickson (1971).

9. Less-skilled workers are defined as those with a high-school diploma or less. Idle men are defined as men who are not employed and not in school.

areas, each with a fixed group of families that are heterogeneous in income and tastes for neighborhood attributes. Residential markets in the two cities are in a competitive equilibrium and identical to each other. Thus the observed level of income segregation is the same in the two cities. At some point, an exogenous force widens the distribution of income in only one city, the so-called *treatment city,* by changing the amount of income associated with each family income percentile but preserving each family's rank in the metropolitan area income distribution. If no family moves in response to the change in the income distribution, income segregation is unchanged.

Given the scenario described above, one might ask what level of income segregation would emerge if the supply of housing were perfectly elastic in the treatment city. The income segregation level under this hypothetical costless competitive equilibrium is the result of market pressure for segregation. In other words, even if no family cares explicitly about the incomes of its neighbors, factors such as income inequality affect the willingness of different income groups to pay for various attributes of neighborhoods. Divergence in the valuation of neighborhood attributes across income groups leads to competitive pressure for income segregation. The difference in equilibrium segregation levels in the treatment and control cities in the absence of adjustment costs is the effect of inequality on the market pressure for segregation.

Adjustment Costs

In practice, adjustment costs in the housing market are likely to be quite important. Glaeser and Gyourko (2005) develop a "bricks-and-mortar" model of metropolitan growth and decline. Population is slow to fall in economically distressed metropolitan areas because the housing stock remains after employment disappears. Housing prices often fall below the price of new construction, attracting some residents to the area despite labor-market conditions. Adjustments to labor demand shocks across metropolitan areas are likely to be slow because housing is durable.

Similarly, the durable nature of housing prevents an immediate market response to changes in relative willingness to pay for neighborhood amenities within metropolitan areas. The financial and regulatory costs of retrofitting or building new housing imply that it may take many years to respond to a demand-side shock in the housing market. Indeed, if the residential market evolves sufficiently slowly, there may be coordination failures that preclude the hypothetical costless equilibrium from ever being realized.

Rapidly and slowly growing metropolitan areas differ in their adjustment costs and, therefore, in their responsiveness to housing market pressures. Glaeser and Gyourko (2005) report that existing housing stock is priced lower than new construction in many declining cities, making it relatively costly to develop new neighborhoods. Similarly, regulatory or zoning barriers may make the supply of housing inelastic. As Gyourko, Mayer, and Sinai (2006) point out, some highly desirable "superstar" cities have very inelastic supply responses to increases in demand over recent decades. Within metropolitan areas, there may be superstar suburbs or neighborhoods as well. In supply-constrained metropolitan areas, demand-side forces generate rapid house price appreciation with little population growth or new construction. In both distressed and supply-constrained metropolitan areas, slow population growth is associated with high costs of adjustment in the housing market.

Americans frequently move from one house to another, suggesting that the financial costs of moving are not prohibitive.[10] The adjustment costs described here are the bricks-and-mortar costs of constructing and retrofitting housing. These costs are likely to be substantial in a city with a preexisting housing stock.

In rapidly growing cities, on the other hand, newly constructed housing can easily respond to current consumer preferences. Developers of new neighborhoods can also overcome coordination problems that might persist in cities with a preexisting housing stock. Thus for a comparable shock affecting demand for different types of housing in different neighborhoods, the transition to a new equilibrium occurs more quickly and cheaply in a rapidly growing metropolitan area.

In sum, an empirically observed change in the level of segregation represents the effect of a change in market pressure toward segregation, tempered by incomplete adjustment. Holding other factors constant, it is expected that income segregation in rapidly growing cities has greater sensitivity to changes in inequality because the housing stock in growing cities adjusts more quickly to changing consumer preferences.

Simple Model

A simple model formalizes the intuition described above. This is not meant to be a complete model of residential location choice, but rather a starting

---

10. In 1970 about 48 percent of metropolitan household heads reported having lived in a different house five years earlier. In 2000 the number was about 45 percent (IPUMS 2004).

point for the empirical analysis that follows. The model abstracts from many of the complex features of urban housing markets.[11]

Suppose that there are two neighborhoods, G and B. The good neighborhood, G, is more desirable because residency includes access to an unspecified local public good such as a good view, but the two neighborhoods are otherwise identical. As the city is built, the housing supply in each neighborhood is upward-sloping, reflecting the fact that it is more expensive to build on some lots in the neighborhood. Let $S_q(p_q)$ describe the supply of housing in neighborhood of quality $q \in \{G,B\}$. Assume $S_q'(p_q) > 0$ and the supply function S_q is the same in both neighborhoods.

The willingness to pay for housing in each neighborhood is described by $D_q(p_q)$, where $D_q'(p_q) < 0$. In neighborhood G this includes the valuation of the local public good. In equilibrium:

$$D_b(p_b) = S_b(p_b),$$

$$D_g(p_g) = S_g(p_g), \text{ and}$$

$$p_g = p_b + a^*,$$

where $a^* > 0$ represents the valuation that the marginal resident assigns to the local public good. Note that in equilibrium it must be the case that $p_g > p_b$.

Suppose a fraction r of the metropolitan area residents are rich, while $1 - r$ are poor. Residents each live on a plot of land of a fixed size, but rich residents always build a high-amenity house and poor residents always build a low-amenity house. Rich and poor residents have different distributions of willingness to pay to live in the good neighborhood, represented by $f_r(a)$ and $f_p(a)$, respectively. The distribution $f_r(a)$ stochastically dominates the distribution $f_p(a)$.

Let a^* be the equilibrium difference in prices between the two neighborhoods, as described above. The fraction of rich residents with valuations $a > a^*$ in equilibrium is $1 - F_r(a^*)$. This is, therefore, the fraction of rich residents who live in neighborhood G. The fraction of poor residents with valuations $a > a^*$ in equilibrium is $1 - F_p(a^*)$. Assume, as in the Epple and Platt model,

---

11. For example, the model does not consider distance to the city center, elasticity of demand for land, crime, racial segregation, discrimination in housing markets, transportation costs, filtering down of old housing, or local public finance. It also abstracts from the question of what drives demand for housing across metropolitan areas, and considers only the effect of these demand shocks on metropolitan area housing prices and population.

some residents of each type have valuations above and below a^*, so $0 < (1 - F_p(a^*)) < (1 - F_r(a^*)) < 1$. It follows that both neighborhoods contain both rich and poor residents, but rich residents are disproportionately represented in neighborhood G and poor residents are disproportionately represented in neighborhood B. The housing in each neighborhood is constructed as a mix of high-amenity and low-amenity houses, reflecting the incomes of residents.

It is instructive to consider the effect of inequality on the distribution of residents across neighborhoods as the metropolitan area is built. Suppose the income of the rich is higher while the income of the poor is unchanged. The distribution of the willingness of the rich to pay for the local public good, $f_r(a)$, shifts upward, while the distribution of the willingness to pay of the poor, $f_p(a)$, remains the same. Let a^{**} represent the marginal valuation of the public good in this new scenario. In the new equilibrium $a^{**} > a^*$, $(1 - F_p(a^{**})) < (1 - F_p(a^*))$, and $(1 - F_r(a^{**})) > (1 - F_r(a^*))$. That is, with rising inequality, poor residents are less likely to live in the good neighborhood and rich residents are more likely to live in the good neighborhood. Because rich residents become increasingly concentrated in the good neighborhood, residential segregation by income increases relative to a situation in which income is distributed equally (see figure 2).

A similar result is obtained if inequality rises at the bottom of the distribution. Poor residents are willing to pay less to live in the good neighborhood. The relative valuation of the rich rises. As a result, rich residents disproportionately construct their homes in the good neighborhood and segregation increases.

Model Applied to Three Types of Metropolitan Areas

Suppose a city is built at a time of relative equality and neighborhoods are characterized by moderate segregation, with a mix of high- and low-amenity houses in each neighborhood. In equilibrium,

$$p_{hg} = p_{hb} + a_r^*, \text{ and}$$

$$p_{lg} = p_{lb} + a_p^*,$$

where h and l represent high-amenity and low-amenity houses, respectively, and a_r^* and a_p^* represent the marginal willingness to pay for the local public good of each type of resident. If the metropolitan area is growing, $a_r^* = a_p^*$ because both groups are simultaneously bidding on empty lots.

Fig 2a. Hypothetical Distributions $f(a)$ under Relative Equality

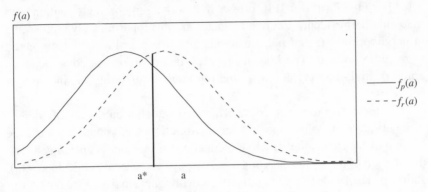

Fig 2b. Hypothetical Distributions $f(a)$ under Relative Inequality

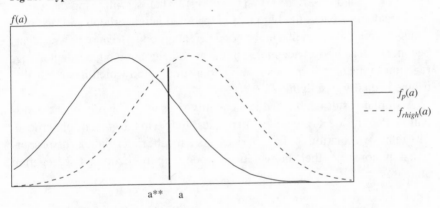

Given this set of initial conditions, consider three types of metropolitan areas. First, consider cities that peak at a time of relative equality and then fall into economic decline with stagnant or falling population and housing prices. Second, consider cities that continue to experience rising demand for housing overall, but supply is restricted due to natural or regulatory barriers, or both. Third, consider metropolitan areas that continue to grow rapidly with an elastic housing supply.

A metropolitan area's economic decline makes it less attractive to potential migrants. The demand for housing in the metropolitan area falls, housing prices drop, and population stagnates or declines. As noted by Glaeser and Gyourko (2005), the housing supply curve is inelastic for prices below the cost of

Figure 3. Housing Market with Kinked Supply Curve

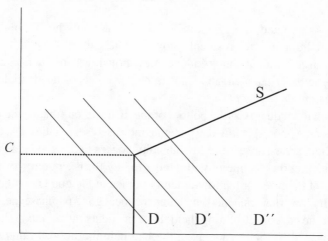

Source: Glaeser and Gyourko (2005).
C = cost of new construction; D = demand for housing; S = supply of housing.

new construction and upward sloping above the cost of new construction (see figure 3).

What is the impact of rising inequality in a declining metropolitan area? As a first case, imagine that inequality increases at the top of the distribution. An exogenous force raises incomes of the rich in the declining metropolitan area. This change increases the willingness to pay of rich residents, but not poor residents. In the new equilibrium,

$$p_{hg} = p_{hb} + a_r^{***},$$

where $a_r^{***} > a_r^*$ represents the marginal valuation of the public good of the new marginal resident. The market pressure for segregation has increased because rich residents are willing to pay more to live in the good neighborhood. However, if the new price $p_{hg} < c_h$ (the cost of new construction for a high-amenity house), then no new high-amenity houses are built in neighborhood G. Similarly, if the new price p_{hg} is sufficiently low relative to the fixed cost of retrofitting, low-amenity homes are not converted into high-amenity homes. The inequality shock raises the demand for high-amenity houses in neighborhood G, but the housing supply remains fixed at its historical level. Because the housing stock is tied to the income levels of residents, no rich residents move into the good neighborhood, and segregation remains constant.

On the other hand, if $p_{hg} > c_h$, then new high-amenity houses in neighborhood G are built and rich residents move into neighborhood G.[12] Thus a sufficiently large demand shock induces new housing construction even in a stagnant metropolitan area, and leads to higher levels of residential segregation by income.

A shock to inequality at the bottom of the distribution (that is, the poor residents become poorer) could also generate increased segregation in a declining metropolitan area. The price of low-amenity houses in the good neighborhood falls, reflecting the decline in willingness to pay for the public good of poor residents. If the price of the low-amenity homes in the good neighborhood is sufficiently low, rich residents who value the local good purchase these homes, and incur the cost of retrofitting them. Poor residents move into high-amenity homes vacated by rich residents in the bad neighborhood. In this scenario, increased segregation occurs as the existing housing stock is retrofitted or replaced to accommodate the rising market pressure for segregation.

Alternatively, an increase in poverty may make neighborhood B a less attractive place to live. The good neighborhood becomes more desirable, especially for rich residents if they are particularly averse to living in a very low-quality neighborhood. Depending on underlying preferences, rich residents may be willing to pay to finance new construction or retrofitting in the good neighborhood. A sufficiently large change in the quality of the bad neighborhood could induce new housing construction and lead to higher levels of residential segregation by income.

To summarize, a distressed metropolitan area is characterized by economic decline, stagnant or negative population growth, and housing prices below the cost of new construction. The durable nature of housing combined with the low market price for housing implies that the supply is fixed in the absence of a large shock. If there is a moderate increase in inequality, the relative prices of high-amenity and low-amenity houses in the good neighborhood change. However, the change is not sufficient to generate retrofitting or new construction. The distribution of rich and poor residents across neighborhoods remains constant and the observed level of income segregation remains unchanged.

---

12. According to a strict interpretation of the model, in which it is assumed poor residents only live in small houses, rich residents leave vacant large homes in the bad neighborhood. More realistically, some poor residents would move into those vacated properties, leaving small homes vacant in neighborhood B.

On the other hand, the economic decline may be accompanied by a very large shift in relative demand for high-amenity houses in the good neighborhood. If the demand shock is sufficiently large, the market price of high-amenity houses exceeds the cost of new construction or retrofitting, and high-amenity houses are built in the good neighborhood. The fraction of rich residents living in the good neighborhood rises and segregation increases. In sum, a declining metropolitan area experiences an increase in segregation and new housing construction (or retrofitting) only if the underlying demand for housing in particular neighborhoods is very high. According to the model, an increase in segregation is not observed without a contemporaneous change in the housing stock.

As a second case consider the implications of the model for supply-constrained, economically vibrant cities. Like the superstar cities in Gyourko, Mayer, and Sinai (2006), these metropolitan areas experience high overall demand for housing, coupled with natural or regulatory supply constraints in the housing market. Rising inequality in a supply-constrained metropolitan area raises the relative valuation of high-amenity houses in the good neighborhood. If construction is very expensive due to natural boundaries or zoning, only a substantial change in the willingness of the rich to pay for the good neighborhood induces a supply response. If supply constraints are severe, little new construction or population growth is expected. In constrained, economically vibrant cities, rising inequality induces rising segregation through retrofitting or replacement of existing housing stock.

In contrast to the two types of slowly growing areas described above, consider a hypothetical, rapidly growing metropolitan area. Rapid population growth typically implies that new homes are priced above the cost of construction. Housing supply is somewhat elastic for both high- and low-amenity houses. If income inequality remains constant as the number of residents grows, market forces yield a distribution of new houses that is similar to the initial distribution of houses. New homes are built, but segregation remains at a constant level in this case.

The housing market in a booming metropolitan area is very responsive to changes in inequality. If inequality is rising as the population expands, the increased demand for high-amenity houses in the good neighborhood is easily accommodated. New construction reflects the contemporary market pressure for segregation. Thus even a minor increase in inequality translates into homogeneous neighborhoods and rising segregation levels in a rapidly growing metropolitan area.

This simple model suggests that it is the interaction between the change in inequality and population growth of a city that determines a metropolitan area's segregation level. In a rapidly growing city, the housing stock and observed

Table 1. Theoretical Predictions Regarding Relationship between Metropolitan Area Growth and Segregation

	Metropolitan area	
Inequality	*Rapid growth*	*Slow growth*
Rising	Increase in observed segregation. New housing construction as predicted by population growth.	Increase in observed segregation only if inequality shock is sufficient to induce higher-than-expected housing construction or retrofitting.
Not rising	No increase in observed segregation. New housing construction as predicted by population growth.	No increase in observed segregation. Little or no new housing construction.

segregation reflect residents' current preferences. In a slowly growing metropolitan area, observed segregation reflects residents' historical preferences, unless the inequality shock is sufficient to induce the construction of new housing or retrofitting that would not have occurred otherwise.

The model generates several predictions, which are summarized in table 1:

—Factors raising the relative willingness of the rich to pay to live in a good neighborhood, such as income inequality, tend to raise residential sorting by income in metropolitan areas.

—The extent to which observed levels of segregation reflect changes in inequality depends on a metropolitan area's population growth.

—Rising segregation is accompanied by higher than expected levels of new housing construction in distressed cities, but not in economically vibrant cities.

—New housing in a metropolitan area reflects the market pressure for segregation at the time it is built. Because the housing stock is durable, market forces generating economic segregation have persistent effects on segregation levels even after the forces themselves have disappeared. Segregation levels are more persistent in cities with a slowly evolving housing stock.

The final prediction is somewhat analogous to Glaeser and Gyourko's (2005) bricks-and-mortar view of metropolitan growth and decline, applied to residential choice within metropolitan areas. Neighborhoods are developed to reflect the heterogeneity of their expected residents in terms of desired housing attributes. Because housing is durable, segregation by income tends to reflect the market pressure for segregation at the time housing is built in a metropolitan area. In slowly growing metropolitan areas, segregation rises only if the market pressure for segregation is sufficient to induce retrofitting or new housing construction that would not otherwise be expected. Changes in the housing stock enable the resorting of income groups across neighborhoods.

Measurement of Income Segregation

The consensus of the empirical literature is that neighborhood income segregation rose between 1970 and 2000. Jargowsky (1996a) reports that economic segregation within racial groups increased in both the 1970s and 1980s. Mayer (2001) finds a slight decline in overall tract-level segregation over the 1970s and a substantial rise in the 1980s, while Massey and Fischer (2003) report an increase in the concentration of poverty between 1970 and 2000 in large metropolitan areas, with a large rise in the 1980s and a decline in the 1990s.[13] Using a measure of income sorting developed in Watson (2006), this paper also documents an increase in economic segregation between 1970 and 2000.

The empirical analysis presented here is based on census tract-level family income data from the 1970, 1980, 1990, and 2000 U.S. censuses.[14] Tract-level data on household income are not available for 1970, so information on family income is used throughout the analysis.[15] As is common in the literature, this

13. Jargowsky (1995, 1996a) reports that economic segregation within racial groups increased during both the 1970s and 1980s. Mayer (2001) finds a slight decline in overall tract-level segregation during the 1970s and a substantial rise in the 1980s. Both Jargowsky and Mayer use the Neighborhood Sorting Index, a measure of overall economic segregation developed by Jargowsky. The index is the square root of the ratio of the between-tract income variance to the total income variance. Massey and Fischer (2003) also measure the concentration of affluence and find rising residential segregation of the rich between 1970 and 2000. Affluence is defined as four times the poverty line. Concentration of affluence declined in the 1970s and 1990s, but rose in the 1980s. When Massey and Fischer instead use the top-income quintile as a measure of affluence, there is no overall change between 1970 and 2000.

14. The tract-level family income data are provided by the census in fifteen income bins for 1970, seventeen for 1980, twenty-five for 1990, and sixteen for 2000. The implications of this fact are discussed at length in appendix A. Information on family income (rather than household income) is used to construct measures of inequality and segregation. Tract-level data on household income are not available for 1970.

15. Families are defined by the census as two or more individuals related by blood or marriage, and they constitute about three-quarters of all households. Families have slightly higher segregation levels than all households in years when both can be observed, but follow similar trends in segregation. The measure of family income is not adjusted for household size or family structure and reflects reported total income, which for most respondents is pretax income. The data do not reflect permanent or lifetime income. Therefore measured family income inequality may not accurately reflect differences in well-being. Similarly, measured segregation is a measure sorting by income rather than a measure of sorting by well-being.

paper uses the census tract (an area of roughly 4,000 people defined by the Census Bureau) as the definition of a *neighborhood.*[16] Information at the tract level is aggregated to construct indicators of income segregation and income inequality at the metropolitan area level, and to calculate several other metropolitan area variables. The tract-level information is supplemented with data collected by the census at the county level, county data in the City and County Data Books, and national industrial employment trends in the Integrated Public Use Microdata Series (IPUMS 2004).[17] The metropolitan areas are based on the 2003 U.S. Census county-based metropolitan area definitions, so they represent a constant geographic area over time to the extent that the counties were tracted in 1970. The sample includes 216 of the 217 metropolitan areas that had at least one tracted county in 1970.[18]

Table 2 presents some basic facts about the sample. On average, the 216 metropolitan areas experienced substantial increases in population, income, and income inequality. Land area increased, reflecting the fact that counties became tracted over the 1970–2000 period. New housing construction slowed in the 1980–2000 period relative to the 1960–80 period. Racial segregation fell between 1970 and 2000, as has been documented elsewhere.[19]

To analyze the changes in residential segregation by income over time, Watson (2006) introduces an index of segregation that is not directly related to the shape of income distribution in a metropolitan area. The Centile Gap Index (CGI) estimates how far the average family income within a tract deviates in percentile terms from the median family income in the tract, compared to how far it would deviate under perfect integration. Because the CGI is based on income percentiles, it is theoretically sensitive to rank-preserving spreads in the income distribution.[20] In other words, if the income distribution widens but families do not move, measured segregation is unchanged. This feature

16. The primary disadvantage to defining a neighborhood as a census tract is that a neighborhood is a much smaller geographic unit in a dense urban area than in a sprawling suburb. It is likely that much of the true segregation in suburban areas is due to within-tract sorting and is not picked up by a tract-based measure. Because both the physical proximity and nearest neighbors matter (for example, a neighbor living a quarter mile away has less relevance in a dense urban area than in a suburb), the ideal measure of neighborhood segregation is unclear.

17. Available at www.ipums.org.

18. Gainesville, Florida, is excluded from the analysis due to missing data. The definition of metropolitan areas is discussed in appendix B.

19. For example, Cutler, Glaeser, and Vigdor (1999).

20. In practice, income percentiles must be estimated using the income bins reported by the census, so that measured CGI may change slightly if the income distribution changes. An extensive discussion of this issue can be found in Watson (2006).

Table 2. Sample Means of Metropolitan Area Characteristics: Population, Income, and Income Inequality, 1970–2000[a]

Characteristic	1970	1980	1990	2000	Change 1970–2000
Metropolitan area					
Number of families	164,878	188,255	219,737	244,766	79,888
Number of tracts	151	171	196	220	69
Population (000s)	661	754	851	967	306
Family income last year (in 2000 dollars)					
Mean	50,604	54,330	57,750	63,940	13,336
Median	44,789	47,597	48,188	51,659	6,870
Family income ratio					
80-20	2.83	3.10	3.34	3.39	0.55
90-50	1.94	2.00	2.13	2.23	0.28
50-10	2.99	3.10	3.32	3.21	0.21
Predicted employment					
Relative to 1970	1.00	1.28	1.54	1.73	0.73
Of less-skilled men relative to 1970 total employment	0.44	0.43	0.38	0.38	−0.06
Predicted central city share of employment	0.57	0.52	0.52	0.48	−0.09
Race, education, and age					
Fraction black	0.10	0.10	0.11	0.12	0.02
Fraction Hispanic	0.05	0.06	0.07	0.10	0.05
Fraction foreign-born	0.03	0.04	0.05	0.07	0.04
Fraction aged 25 and older who are high school graduates[b]	0.55	0.68	0.71	0.85	0.30
Fraction aged 25 and older who are college graduates[c]	0.11	0.16	0.20	0.24	0.12
Fraction under age 18	0.35	0.29	0.26	0.25	−0.10
Fraction under age 65	0.91	0.90	0.86	0.88	−0.03
Racial segregation index[d]	0.38	0.32	0.28	0.22	−0.16
Land area (square miles)	1,894	2,469	2,844	2,843	949
New housing construction[e]	0.40	0.41	0.27	0.22	−0.18

Source: Tract-level and county-level census data from the U.S. Census Bureau, Census CD; Urban Institute Underclass Database; IPUMS; and author's calculations.

a. Means of 216 metropolitan areas (unweighted). Median family income and family income ratios are estimated. Inflation adjustment based on CPI-U, 1982–84 base year. Predicted variables based on 1970 industry mix interacted with national trends. For some cities 1970 black and Hispanic populations are imputed.

b. High school graduates include GED graduates in 1990 and 2000.

c. College graduates include those with four or more years of college in 1970 and 1980.

d. Racial segregation refers to the isolation of blacks from whites, adjusting for group populations.

e. New housing construction is the percentage of homes built within the last ten years relative to the percentage built ten or more years ago.

distinguishes the CGI from other measures of income sorting used in the literature.[21] The CGI is particularly well-suited to studying the relationship between income inequality and residential choice.

The family income data at the census tract level are presented using fifteen to twenty-five income bins defined by the U.S. Census Bureau. The information can be aggregated to the metropolitan area level and, to the extent that income is accurately reported, one can determine the actual range of family income percentiles in a metropolitan area represented by each income bin. This strategy eliminates the need for any assumptions about the income distribution in a metropolitan area and thereby overcomes a potential source of bias.[22] Family income groups within a census tract are known to be within a narrow range of income percentiles, but the exact income ranks are not known. To estimate the likelihood that a family is in a given percentile within the narrow range, this paper assumes that families in a particular income bin in a particular tract are uniformly distributed among the percentiles represented by the bin.[23]

The formula for the Centile Gap Index of metropolitan area m is

$$CGI_m = \left(0.25 - \left(1/J_m\right)\sum_j \left|P_j - P_{medtj}\right|\right)/0.25,$$

where

CGI_m : CGI in metropolitan area m,

J_m : number of families in metropolitan area m,

P_j : estimated percentile in the metropolitan area m income distribution of family j,

and P_{medtj} : estimated income percentile of median family in the tract of family j.

That is, the term $\left|P_j - P_{medtj}\right|$ represents the estimated income percentile distance of a given family from the median family in their tract. If a metropolitan area were fully integrated by income, each census tract would contain the full income distribution (defined from 0 to 1). In this case, the median family in the tract would be in the 50th percentile of the metropolitan area income distribution and the average centile difference between a family and

---

21. The Neighborhood Sorting Index, developed by Jargowsky (1995, 1996a), is a commonly used measure of income sorting that is not invariant to rank-preserving spreads in the income distribution. See Watson (2006) for details.

22. For more information about measurement of the income distribution, see Watson (2006).

23. Watson (2006) uses simulation to demonstrate that the bias introduced by the uniformity assumption is likely to be small with fifteen or more income bins.

the median family in the tract would be 0.25. Therefore, under perfect integration, the CGI equals zero. In contrast, a completely segregated city would consist of homogeneous neighborhoods. The average percentile difference between a family and the median family in the tract would be zero, yielding a CGI of 1 under perfect segregation.[24]

Conceptually, it is worth distinguishing between two different notions of neighborhood income segregation. The neighborhood distribution of income is plausibly important to outcomes. The isolation of the poor, a measure of segregation used in some studies, focuses on the income distribution of a typical poor family's neighborhood. In contrast, the CGI is a measure of the distribution of income rank groups across neighborhoods, not of the distribution of income across neighborhoods. Thus if neighborhoods are segregated and fixed, a rise in income inequality could make the poor worse off because average neighborhood income might fall. This effect is not captured by the CGI. Rather, a rank-preserving spread of the income distribution induces a systematic change in the CGI only if it induces a change in the residential location choices of different income groups. Because this study investigates the relationship between income inequality and residential choice, the CGI is an appropriate measure to use.

This paper uses an additional percentile-based segregation measure to examine segregation at different parts of the income distribution. The families in each metropolitan area are divided into five income quintiles. The exposure of quintile x to quintile y is the fraction of quintile y families in a typical quintile x family's census tract.[25] For example, the exposure of the bottom quintile to the top quintile represents the fraction of top-quintile families in a typical bottom-quintile family's census tract. The exposure of an income group to itself is referred to as the *isolation* of that income quintile.

Trends in Segregation by Income

As shown in table 3, economic segregation in metropolitan areas increased between 1970 and 2000. The average CGI rose from 0.110 to 0.120 over the period, decreasing slightly over the 1970s and the 1990s, and rising substantially over the 1980s. Income segregation grew earlier and more substantially in

---

24. With a finite number of income bins, perfect segregation cannot be observed. See Watson (2006) for a discussion.

25. The formula for the Exposure Index is reported in appendix A.

Table 3. Sample Means of Metropolitan Area Characteristics: Economic Segregation, 1970–2000

Measure	1970	1980	1990	2000	Change 1970–2000[a]
Family income segregation					
CGI	0.110	0.106	0.123	0.120	0.009
Isolation of bottom quintile	0.263	0.267	0.281	0.276	0.013
Isolation of top quintile	0.275	0.271	0.286	0.283	0.007
Family suburbanization (210 metropolitan areas)					
Fraction of all families in central city	n.a.	0.464	0.425	0.439	−0.026
Fraction of bottom quintile in central city	n.a.	0.528	0.499	0.519	−0.008
Fraction of top quintile in central city	n.a.	0.439	0.399	0.408	−0.031
Fraction of central city in bottom quintile	n.a.	0.239	0.249	0.253	0.015
Fraction of central city in top quintile	n.a.	0.184	0.182	0.178	−0.006
Within central city versus suburb segregation (210 metropolitan areas)					
CGI within central city	n.a.	0.125	0.147	0.138	0.013
Isolation of bottom quintile in central city	n.a.	0.390	0.444	0.445	0.055
Isolation of top quintile in central city	n.a.	0.253	0.268	0.254	0.001
CGI within suburbs	n.a.	0.067	0.082	0.079	0.012
Isolation of bottom quintile in suburbs	n.a.	0.191	0.195	0.187	−0.004
Isolation of top quintile in suburbs	n.a.	0.276	0.286	0.286	0.010

Source: Tract-level census data, U.S. Census Bureau, Census CD; Urban Institute Underclass Database; and author's calculations.
n.a. Not available.
CGI = centile gap index.
a. Change reflects 1980–2000 changes when 1970 information is unavailable.

larger cities. Sorting declined in southern metropolitan areas, but increased in other regions. Trends in the CGI for different types of metropolitan areas are shown in table 4.[26]

Is the change in the CGI large or small? To get a sense of this, consider a hypothetical metropolitan area with many neighborhoods of equal population. If each neighborhood is representative of the metropolitan income distribution, the CGI is zero. Suppose some neighborhoods become moderately segregated. They contain 20 percent of their population from each of the three middle-income quintiles, and the remaining 40 percent of their population from either just the top- or bottom-income quintile. If 69 percent of neighborhoods are segregated as described and 31 percent of neighborhoods are representative of the whole population, the CGI is about 0.110, the sample mean CGI

26. The Neighborhood Sorting Index also shows an increase in income segregation between 1970 and 2000, but the index rose in all three decades. See Watson (2006) for a discussion of the differences between alternative measures of income sorting.

Table 4. CGI by Metropolitan Area Characteristics, 1970–2000

Category	CGI 1970	1980	1990	2000	Change 1970–2000
All metropolitan areas (216)	0.110	0.106	0.123	0.120	0.009
All metropolitan areas (weighted by 2000 population, $N = 216$)	0.130	0.137	0.157	0.158	0.028
By region					
East (33)	0.082	0.091	0.106	0.115	0.033
Midwest (63)	0.090	0.097	0.118	0.110	0.020
South (83)	0.139	0.119	0.130	0.123	−0.016
West (37)	0.104	0.109	0.128	0.131	0.027
By growth in inequality (80-20 family income ratio)					
Slowest (72)	0.118	0.104	0.113	0.109	−0.010
Moderate (72)	0.111	0.106	0.124	0.121	0.010
Fastest (72)	0.101	0.110	0.131	0.129	0.028
By population growth					
Slowest (72)	0.088	0.095	0.114	0.111	0.023
Moderate (72)	0.117	0.110	0.125	0.120	0.003
Fastest (72)	0.125	0.114	0.129	0.128	0.002
By growth in inequality (80-20 family income ratio), in slow population growth areas					
Slowest (24)	0.083	0.097	0.098	0.087	0.004
Moderate (24)	0.075	0.084	0.103	0.098	0.023
Fastest (24)	0.103	0.119	0.142	0.146	0.043
By growth in inequality (80-20 family income ratio), in rapid population growth areas					
Slowest (24)	0.124	0.108	0.117	0.112	−0.012
Moderate (24)	0.118	0.110	0.121	0.122	0.004
Fastest (24)	0.133	0.125	0.157	0.148	0.015
By 2000 population					
< 250,000 (66)	0.094	0.086	0.098	0.091	−0.003
250,000–499,000 (64)	0.105	0.100	0.114	0.111	0.006
500,000–1 million (37)	0.118	0.114	0.132	0.132	0.014
>1 million (49)	0.133	0.136	0.160	0.161	0.028
By predicted employment growth					
Slowest (72)	0.080	0.084	0.101	0.098	0.018
Moderate (72)	0.128	0.118	0.134	0.131	0.003
Fastest (72)	0.123	0.118	0.132	0.129	0.007

Source: Tract-level census data, U.S. Census Bureau, Census CD; Urban Institute Underclass Database; and author's calculations.
CGI = centile gap index.

value for 1970. If 75 percent of neighborhoods are segregated as described and 25 percent of neighborhoods are representative of the whole population, the CGI is about 0.120, the sample mean for 2000.

Average segregation levels peaked in 1990. A CGI of 0.123, the sample mean in 1990, would be generated if 77 percent of neighborhoods are segregated as described above and 23 percent of neighborhoods are representative. Indeed, in 1990 a quarter of the metropolitan areas in the sample had CGIs exceeding 0.160, a statistic that would be generated if 100 percent of neighborhoods were segregated as described above. Thus the change in segregation over time is economically meaningful.

Nevertheless, changes in segregation over time are not particularly large compared to variation across metropolitan areas. The metropolitan area with the median CGI in 1990 would have placed at the 64th percentile of segregation in 1970. The 1990 mean CGI is 0.3 of a standard deviation higher than the 1970 mean CGI (using the 1970 standard deviation).

To get a better sense of neighborhood composition, it is helpful to examine the typical experience of family income quintile groups. The top and bottom income groups were more isolated in 2000 than 1970. Families in the bottom quintile of their metropolitan area family income distribution had neighborhoods that were 26.3 percent bottom quintile in 1970 and 27.6 percent bottom quintile in 2000. Top-quintile families also became more likely to live with other top-income quintile families. In 2000 the typical family in the bottom quintile lived in a neighborhood that was about 28 percent bottom-quintile residents and 14 percent top-quintile residents, while the proportions were roughly reversed for top-quintile families.

This paper focuses on income segregation at the neighborhood level. However, there is a mechanical relationship between central city-suburb sorting and neighborhood sorting. The 1970–2000 period was characterized by disproportionate suburbanization of the rich. Empirically, however, income sorting between the central city and suburbs does not explain the bulk of neighborhood income segregation. The growth in neighborhood income segregation is not primarily due to differential suburbanization rates, but rather sorting both within the suburbs and central city.

Trends by Metropolitan Area Growth

Slowly growing metropolitan areas are those in the bottom third of population growth. These include economically distressed cities as well as some economically vibrant cities (such as Boston and New York) with housing supply constraints. Rapidly growing metropolitan areas are those in the top third of the population growth distribution. Table 4 shows trends in income segregation by population growth rates.[27] The most slowly growing metropolitan areas had the largest changes in segregation.

Table 5 summarizes the changes that took place in slowly growing cities between 1970 and 2000. About a third of slow-growth metropolitan areas lost population between 1970 and 2000. Slow growth areas also experienced large increases in inequality. These areas faced a strong trend toward suburbanization of the rich and middle class. Residential segregation by income also increased within central cities and suburbs. The net result was a large increase in the concentration of bottom-quintile families in the central city. By 2000 a typical bottom-quintile central-city family in a slow-growth metropolitan area lived in a neighborhood that was composed of 55 percent bottom-quintile family residents.

The pattern in booming metropolitan areas, also shown in table 5, was quite different. Growth in inequality was relatively modest, and average segregation levels were nearly flat over the period. There was also greater variation in segregation trends in these areas. More than 40 percent of rapid-growth metropolitan areas had declining segregation, while a number of other areas had large increases in segregation. Unlike slow-growth areas, high-growth areas were not characterized by disproportionate suburbanization of the rich, even among those with rising segregation. Rising segregation in booming metropolitan areas, where it occurred, was driven by the fact that the rich were becoming increasingly isolated within the suburbs and central cities. It was the growing isolation of the rich that drove segregation in a subset of rapidly growing metropolitan areas.

Testing the Model's Implications

The CGI is well suited to investigating the relationship between inequality and residential choice. This section presents empirical evidence regarding the implications of the model using a panel of 216 metropolitan areas over four decennial censuses spanning thirty years.

---

27. Table 4 also shows segregation trends by predicted employment growth rates. Predicted employment is based on 1970 industrial composition interacted with national industry-specific employment trends. The variable is discussed later in this paper. Predicted employment growth serves as a proxy for economic growth.

Table 5. Sample Characteristics for Slowly and Rapidly Growing Metropolitan Areas, 1970–2000[a]

| | Metropolitan areas | | | | | |
| | Slow growth[b] | | | Rapid growth[c] | | |
Characteristic	1970	2000	Fraction positive change	1970	2000	Fraction positive change
Metropolitan area						
Population (000s)	995	1,083	0.67	436	998	1.00
Family income ratio						
80-20	2.58	3.31	1.00	3.04	3.48	0.96
90-50	1.86	2.17	1.00	2.02	2.29	1.00
50-10	2.80	3.18	0.89	3.12	3.25	0.71
Racial segregation index	0.389	0.310	0.29	0.353	0.137	0.18
Land area (square miles)	1,558	1,866	0.49	2,529	4,159	0.78
New housing construction	0.25	0.13	0.01	0.55	0.32	0.09
Family income segregation measures						
CGI	0.088	0.111	0.83	0.125	0.128	0.57
Isolation of bottom quintile	0.253	0.281	0.92	0.268	0.272	0.61
Isolation of top quintile	0.259	0.271	0.71	0.289	0.293	0.61
Family suburbanization measures (210 metropolitan areas, 1980–2000)						
Fraction of all families in central city	0.412	0.373	0.19	0.473	0.458	0.39
Fraction of bottom quintile in central city	0.511	0.502	0.43	0.513	0.503	0.44
Fraction of top quintile in central city	0.357	0.298	0.15	0.472	0.463	0.36
Fraction of central city in bottom quintile	0.262	0.288	0.89	0.225	0.230	0.65
Fraction of central city in top quintile	0.166	0.150	0.21	0.197	0.198	0.49
Within central city versus suburb segregation (210 metropolitan areas, 1980–2000)						
CGI within central city[d]	0.107	0.121	0.81	0.139	0.151	0.67
Isolation of bottom quintile in central city	0.449	0.548	0.88	0.355	0.373	0.69
Isolation of top quintile in central city	0.199	0.178	0.28	0.293	0.310	0.58
CGI within suburbs[d]	0.057	0.067	0.72	0.075	0.091	0.74
Isolation of bottom quintile in suburbs	0.166	0.154	0.31	0.209	0.218	0.53
Isolation of top quintile in suburbs	0.286	0.314	0.92	0.267	0.261	0.67

Source: Tract-level census data, U.S. Census Bureau, Census CD; Urban Institute Underclass Database; and author's calculations.
CGI = centile gap index.
a. Suburbanization measures reported for 1980 rather than 1970; suburbanization variables not available for 1970. Changes for population, number of families, and land area reported in percentage terms. See text and appendix A for description of segregation measures.
b. Bottom third of the population growth rate distribution.
c. Top third of the population growth rate distribution.
d. Computed using city or suburb income percentiles.

Figure 4. Relationship between Changes in Family CGI and Family Income Ratio (80-20), 1970–2000

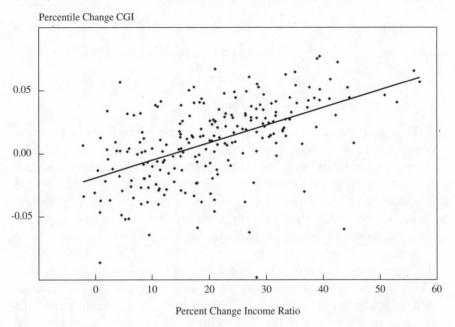

Percentile Change CGI

Percent Change Income Ratio

Inequality and Segregation

The model's first implication is that factors that raise the relative willingness of the rich to pay to live in a good neighborhood tend to increase a metropolitan area's income segregation. Though a number of factors are likely to contribute to market pressure for segregation, this paper focuses on rising income inequality. As suggested by the model, rising inequality is likely to affect the relative willingness of high- and low-income families to pay for certain neighborhood attributes.

The data show a strong relationship between income inequality and segregation by income percentile. A one standard deviation increase in inequality raises income segregation by 0.4 standard deviations. This result is foreshadowed by figure 4, which plots the relationship between growth in income segregation and growth in income inequality between 1970 and 2000.

A fixed effects specification using four decennial censuses (1970–2000) controls for any unobserved attributes of metropolitan areas that do not change over time and that could be correlated with both inequality and segregation levels. I estimate the following reduced form model:

$$\text{Segregation}_{mt} = \beta_1 * \text{Inequality}_{mt} + \beta_2 * \text{Predicted Employment}_{mt}$$
$$+ \beta_3 * \text{Predicted Employment for Less-Skilled Men}_{mt}$$
$$+ \beta_4 * \text{Predicted Central-City Employment Share}_{mt}$$
$$+ \text{other MSA characteristics}_{mt} * \beta_5 + \alpha_m + \delta_t + \mu_{mt}.$$

Three industrial composition variables—predicted employment, predicted employment for less-skilled men, and predicted central-city employment share—are constructed using 1970 industrial shares in each metropolitan area interacted with national industry trends.[28] It is important to control for the industrial composition variables because metropolitan areas with different economic bases are likely to have differentially changing residential patterns independent of differential changes in the income distribution.

Metropolitan areas may have long-standing differences in residential patterns that are correlated with the income distribution in those areas. Metropolitan area fixed effects, α_m, are included in the model to control for time-invariant differences across metropolitan areas. Year fixed effects, δ_t, control for national trends in preferences common to all metropolitan areas that could influence segregation levels. Additional time-varying metropolitan area characteristics are included as well.[29]

Results of the fixed effects model are shown in table 6. In the table's first column, a baseline model is presented in which the log of the 80-20 ratio is the measure of inequality and the CGI is the measure of segregation. As predicted by theory, income inequality is highly correlated with observed income segregation. After the model has controlled for the effects of industrial composition and a number of other factors, the coefficient on inequality is 0.108. This number implies that a 1 standard deviation increase in income inequality raises income segregation by 0.4 standard deviations.

To put the effect's size into perspective, recall the hypothetical metropolitan area discussed above. Some neighborhoods are representative of the metropolitan area population. Others are moderately segregated, with 20 percent

---

28. The construction of these variables is described in appendix B.

29. Time-varying metropolitan area characteristics include log of population, racial and ethnic composition variables, educational composition variables, age composition variables, and land area. Land area changes if a county eventually included in a metropolitan area was not tracted in 1970.

of their population from each of the three middle-income quintiles, and the remaining 40 percent of their population from either just the top- or bottom-income quintile. The mean CGI for 1970 (0.110) is consistent with a hypothetical metropolitan area in which 69 percent of neighborhoods are segregated as described and 31 percent of neighborhoods are representative of the whole population. Between 1970 and 2000, the increase in the average of the log 80-20 ratio was 0.18. According to the regression model, this change predicts an increase in the CGI of 0.020. The resulting level of segregation would be achieved if 81 percent of neighborhoods were segregated as described and 19 percent were representative of the population. The estimated effect of rising inequality more than fully accounts for the observed growth in income segregation between 1970 and 2000.

Differences in family income across income quintile groups are associated with different neighborhood choices by those groups. For example, inequality at the top of the income distribution is associated with residential isolation of the top quintile. An increase in the log 90-50 ratio equivalent to the change in the sample mean between 1970 and 2000 predicts an increase in isolation of the rich of 0.022. In 2000, holding all else equal, the typical top-quintile family is predicted to live in a neighborhood consisting of an additional 2.2 per 100 top-quintile families (from a base of 27.5 per 100 in 1970).

Similarly, inequality at the bottom of the income distribution is associated with isolation of the bottom quintile. The coefficient on the isolation of the poor and the actual change in inequality are both smaller than for the top quintile, so that the predicted increase in isolation of the bottom quintile is a modest 0.003. In 2000 the typical bottom-quintile family is predicted to live in a neighborhood consisting of an additional 0.3 per 100 top-quintile families (from a base of 26.3 per 100 in 1970), holding industrial composition and other factors fixed.

Some of the effect of inequality at the bottom on residential sorting is likely captured by the industrial mix variables. The data indicate a strong negative relationship between predicted employment demand for less-skilled men and segregation, after the model has controlled for employment decentralization and overall employment levels. In particular, declining employment for less-skilled men is associated with rising isolation of families in the bottom-income quintile. This is suggestive evidence that manufacturing job loss may cause a change in the relative desirability of high- and low-quality neighborhoods, leading all but the lowest-income groups to exit low-quality neighborhoods. Also, fewer jobs for less-skilled men may affect variation in permanent incomes, in which case measured income inequality does not fully capture the differences in economic well-being that affect residential choices.

Table 6. Fixed Effects Analysis of Income Segregation, 1970–2000[a]

Dependent variable	CGI		Isolation			
			Of bottom quintile		Of top quintile	
	I	II	III	IV	V	VI
Log (80-20 family income ratio)	0.108**		0.060**		0.084**	
	(0.020)		(0.015)		(0.015)	
Log (90-50 family income ratio)		0.115**		0.010		0.163**
		(0.028)		(0.026)		(0.025)
Log (50-10 family income ratio)		0.040**		0.055**		0.007
		(0.013)		(0.011)		(0.009)
Predicted employment	0.197**	0.200**	0.188**	0.178**	0.086	0.100*
	(0.073)	(0.071)	(0.062)	(0.062)	(0.055)	(0.053)
Predicted employment of less-skilled men	-0.894**	-0.927**	-0.812**	-0.801**	-0.321	-0.378*
	(0.281)	(0.281)	(0.238)	(0.238)	(0.199)	(0.194)
Predicted central city employment	-1.082**	-1.127**	-0.803**	-0.847**	-0.593**	-0.593**
	(0.364)	(0.350)	(0.327)	(0.327)	(0.215)	(0.202)
Log (population)	0.018*	0.016*	0.007	0.006	0.008	0.007
	(0.010)	(0.010)	(0.007)	(0.007)	(0.007)	(0.006)
Fraction black	0.083	0.107	0.133**	0.117*	0.047	0.083
	(0.079)	(0.080)	(0.063)	(0.062)	(0.055)	(0.054)
Fraction Hispanic	0.013	0.037	0.000	-0.002	0.041	0.061*
	(0.057)	(0.057)	(0.050)	(0.050)	(0.036)	(0.031)
Fraction foreign-born	-0.051	-0.063	-0.079*	-0.069	0.038	-0.003
	(0.053)	(0.052)	(0.047)	(0.049)	(0.037)	(0.032)

	(1)	(2)	(3)	(4)	(5)	(6)
Log (mean family income in 2000 dollars)	−0.036**	−0.054**	−0.012	−0.014	−0.029*	−0.043**
	(0.016)	(0.016)	(0.014)	(0.013)	(0.015)	(0.015)
Fraction aged 25 and older who are high school graduates	−0.033**	−0.030**	−0.007	−0.010	−0.029**	−0.026**
	(0.014)	(0.014)	(0.012)	(0.012)	(0.010)	(0.010)
Fraction aged 25 and older who are college graduates	0.194**	0.223**	0.071	0.086*	0.214**	0.219**
	(0.056)	(0.056)	(0.046)	(0.045)	(0.050)	(0.050)
Fraction under age 18	0.194**	0.171**	0.193**	0.180**	0.012	−0.012
	(0.082)	(0.084)	(0.077)	(0.079)	(0.066)	(0.065)
Fraction under age 65	0.199**	0.219**	0.091	0.070	0.102	0.170**
	(0.096)	(0.100)	(0.079)	(0.080)	(0.071)	(0.073)
Log (square miles)	−0.015**	−0.014**	−0.014**	−0.013**	−0.005*	−0.005*
	(0.005)	(0.005)	(0.003)	(0.004)	(0.003)	(0.003)
Year fixed effects	yes	yes	yes	yes	yes	yes
MSA fixed effects	yes	yes	yes	yes	yes	yes
Observations	864	864	864	864	864	864
Number of metropolitan areas	216	216	216	216	216	216
R-squared	0.93	0.93	0.91	0.91	0.92	0.92

Source: Author's calculations based on U.S. Census data.
CGI = centile gap index; MSA = metropolitan statistical area.
*Significant at the 10 percent level; **significant at the 5 percent level.
a. Analysis is unweighted. Standard errors clustered on metropolitan area are in parentheses. See notes in table 2 and text for variable descriptions.

Overall, the evidence is consistent with a model in which income inequality affects the relative willingness to pay for neighborhood attributes across income groups.[30] It is worth noting that an exogenous change in residential patterns could lead to inequality in educational or labor-market opportunities. A change in educational opportunities would likely be reflected in family income inequality with a substantial lag, but a change in labor-market opportunities could generate an immediate effect on the income distribution. Although there is no way to definitively reject the possibility of reverse causality, the effects are assumed to be small relative to the direct effect of income on residential choice.

Segregation and Growth

The model's second prediction is that the extent to which observed levels of segregation respond to a similar inequality shock depends on the population growth of a metropolitan area. That is, a comparable change in inequality should have a larger impact on observed segregation in a growing metropolitan area than in a stagnant metropolitan area. Rapidly growing metropolitan areas without supply constraints in the housing market can easily accommodate changing demand for different types of housing. Slowly growing metropolitan areas, on the other hand, require a large shock to induce retrofitting of existing housing or new construction.

The fixed effects analysis described above is repeated separately for three groups of cities categorized by population growth. Table 7 shows these regressions for both the most rapidly and most slowly growing cities. The empirical evidence supports the hypothesis for the effect of inequality at the top of the distribution, but not at the bottom of the distribution. That is, slow-growth metropolitan areas have larger responses to a given change in the 50-10 family income ratio, while rapid-growth metropolitan areas are more responsive to a given change in the 90-50 family income. It may be the case that the economic prospects of the poor affect demand for segregation differentially in stagnating cities, where a given observed change in inequality may be associated with a variety of social ills.[31]

---

30. Decentralization of employment also contributes to rising segregation. Several other metropolitan area characteristics are also important. See Watson (2006) for a further discussion.

31. Results categorizing metropolitan areas by predicted employment growth rather than population growth support this interpretation. The pattern of coefficients is qualitatively similar, but the coefficient on the log of the 50-10 ratio on isolation of the bottom quintile is 0.119. This suggests that there is a particularly large effect of inequality at the bottom in economically depressed metropolitan areas.

If a given change in the 90-50 ratio represents a similar demand shock across different types of cities, then the larger coefficient for rapidly growing cities is consistent with the model. The estimated coefficients imply that a 1.00 standard deviation change in the log of the 90-50 ratio is associated with a 0.21 standard deviation increase in isolation of the top quintile in a slow-growth city, but a 0.70 standard deviation increase in isolation in a rapid-growth metropolitan area. The difference is statistically significant.

The results suggest that residential patterns in rapidly growing areas are particularly sensitive to the expanding right tail of the income distribution. The growth in the average log 90-50 ratio was smaller in rapidly growing cities than in slowly growing cities between 1970 and 2000 (0.125 compared to 0.153). However, because rapidly growing metropolitan areas are more sensitive to any given change in inequality, a smaller change in inequality yields a substantially larger predicted change in the isolation of the rich, holding other factors constant. In a booming metropolitan area, the typical top-quintile family in 2000 is predicted to live in a neighborhood consisting of an extra 3.0 per 100 top-quintile families (from a base of 25.9 per 100 in 1970), holding all else equal. In contrast, despite greater inequality growth in the slowest-growing cities, the typical top-quintile family is predicted to live in a neighborhood consisting of an extra 1.1 per 100 top-quintile families (from a base of 25.3 per 100 in 1970). The evidence is consistent with the notion that rapidly growing cities quickly develop neighborhoods of homogeneous, high-amenity housing when inequality rises. It is more costly for slowly growing cities to adjust their housing stocks to meet changing demand induced by a comparable change in inequality.

If rapid growth areas are sensitive to rising inequality, why did they experience modest increases in segregation, on average, over the period? The answer is that a number of rapidly growing areas had negligible changes in income inequality. Indeed, a quarter of rapidly growing areas experienced net declines in the 50-10 ratio between 1970 and 2000, and these areas experienced average declines in segregation as well (analysis not shown). Furthermore, the expanding land area of rapidly growing areas tends to reduce measured income segregation.[32] Nevertheless, a subset of rapidly growing areas did experience sizable increases in inequality, especially at the top of the income distribution. In those areas, such as Tucson and Reno, where the market pressure for segregation rose, the flexible housing market allowed substantial increases in residential sorting by income.

---

32. A census tract represents a larger land area in a low-density metropolitan area. In general there is more heterogeneity in these geographically larger tracts.

Table 7. Fixed Effects Analysis by Metropolitan Area Population Growth Rate, 1970–2000[a]

| | Metropolitan areas | | | | | |
| | Slow growth[b] | | | Rapid growth[c] | | |
Dependent variable	CGI	Isolation bottom quintile	Isolation top quintile	CGI	Isolation bottom quintile	Isolation top quintile
Log (90-50 family income ratio)	0.050	0.028	0.073**	0.142**	-0.019	0.239**
	(0.039)	(0.030)	(0.036)	(0.053)	(0.049)	(0.045)
Log (50-10 family income ratio)	0.038**	0.062**	0.006	-0.012	0.001	-0.014
	(0.015)	(0.013)	(0.013)	(0.029)	(0.022)	(0.019)
Predicted employment	0.254**	0.229**	0.262**	0.185	0.139	0.088
	(0.099)	(0.083)	(0.103)	(0.111)	(0.086)	(0.079)
Predicted employment of less-skilled men	-1.409**	-1.114**	-1.200**	-0.695	-0.457	-0.348
	(0.397)	(0.345)	(0.402)	(0.458)	(0.352)	(0.290)
Predicted central city employment	-1.283**	-0.937**	-1.092**	-0.847	-0.460	-0.513*
	(0.336)	(0.274)	(0.341)	(0.558)	(0.508)	(0.291)
Log (population)	-0.010	-0.012	-0.006	0.018	0.005	0.019*
	(0.020)	(0.023)	(0.016)	(0.016)	(0.014)	(0.011)
Fraction black	0.169*	0.285**	0.104**	0.067	0.107	0.028
	(0.085)	(0.095)	(0.052)	(0.122)	(0.088)	(0.079)
Fraction Hispanic	0.049	-0.000	0.026	-0.082	-0.057	-0.042
	(0.060)	(0.102)	(0.066)	(0.109)	(0.088)	(0.067)
Fraction foreign-born	-0.161*	-0.194**	-0.060	0.166	0.106	0.081
	(0.081)	(0.094)	(0.089)	(0.130)	(0.115)	(0.081)

Log (mean family income in 2000 dollars)	-0.046**	-0.014	-0.047**	-0.064**	-0.040	-0.021
	(0.020)	(0.017)	(0.017)	(0.031)	(0.030)	(0.038)
Fraction aged 25 and older who are high school graduates	0.022	0.016	0.005	-0.039*	-0.016	-0.033**
	(0.025)	(0.020)	(0.020)	(0.021)	(0.018)	(0.017)
Fraction aged 25 and older who are college graduates	0.326**	0.101	0.292**	0.162	0.134*	0.067
	(0.065)	(0.066)	(0.057)	(0.103)	(0.071)	(0.102)
Fraction under age 18	0.051	-0.014	0.045	0.229	0.263*	-0.016
	(0.098)	(0.088)	(0.078)	(0.148)	(0.137)	(0.115)
Fraction under age 65	0.340**	0.309*	0.248**	0.260	0.089	0.262*
	(0.134)	(0.165)	(0.115)	(0.188)	(0.123)	(0.136)
Log (square miles)	-0.009	-0.004	0.000	-0.009	-0.006	-0.005
	(0.007)	(0.009)	(0.006)	(0.007)	(0.004)	(0.004)
Year fixed effects	yes	yes	yes	yes	yes	yes
MSA fixed effects	yes	yes	yes	yes	yes	yes
Observations	288	288	288	288	288	288
Number of metropolitan areas	72	72	72	72	72	72
R-squared	0.97	0.96	0.96	0.90	0.88	0.90

Source: Author's calculations based on U.S. Census data.

CGI = centile gap index; MSA = metropolitan statistical area.

*Significant at the 10 percent level; **significant at the 5 percent level.

a. Analysis is unweighted. Standard errors clustered on metropolitan area are in parentheses. Growth rates are defined by metropolitan area population growth rate 1970–2000. See notes in table 2 and text for variable descriptions.

b. Bottom third of growth.

c. Top third of growth.

· *New Housing Construction*

The model predicts that rising segregation is accompanied by higher than expected levels of new housing construction and retrofitting in economically declining cities. Because of the durable nature of housing, the housing supply does not adjust immediately to changing preferences. In distressed metropolitan areas, rising segregation is observed if the market pressure for segregation is sufficient to induce the construction of new housing or the retrofitting of old housing. Economically vibrant cities with binding supply constraints are likely to respond to inequality shocks by retrofitting existing housing. In growing cities, population growth induces housing construction regardless of whether inequality is rising or falling.

To test the model's prediction, a fixed effects analysis investigates the relationship between the date of housing construction and economic segregation across different types of metropolitan areas.[33] The dependent variable is the new construction relative to the previously existing housing stock—that is, housing units built in the previous ten years divided by housing units built ten or more years ago. I control for the previous ten-year population growth rate and its square, as well as metropolitan area fixed effects and year effects. The key independent variable of interest is the CGI interacted with categories of metropolitan area predicted employment growth (a proxy for economic growth). The theory predicts that, after the model has controlled for flexibly for population growth, segregation should be positively correlated with new housing construction in economically stagnating areas but not in economically vibrant areas.

The empirical evidence presented in table 8 is consistent with the hypothesis. Slow-growth metropolitan areas show a significant positive relationship between segregation and new construction. A one standard deviation increase in the CGI is associated with an extra 5 percentage points in new construction in an economically distressed metropolitan area. As expected, rapidly growing metropolitan areas show no significant positive relationship between segregation and housing construction. Indeed, the correlation is weakly negative. The difference in coefficients across economic growth categories is statistically significant. In sum, slowly growing metropolitan areas have a positive association between segregation and excessive housing construction, while rapidly growing areas do not.

One concern with the above analysis is that an unobserved third factor might be influencing the housing market such that both segregation and construction

---

33. Retrofitting cannot be inferred from the census data unless it changes the reported date of construction of the dwelling.

Table 8. New Construction and Segregation[a]

Dependent variable: New construction (previous ten years) relative to old construction

Variable	By predicted employment growth category		By population growth category	
	OLS	2SLS	OLS	2SLS
CGI	1.192**		1.209**	
	(0.288)		(0.270)	
CGI × intermediate growth	−0.732		−0.570	
	(0.473)		(0.551)	
CGI × rapid growth	−1.943**		−1.909**	
	(0.629)		(0.545)	
CGI (predicted)		1.623**		1.882**
		(0.411)		(0.374)
CGI (predicted) × intermediate growth		−0.805		−0.991*
		(0.599)		(0.590)
CGI (predicted) × rapid growth		−3.479**		−2.779**
		(0.776)		(0.825)
Previous ten-year population growth rate	0.555**	0.573**	0.551**	0.574**
	(0.084)	(0.083)	(0.080)	(0.080)
Previous ten-year population growth rate squared	−0.041	−0.079	−0.044	−0.076
	(0.125)	(0.124)	(0.120)	(0.118)
Year fixed effects	yes	yes	yes	yes
MSA fixed effects	yes	yes	yes	yes
Observations	864	864	864	864
Number of metropolitan areas	216	216	216	216
R-squared	0.88	—	0.88	—

Source: Author's calculations based on U.S. Census data.

CGI = centile growth index; MSA = metropolitan statistical area; OLS = ordinary least squares model; 2SLS = two-stage least squares model.

*Significant at the 10 percent level; **significant at the 5 percent level.

a. Analysis is unweighted. Standard errors clustered on metropolitan area are in parentheses. Intermediate growth is a dummy indicating the metropolitan area is in the middle third of thirty-year population growth rates; rapid growth is a dummy indicating the metropolitan area is in the top third of thirty-year predicted employment growth or population growth rates. In the two-stage least squares model, the CGI is predicted using the following variables: log of 90-50 family income ratio, log of 50-10 family income ratio, predicted employment, predicted demand for less-skilled men, predicted central-city employment, percentage black, percentage Hispanic, percentage foreign-born, log mean family income, percentage high school, percentage college, percentage under age 18, and fraction under age 65, all interacted with the growth category dummy variables.

rise in some cities. Therefore a two-stage least squares analysis is considered. In the first stage, segregation is predicted by a number of demand-side factors including inequality, industrial composition, and other metropolitan area characteristics. In the second stage, the predicted level of segregation is interacted with categories of economic growth. The results are quite similar; predicted market pressure for segregation is positively correlated with unexpectedly high levels of new construction in distressed metropolitan areas but not in economically healthy areas. Metropolitan areas with almost no economic growth appear to construct new housing in response to market pressure for segregation.

The analysis is repeated using categories of population growth rather than predicted employment growth. Results are qualitatively similar. Metropolitan areas with slow population growth and competitive pressure for segregation have higher than expected rates of new construction. The small differences between the categorizations based on predicted employment versus population stem in part from supply-constrained, economically healthy metropolitan areas. Areas with severe supply constraints are likely to respond to market pressure by retrofitting existing housing rather than constructing new housing. As expected, segregation and new construction are particularly correlated in economically distressed areas.

The relationship between new construction and segregation in distressed cities suggests that resorting of income groups across neighborhoods may require adjustments to the housing stock. Americans are highly mobile, but the neighborhoods in which different income groups reside are somewhat determined by the housing stock. In metropolitan areas with population growth too meager to induce housing construction, a sufficient level of market pressure for income resorting may itself drive new housing.

Persistence of Segregation by Income

The model suggests that the housing stock of a metropolitan area tends to reflect the underlying demand for segregation at the time it was built. Thus market forces that generate economic segregation, such as inequality, have persistent effects on segregation levels even after the forces themselves have disappeared. This is particularly true in slowly growing cities; the model suggests that levels of segregation are more persistent if the housing stock is older.

Segregation appears to be quite persistent in the sample. The raw correlation between the CGI in 1970 and 2000 is 0.69 across metropolitan areas. The cross-sectional regressions in the first two columns of table 9 show a sizable and statistically significant effect of the 1970 segregation level on 2000 segregation levels. The 1970 income segregation level can explain about half of the variation in segregation even after controlling for 2000 inequality and a large number of other factors likely to affect 2000 segregation levels.

The third and fourth columns of table 9 test the hypothesis that the persistence of segregation is related to the durability of housing. In a cross-section of metropolitan areas in 2000, a variable indicating the fraction of homes built before 1970 is included and interacted with the 1970 segregation index. As expected, the predictive power of the 1970 segregation level rises with a higher fraction of homes built before 1970. In metropolitan areas with a large fraction

Table 9. Persistence of Segregation[a]

Dependent variable: 2000 CGI

Variable	I	II	III	IV
1970 CGI	0.668**	0.449**	0.072	0.168
	(0.047)	(0.054)	(0.183)	(0.210)
Fraction of housing units built before 1970			−0.106**	0.420
			(0.042)	(1.570)
1970 CGI × fraction of units built before 1970			1.374**	0.625
			(0.370)	(0.465)
2000 log (80-20 family income ratio)		0.079**		0.058
		(0.021)		(0.088)
2000 log (80-20 family income ratio) × fraction built before 1970				0.011
				(0.174)
Other 2000 metropolitan area characteristics	no	yes	no	yes
Other 2000 metropolitan area characteristics × fraction built before 1970	no	no	no	yes
Observations	216	216	216	216
Number of metropolitan areas	216	216	216	216
R-squared	0.49	0.53	0.82	0.87

Source: Author's calculations using U.S. Census data.

CGI = centile growth index.

*Significant at the 10 percent level; **significant at the 5 percent level.

a. Analysis is unweighted. Standard errors clustered on metropolitan area are in parentheses. Control variables include all variables in table 6, column I for 2000.

of their housing built since 1970, the 1970 segregation level is less correlated with the 2000 segregation level. When all control variables and interactions are included, the coefficient on the interaction term is statistically significant only at the 20 percent level, but the pattern of coefficients is similar.

The evidence is largely consistent with a bricks-and-mortar view of segregation in metropolitan areas. That is, segregation (or integration) persists in part because the housing stock reflects consumer preferences at the time it is built. It is costly to change the housing stock once the infrastructure of a metropolitan area has been developed, inducing hysteresis in the residential patterns of income groups. When residential patterns do change in an older city, it is because there are large shocks to inequality and other forces creating market pressure for resorting of income groups. Extreme market pressure is sufficient to induce retrofitting or to induce new construction in areas without population growth. Changes to the housing stock enable the desired resorting of income groups across neighborhoods to take place.

Racial Segregation and Income Segregation

A discussion of residential segregation in metropolitan areas is incomplete without mention of racial segregation. Racial segregation has been declining since its peak in 1970.[34] The paper's main results are qualitatively unaffected by controlling for racial segregation in the analysis (results not shown).

Although the model does not explicitly consider racial segregation, the framework may have some relevance for sorting by race. In the context of the model, market pressure for racial segregation could be viewed as stemming from racial differences in the willingness to pay for various neighborhood attributes, which could include the neighborhood's racial composition. The housing market in rapidly growing metropolitan areas may be responsive to changing preferences with regard to racial segregation.

The three metropolitan area population growth categories had similar levels of racial segregation in 1970, as measured by the exposure of blacks to nonblacks.[35] By 2000, however, rapid-growth metropolitan areas had witnessed much larger drops in racial segregation, as shown in table 5. Furthermore, racial and economic segregation are positively correlated in slowly growing metropolitan areas, but not in rapidly growing areas (analysis not shown). This is consistent with the notion that some metropolitan areas may be moving more quickly than others to a new equilibrium—one in which racial segregation is replaced by economic segregation. The relationship between income and race is complicated and a full analysis is beyond this paper's scope.

Conclusion

Divergence in the valuation of neighborhood attributes across income groups leads to competitive pressure for segregation. Although individuals are highly mobile, the housing stock is expensive to change once it is built. It may take years for residential markets to fully respond to changes in demand for segregation. Observed segregation depends both on the underlying pressure for segregation and the adjustment costs associated with changing the housing stock. Rapidly growing metropolitan areas have low adjustment costs and accommodate changing preferences easily, but slowly growing metropolitan areas witness rising segregation only if market pressure is sufficient to induce retrofitting or new construction.

34. Cutler, Glaeser, and Vigdor (1999).
35. The exposure index used here adjusts for relative group size. See Cutler, Glaeser, and Vigdor (1999) for details.

The empirical findings are generally consistent with the model. First, higher levels of income inequality are associated with higher levels of residential segregation by income. Second, inequality at the top of the distribution (though not the bottom of the distribution) has a bigger effect on segregation in rapidly growing areas than in slowly growing areas. Third, among slowly growing metropolitan areas, large increases in segregation are coupled with higher than expected housing construction. This is not the case in rapidly growing areas. Finally, segregation levels are persistent. The 1970 level of segregation affects current segregation even after one has controlled for contemporaneous factors likely to affect segregation. The persistence is more pronounced in cities with older housing stocks.

The bricks-and-mortar framework explains the U-shaped relationship between a metropolitan area's population growth and its growth in income segregation. In cities facing industrial decline, the market pressure for income segregation rose between 1970 and 2000 because of growth in inequality and falling labor-market demand for less-skilled men. Despite the fact that existing housing was cheap, middle-class and rich residents were willing to pay to construct new housing in good suburban neighborhoods. Thus economically distressed metropolitan areas witnessed rising segregation and higher than expected new housing construction.

Economically vibrant, supply-constrained superstar cities also witnessed growth in segregation. These areas experienced large increases in inequality.[36] New construction and population growth were muted by regulatory constraints in these areas, but segregation did rise, presumably through the retrofitting of existing housing.

Rapidly growing metropolitan areas as a group did not face the same growth in inequality as other areas. Indeed, a number of booming areas experienced declines in the 50-10 family income ratio over the time period, and these areas also tended to experience declines in segregation. On the other hand, some rapidly growing cities did experience growth in inequality. These boom towns had cheap adjustment costs—the housing market was able to adapt quickly to changing consumer preferences. In rapidly growing areas, the isolation of the rich is very responsive to inequality at the top of the distribution. Thus a subset of rapidly growing areas with moderate to large increases in inequality had substantial growth in segregation.

The work presented here has implications for redistributive policy. Family income inequality generates residential segregation by income within American

36. Discussed in Gyourko, Mayer, and Sinai (2006).

metropolitan areas. To the extent that income sorting adversely affects the outcomes of those families at the bottom of the economic ladder, it follows that relative income matters to absolute outcomes. Furthermore the results suggest that a short period of high inequality could affect the shape of American metropolitan areas in the long run. Neighborhoods are built to reflect contemporary preferences for residential sorting by income. The housing stock built during high-inequality periods will tend to reflect market pressures for segregation. Because housing is durable, neighborhoods with low-amenity (or high-amenity) housing will continue to attract low-income (or high-income) families unless market forces are sufficient to drive retrofitting or new housing construction. Thus the legacy of income inequality could persist into the next generation even if inequality itself fades.

APPENDIX A

Income Segregation Measures

The centile gap index (CGI) estimates how far the average family income within a tract deviates in percentile terms from the median tract family income, compared to how far it would deviate under perfect integration.[37]

As noted in the text, the formula for CGI is:

$$CGI_m = \left(0.25 - \left(1/J_m\right)\sum_j \left|P_j - P_{medtj}\right|\right)/0.25,$$

where

CGI_m : centile gap index in metropolitan area m,
J_m : number of families in metropolitan area m,
P_j : estimated percentile in the metropolitan area m income distribution of family j,
and P_{medtj} : estimated income percentile of median family in the tract of family j.

That is, the term $\left|P_j - P_{medtj}\right|$ represents the estimated income percentile distance of a given family from the median family in its tract. Note that although this paper refers to income percentiles for clarity, it does not divide families

---

37. See Watson (2006) for details and comparisons to measures of income sorting used elsewhere in the literature.

into 100 discrete groups. Rather, the ranking is continuous on a scale from 0 to 1. In principle, the CGI goes from 0 to 1, with 1 meaning perfect segregation. In practice, perfect segregation could never be observed with a finite number of income bins.

The formula for an exposure index of quintile x to quintile y in metropolitan area m is

$$\text{Exposure}_{xym} = \sum_t \left(X_t / X_m \right) * \left(Y_t / J_t \right),$$

where

X_t : number of quintile X families in tract t,
X_m : number of quintile X families in metro area m,
Y_t : number of quintile Y families in tract t,
and J_t : number of families in tract t.

The exposure of quintile x to quintile y can be interpreted as the average fraction of quintile y families in the typical quintile x family's census tract.[38]

In the present analysis, no adjustment is necessary for group size since all family income quintiles are the same size. Exposure indexes were developed to study segregation between discrete racial groups and are not ideal for analyzing segregation along a continuous dimension such as income. Nevertheless, they are useful as a supplement to overall income segregation measure.

Note that none of the income segregation measures used here are explicitly spatial. That is, this paper does not use geographic information about proximity of neighborhoods to one another.

APPENDIX B

Data and Other Variables

Definitions of terms and measures used in this paper are listed below.

Data Description

Tract-level census data for 1980, 1990, and 2000 are taken from Census CDs. For 1970 they are taken from the Urban Institute Underclass Database. This paper also uses county-level information from the Census CDs and City

38. See also Cutler, Glaeser, and Vigdor (1999).

and County Data Books. The IPUMS data are used to estimate national trends in industrial mix and job centralization. The income data for families in the tract-level data sets is the number of families in different income bins in the year previous to the census year. There are fifteen income bins in the 1970 data, seventeen in the 1980 data, twenty-five in the 1990 data, and sixteen in the 2000 data.

Gainesville, Florida, is excluded from the analysis due to missing data. There are 216 metropolitan areas in the analysis.

Metropolitan Area Definitions

The boundaries of metropolitan areas change over time and a researcher must decide how to deal with this fact in the analysis. One values consistency, but at the same time wants to capture genuine changes in the area of the residential market. This paper pursues an intermediate approach, using the consolidated metropolitan areas defined by the Census Bureau as of 2003, including all of the counties that were tracted in a particular year. Therefore, the boundaries of about half of the metropolitan areas in the sample change over time. The analysis excludes metropolitan areas that had no tracted counties in 1970. For New England, the county-based metropolitan area definitions developed by the Census (New England County Metropolitan Areas) are used, rather than the standard town-based definitions. Metropolitan areas outside of New England are based on counties or county-equivalents as usual.

Families versus Households

Data for families are used because they are available for all four Census years. Families, which are households in which at least two residents are related by blood or marriage, make up a large fraction (ranging from 68 percent in 2000 to 75 percent in 1980) of households. In the 1980–2000 period, families had higher segregation levels than all households. Comparing the baseline regression relating family segregation and family income inequality for 1980–2000 to the analogous model using households, the main results are very similar and highly significant.

Industrial Mix Variables

Ten initial metropolitan area industry shares are interacted with national industry changes over time to predict the level of total employment relative to 1970 total employment, the level of employment of less-skilled men relative to 1970 total employment, and the fraction of metropolitan employment in the central city. Less-skilled workers are defined as those with a high-school diploma or less education. The national trends for centralization and skill level are computed using IPUMS data on eighteen- to sixty-five-year olds in metropolitan areas who worked at least fifteen hours in the previous week. Predicted variables are used rather than direct measures of employment growth, demand for less-skilled men, and job centralization because these characteristics may be endogenous to segregation. Therefore the industrial mix variables in some sense undercontrol because they do not capture the effect of idiosyncratic changes in industrial composition.

The formula for Predicted Employment is

$$PredEmp_{mt} = \sum_i \left(Emp_{im70}/Emp_{m70}\right) * \left(NatEmp_{it}/NatEmp_{i70}\right),$$

where

$PredEmp_{mt}$: predicted employment level in metropolitan area m at time t,
Emp_{im70} : employment in metropolitan area m in 1970 in industry i (from aggregated county-level data),
Emp_{m70} : total employment in metropolitan area m in 1970 (from aggregated county-level data),
$NatEmp_{it}$: total employment in all metropolitan areas in industry i at time t (from aggregated county-level data),
and $NatEmp_{i70}$: total employment in all metropolitan areas in industry i in 1970 (from aggregated county-level data).

It is clear from the formula that all metropolitan areas have a predicted employment of 1 in 1970.

The formula for Predicted Employment of less-skilled men is:

$$PredEmpLSM_{mt} = \sum_i \left(Emp_{im70}/Emp_{m70}\right) * \left(Nat2LSM_{it}/Nat2Emp_{it}\right)$$
$$* \left(NatEmp_{it}/NatEmp_{i70}\right),$$

where

$PredEmpLSM_{mt}$: predicted employment of less-skilled men in metropolitan area m at time t,
$Nat2LSM_{it}$: employment of less-skilled men in all metropolitan areas at time t in industry i (from the PUMS),
$Nat2Emp_{it}$: total employment of less-skilled men in all metropolitan areas at time t (from the PUMS), and other variables are as above.

The variable is a prediction of employment of less-skilled men in year t relative to total metropolitan area employment in 1970.

The formula for Predicted Job Centralization is

$$PredCent_{mt} = \sum_i (PredFrac_{imt}) * (Nat2CC_{it} / Nat2Emp_{it}),$$

where

$PredCent_{mt}$: predicted fraction of employment in the central city,

$Nat2CC_{it}$: employment in industry i at time t in all central cities (from the PUMS),

$Nat2Emp_{it}$: employment in industry i at time t in all metropolitan areas (from the PUMS),

and $PredFrac_{imt}$: predicted fraction of employment in industry i in metropolitan area m at time t and is defined by:

$$PredFrac_{imt} = Emp_{im70} * (Nat2Emp_{it} / Nat2Emp_{i70})$$
$$/ \sum_i [Emp_{im70} * (Nat2Emp_{it} / Nat2Emp_{i70})].$$

In the formula, Emp_{im70} is the employment in industry i in metropolitan area m in 1970 (from aggregated county-level data), $Nat2Emp_{i70}$ is the employment in industry i in 1970 in all metropolitan areas (from the IPUMS), and other variables are defined as above.

Racial Segregation Measures

The measure of racial segregation used in the paper is a person-based measure (rather than family-based), similar to that used by Cutler, Glaeser, and Vigdor (1999). It is an exposure (isolation) index of black residents to other black residents, adjusted for the exposure that would be expected given the number of black residents and white residents in the metropolitan area.[39] Note, however, that they consider isolation of black residents from all other residents while this paper considers the isolation of black residents from white residents.

Hispanic families may be of any race. Some of the rise in exposure of black residents to white residents may be due to an increase in exposure to white Hispanic residents.

---

39. For details, see Cutler, Glaeser, and Vigdor (1999, p. 459).

Measurement of Metropolitan Area Income Inequality

The construction of metropolitan area income inequality measures is based on a methodology described and tested in Jargowsky (1995). In particular, metropolitan area income is assumed to be distributed with a linear distribution below the mean and a Pareto distribution above the mean.[40]

Central City and Suburbs

Central cities are those places identified by the U.S. Census Bureau as such in 2003 based on metropolitan area residential and commuting patterns, and represent a consistent geographic area over time. There may be more than one central city in a metropolitan area; these are combined for the purpose of the analysis. The suburbs include all remaining tracted portions of the metropolitan area in a given year. Suburbs are also combined for the purpose of the analysis. Census tracts in the 1980–2000 period are matched to places, which in turn are matched to central cities. For cases in which a census tract includes both central city and suburban places, it is considered part of the central city if at least half of the tract area is within the central city. In 1970 neither central cities nor places are identified in the data.

New Construction

New construction is defined as newly constructed housing relative to previously existing housing. The variable in any given year is the number of housing units built in the past ten years divided by the number of housing units built more than ten years ago.

40. See Watson (2006) for more details.

Comments

Gerald Carlino: It is well documented that income inequality has increased in the United States over the past three decades. For example, the variance of the log household income distribution increased nearly 25 percent between 1970 and 2000.[1] Affluent and poor households also have become more geographically segregated in the United States over the past three decades.[2] More importantly, there is evidence that concentration by income has increased in neighborhoods, leading to greater income segregation within metropolitan areas.[3] Tara Watson adds the interesting observation that the interaction between increased income inequality and a city's population growth determines that city's income segregation level. Watson hypothesizes that increasing income inequality creates a demand for income segregation in local housing markets. In her view, income sorting is more easily accomplished in fast-growing cities than in slow-growing ones because the housing stock adjusts more easily in fast-growing cities than in slow-growing cities. That is, observed segregation in cities depends both on the demand for segregation and the adjustment cost associated with changing a city's housing stock. It may take many years for local housing markets to fully adjust to changes in housing demand, especially in distressed cities.

Watson's paper is one of a few recent studies that have stressed the importance of incorporating the adjustment cost associated with the supply of local housing markets. As Glaeser, Gyourko, and Saks have noted, it is "impossible to understand many aspects of urban dynamics without understanding housing supply."[4] For example, a recent study looked at declining U.S. cities and found evidence that urban decline is mediated by a durable housing stock.[5] Gyourko,

1. Wheeler and La Jeunesse (2006).
2. Jargowsky (1996a and 1996b).
3. Massey and Fischer (2003).
4. Glaeser, Gyourko, and Saks (2005).
5. Glaeser and Gyourko (2005).

Mayer, and Sinai define "superstar" locations (which include high-amenity neighborhoods within a metropolitan area) as places that are in fixed or inelastic supply.[6] In the presence of increasing demand, these locations exhibit rising housing prices but little population growth, no new construction, and increased income segregation. While it is possible to quibble with Watson's study on both methodological and empirical grounds, her findings generally support her view that the durability of an area's housing stock is an important determinant of how quickly an area's housing stock adjusts to meet changing demand for neighborhood segregation.

Although Watson mentions the social problems associated with neighborhood segregation, this is not her study's focus, and she does not offer any policy recommendations. Thus I would like to devote some space to these issues. As Watson points out, segregation is problematic since it dramatically limits the accessibility of the city's poorer residents to many public goods and services that ideally should be available to all city residents—good schools, clean and safe streets, cultural and recreational facilities, positive role models, and access to jobs. While neighborhood sorting based on a household's preference for local public goods and tax packages may be efficient, is it equitable? Geographic sorting by income has led to rich households' living in homogeneous suburban neighborhoods and poor families living in central cities. Fiscal or exclusionary zoning has been an important policy instrument used by municipal governments to exclude poor households from suburban neighborhoods. While fiscal zoning is justified on efficiency grounds, it nonetheless denies poor households access to many of the metropolitan area's best neighborhoods and to suburban jobs, and it runs contrary to the egalitarian principles of the United States.

If Watson is correct in her belief that an increase in neighborhood segregation largely occurs with a corresponding change in local housing stock, that view suggests ways in which local governments could reduce segregation. One way is to encourage municipalities to use inclusionary zoning policies that attempt to reduce segregation by requiring that a mix of affluent and less-affluent households be represented in new housing development. Typically, inclusionary zoning programs are the province of local governments and require local developers to build affordable new homes for low-income families in exchange for the right to build a given number of market-rate homes. If Watson is correct, inclusionary zoning policy may be more effective in combating income segregation in the nation's fast-growing metropolitan areas. Currently, only a little more than 200 communities have provisions for

6. Gyourko, Mayer, and Sinai (2006).

inclusionary zoning, a small number given the roughly 40,000 municipalities and townships in the United States. Perhaps state governments could do more to ensure that local municipalities, especially in affluent neighborhoods, make housing available for low- and moderate-income households.

Another promising alternative that has been proposed is *metropolitan federation.* Under metropolitan federation, it would be more difficult for a region's rich households to escape redistribution of income toward the region's lower-income households by sorting into neighborhoods based on income. Lower-income neighborhoods would have more resources to devote to schooling, crime prevention, and so on. Improving the prospects for social mobility and improved economic advancement would mean that future residents of these low-income neighborhoods ultimately might become more productive members of society and improve the economic and social prospects of all residents of our metropolitan areas. In sum, Watson's paper is interesting and makes us think about these important issues.

Ingrid Gould Ellen: This very interesting paper, which examines an important topic, is motivated by two parallel phenomena—the rise in income inequality and the rise in economic segregation in many metropolitan areas around the United States since 1970. The author cleverly explores whether these two phenomena are related, specifically whether the increase in income inequality has led to greater segregation. The mechanism posited is that heightened inequality leads to a greater divergence in the willingness to pay of low- and high-income households for neighborhood amenities, and therefore leads to a desired resorting of households across neighborhoods. This resorting cannot occur instantaneously, however, since the housing stock is durable. It is this emphasis on the friction in the adjustment process, and how it might vary across metropolitan areas, which is the paper's most important contribution.

The theory has intuitive appeal, and the paper's empirical work is done carefully. The unusual attention given to the various indexes is commendable. My comments center on some alternative explanations that might be explored productively in future work.

First, to the extent that neighborhood effects exist, they suggest the possibility of reverse causality—that increases in economic segregation lead to widening income disparities, since the poor will be disadvantaged by living in lower-income neighborhoods, and the wealthy will benefit from living in higher-income areas. The neighborhood effects hypothesis (if one thinks neighborhood effects are more paramount in stagnating cities) might also help to explain the paper's finding that widening income inequality at the low end is more correlated with economic segregation in slow-growth metropolitan areas than in fast-growth areas.

Second, the paper focuses on a single explanation for rising economic segregation—sorting on tastes for neighborhood amenities. Yet drawing on the racial segregation literature, we can identify several other possibilities with different normative implications. In particular, income segregation may result not only from varying preferences for neighborhood amenities or characteristics but also from preferences for the characteristics of neighbors. Households may choose neighborhoods based on the income levels of the residents, or alternatively, households may sort on tastes for racial composition. In this latter case, economic segregation may result, but only because whites, on average, have higher incomes than blacks and Hispanics. Finally, while the author notes that regulatory barriers to new construction can slow the pace of increases in segregation, regulatory barriers can also help to facilitate an increase in segregation, by blocking the construction of lower-quality housing in high-amenity neighborhoods.

The relative importance of these different causes has been a central debate in the work on racial segregation, and research suggests that multiple causes are at play. It seems likely that multiple causes contribute here as well, though there has been little corresponding examination. Thus it would be helpful to see this paper's model explicitly distinguished from the kind of tipping models that would be predicted by the assumption that segregation is driven by sorting on neighbor characteristics.

These alternative causes also suggest some alternative explanations for the paper's results. For example, rising crime rates may make wealthy households particularly keen on isolating themselves from the poor, and crime rates have also been shown to be associated with income inequality. Or, perhaps in metropolitan areas where income inequality has been rising, the composition of low-income households might have changed in ways that make them less desirable neighbors in the eyes of higher-income households. This would also naturally have implications for where we would expect to see a greater link between inequality and segregation—given the correlation between immigration and population growth, it might predict that in higher-growth areas, inequality and segregation would be more tightly linked. Another possibility is that regulatory barriers have grown more rapidly in areas where income inequality is rising, because homeowners living in such areas have pushed for greater regulation.

All this said, the paper's public goods sorting model has a lot of appeal. In future work, it would be nice to see the model extended to incorporate local government and governmental structure. For example, the logic of the paper's theory suggests that segregation should increase more rapidly in response to increases in income inequality in metropolitan areas where quality of neighborhoods is more divergent, which would presumably be true in metropolitan areas with greater numbers of school districts or jurisdictions. This would be fairly easy to test and would represent a worthwhile extension.

Finally, it is worth underscoring that the paper focuses on how rising inequality affects segregation. Yet not all metropolitan areas experienced increases in inequality during this period. During the 1990s, the average area experienced a decline in the 50-10 ratio, and the process of residential adjustment to reductions in inequality may be quite distinct. Specifically, exclusionary barriers may make reductions in segregation far more difficult to achieve than increases. Thus friction—of a similar sort to that emphasized in this paper—may be more pronounced in the case of reductions in inequality.

References

Bjorvatn, Kjetil, and Alexander Wright Cappelen. 2003. "Inequality, Segregation, and Redistribution." *Journal of Public Economics* 87 (7–8): 1657–79.

Case, Ann C., and Lawrence F. Katz. 1991. "The Company You Keep: The Effects of Family and Neighborhood on Disadvantaged Youths." Working Paper 3705. Cambridge, Mass.: National Bureau of Economic Research.

Cutler, David M., and Edward L. Glaeser. 1997. "Are Ghettos Good or Bad?" *Quarterly Journal of Economics* 112 (3): 827–72.

Cutler, David M., Edward L. Glaeser, and Jacob L. Vigdor. 1999. "The Rise and Decline of the American Ghetto." *Journal of Political Economy* 107 (3): 455–506.

Ellickson, Bryan. 1971. "Jurisdictional Fragmentation and Residential Choice." *American Economic Review* 61 (2): 334–39.

Epple, Dennis, and Glenn J. Platt. 1998. "Equilibrium and Local Redistribution in an Urban Economy When Households Differ in Both Preferences and Incomes." *Journal of Urban Economics* 43 (1): 23–51.

Glaeser, Edward L., and Joseph Gyourko. 2005. "Urban Decline and Durable Housing." *Journal of Political Economy* 113 (2): 345–75.

Glaeser, Edward L., Joseph Gyourko, and Raven E. Saks. 2005. "Urban Growth and Housing Supply." Working Paper 11097. Cambridge, Mass.: National Bureau of Economic Research.

Glaeser, Edward L., Matthew E. Kahn, and Jordan Rappaport. 2000. "Why Do the Poor Live in Cities?" Working Paper 7636. Cambridge, Mass.: National Bureau of Economic Research.

Gyourko, Joseph, Christopher Mayer, and Todd Sinai. 2006. "Superstar Cities." Working Paper 528. Samuel Zell and Robert Lurie Real Estate Center at Wharton.

Hoxby, Caroline. 2000. "Peer Effects in the Classroom: Learning From Gender and Race Variation." Working Paper 7867. Cambridge, Mass.: National Bureau of Economic Research.

Jargowsky, Paul A. 1995. "Take the Money and Run: Economic Segregation in U.S. Metropolitan Areas." Discussion Paper 1056–95. Institute for Research on Poverty, University of Wisconsin-Madison.

———. 1996a. "Take the Money and Run: Economic Segregation in U.S. Metropolitan Areas." *American Sociological Review* 61: 984–98.

———. 1996b. "Beyond the Street Corner: The Hidden Diversity of High Poverty Neighborhoods." *Urban Geography* 17 (7): 579–603.

Kling, Jeffrey R., Jeffrey B. Liebman, and Lawrence F. Katz. 2007 (forthcoming). "Experimental Analysis of Neighborhood Effects." *Econometrica*.

Massey, Douglas S., and Marry J. Fischer. 2003. "The Geography of Inequality in the United States, 1950–2000." In *Brookings-Wharton Papers on Urban Affairs,* edited by William G. Gale and Janet Rothenberg Pack, pp. 1–40. Brookings.

Mayer, Susan. 2001. "How Growth in Income Inequality Increased Economic Segregation." Working Paper 230. Chicago: Joint Center for Poverty Research.

Oreopoulos, Philip. 2003. "The Long-Run Consequences of Growing Up in a Poor Neighborhood." *Quarterly Journal of Economics* 118 (4): 1533–75.

Ruggles, Steven, and others. 2004. *Integrated Public Use Microdata Series, ver. 3.* Minneapolis, Minn.: Population Center (www.ipums.org).

Tiebout, Charles M. 1956. "A Pure Theory of Local Expenditures." *Journal of Political Economy* 64 (5): 416–24.

Watson, Tara. 2006. "Measuring Income Segregation." Unpublished manuscript.

Wheeler, Christopher H., and Elizabeth A. La Jeunesse. 2006. "Neighborhood Income Inequality." Working Paper 2006-039A. Federal Reserve Bank of St. Louis (June).

Wilson, William J. 1987. *The Truly Disadvantaged: The Inner City, the Underclass, and Public Policy.* University of Chicago Press.

KENNETH A. SMALL
University of California, Irvine

CLIFFORD WINSTON
Brookings Institution

JIA YAN
Hong Kong Polytechnic University

Differentiated Road Pricing, Express Lanes, and Carpools: Exploiting Heterogeneous Preferences in Policy Design

THE U.S. HIGHWAY SYSTEM, largely constructed with public funds from the federal road user tax, could be characterized as a public good if it were rarely congested. But like many public goods that are available at little or no charge, its quality has deteriorated with the intensity of use. Today, the nation's road system has turned into a "tragedy of the commons" as road users experience nearly 4 billion hours of annual delay.[1] Of course, even an efficient road system would force motorists to incur some delays, but the current level is regarded by most observers as excessive.

Historically, the public has had a *status quo* bias against economists' recommendations to use the price mechanism to reduce congestion.[2] Policymakers therefore have pursued other approaches, such as allocating reserved lanes to vehicles carrying two or more people. But recent evidence indicates that these *high-occupancy vehicle* (HOV) lanes sometimes carry fewer people than general-purpose lanes, attract many family members who would ride together anyhow, and shift some travelers from vanpools or buses to low-occupancy carpools.[3] As a result, HOV lanes are losing favor among state transportation departments.

---

1. Schrank and Lomax (2005).
2. Small, Winston, and Evans (1989); Mohring (1999). The papers in Santos (2004) provide recent discussions of road pricing.
3. Orski (2001); Poole and Balaker (2005).

A recent innovation is to fill the reserve capacity not used by HOVs with solo drivers willing to pay a toll. These so-called *high-occupancy toll* (HOT) lanes can be found in the Los Angeles, San Diego, Houston, and Minneapolis–St. Paul metropolitan areas, and they are currently under consideration in other cities including Denver, Seattle, San Francisco, and Washington.

HOT lanes appeal to a broad set of motorists who are sufficiently inconvenienced by congestion to pay a sizable toll to travel on less-congested lanes, either daily or as dictated by their schedules. Although the adoption of HOT lanes in some urban areas indicates that the public is no longer opposed to all forms of congestion pricing, HOT lanes are questionable on welfare grounds for two reasons. First, motorists continue to impose high congestion costs on each other because most of the highway is unpriced. Second, the express lanes are still underused because a big price differential exists between the two roadways.[4] Indeed, simulations show that HOT lanes sometimes lower welfare compared with keeping all lanes in general use, particularly if they are priced high enough to allow motorists to travel at approximately free-flow speeds—a condition that is achieved to promote the service advantages of the lanes among the public.

In short, HOV and HOT policies do not appear to have answered the long-standing call for efficient yet politically viable road pricing policies. In this paper we seek to identify such policies by analyzing the behavior of motorists traveling on California State Route 91 (SR91) in Orange County. These travelers have the option of traveling solo on the general lanes, paying a toll to use the HOT express lanes, or forming a carpool to use the express lanes at a discount. Because travelers are likely to vary in their preferences for speedy and reliable travel, we model the situation accounting for both observed and unobserved preference heterogeneity.[5] We find that users of SR91 have high average values of travel time and travel-time reliability, and that the distributions of these values exhibit considerable dispersion.

We show that by designing differentiated pricing schemes for general and express lanes that cater to such varying preferences, it is possible to capture some of the efficiency that HOV and HOT policies sacrifice while generating welfare disparities among road users that are not only smaller than more-

4. Small and Yan (2001).

5. Previous empirical studies that allow for heterogeneous preferences among motorists include Calfee, Winston, and Stempski (2001); Hensher (2001); Jiang and Morikawa (2004); Steimetz and Brownstone (2005); Hess, Bierlaire, and Polak (2005); Small, Winston, and Yan (2005a). Simulation studies incorporating heterogeneity to analyze pricing scenarios include Small and Yan (2001); Verhoef and Small (2004); De Palma and Lindsey (2004).

efficient pricing policies generate but small enough to be comparable to policies that have actually passed the test of political acceptability in a few urban areas.

Empirical Model of Travel Choices

California State Route 91 is a major limited-access expressway used heavily by long-distance commuters. A ten-mile stretch in Orange County includes four free lanes and two express lanes in each direction. Motorists who wish to use the express lanes must set up a financial account and carry an electronic transponder to pay a toll, which varies hourly according to a preset schedule. Carpools of three or more people could use the express lanes at a 50 percent discount at the time our surveys were conducted.[6] Unlike the regular lanes, the express lanes have no entrances or exits between their end points.

We assembled a data set from surveys of travelers on the corridor, describing the lane choices they actually make and choices they hypothetically would make in different circumstances. In an earlier paper using the same data, we modeled motorists' lane choice only.[7] Here we model three simultaneous decisions by motorists: 1) whether to acquire a transponder, which gives them the flexibility to use the express lanes whenever they desire; 2) whether to travel on the express or free lanes for the trip in question; and 3) how many people to travel with in their vehicle. We include transponder acquisition as a separate choice because it captures a legal requirement to use the express lanes. Whether a motorist decides to meet the requirement may depend on other characteristics than those explaining day-to-day travel choices, and may cause more persistence in travel behavior than would otherwise be the case. We include vehicle occupancy so that we can explore the effects of various policies that depend on it.

The three choices are assumed conditional on related choices including travel mode (car versus public transport), residential location, and time of day of travel. In our context, mode choice is unimportant because public transportation has a very small share of travelers on the corridor served by SR91. Residential location indeed may be important, but it is a longer-run response that introduces complexities that are difficult to capture in a tractable empirical model. We would like to model the choice of what time of day people travel

6. Starting in late May 2003, these carpools could travel for free except when traveling outbound on weekday afternoons (from 4:00 p.m. to 6:00 p.m.), at which time there is a 50 percent discount. Current information is available on the Orange County Transportation Authority's *91 Express Lanes* website (www.91expresslanes.com).

7. Small, Winston, and Yan (2005a).

but are unable to do so because we lack information on how congestion varies on roads that people use besides the SR91 study corridor. Later in this paper we describe some statistical tests that indicate that our results are not particularly sensitive to our assumption that travel occurs at a given time of day.

In the empirical analysis that follows, we combine data that describe motorists' actual decisions for their morning commute with data indicating hypothetical choices between the express and free lanes under varying travel conditions. This strategy permits us to extract information about the distribution of preferences that would otherwise be impossible to extricate from other random influences on behavior. The mechanism at work is that an individual who answered the hypothetical questions provides responses for up to eight different scenarios. Hence we can effectively infer that individual's preferences through his or her unique pattern of responses to trade-offs among cost, time, and reliability. We estimate common coefficients of the trade-offs that are shared among individuals and coefficients of the trade-offs that vary among individuals, enabling us to measure the key distributions of the value of time and reliability in our sample.

Formally, traveler n faces a choice whether to have a transponder (T) or not (N); whether to travel on a general (free) lane (G) or express lane (X); and whether to travel with one, two, or three people in the vehicle (where three means three or more). The three choice dimensions define $2 \times 2 \times 3 = 12$ alternatives, but only nine of them are available because a highway traveler must have a transponder to use the express lane, thereby eliminating combinations $NX1$, $NX2$, and $NX3$.

Following standard discrete-choice modeling, we specify the indirect utility of traveler n choosing an alternative j to be random:

$$(1) \qquad \mathbf{U}_{jn} = \mathbf{X}_{jn}\boldsymbol{\beta}_n + \varepsilon_{jn}.$$

In equation (1), $\mathbf{X}_{jn}$ is a vector of attributes associated with alternative j including the toll, travel time, and reliability that apply to the traveler's trip; $\boldsymbol{\beta}_n$ is a vector of parameters that captures the traveler's preferences for those attributes; and ε_{jn} is an error term capturing unobserved influences. We measure preference heterogeneity by allowing parameter vector $\boldsymbol{\beta}_n$ to vary across individuals according to both observed characteristics and random (that is, unobserved) influences:

$$(2) \qquad \boldsymbol{\beta}_n = \mathbf{W}_n\boldsymbol{\gamma} + \boldsymbol{\mu}_n.$$

In equation (2), $\mathbf{W}_n$ is a vector of explanatory variables relating to traveler n, while $\boldsymbol{\mu}_n$ is a vector of random variables; $\boldsymbol{\gamma}$ is a vector of parameters, to be estimated statistically, describing how preferences depend on observed characteristics. The random terms μ_n are assumed to be independent normal random variables, with variances to be estimated. Thus the term $\mathbf{W}_n\gamma$ describes observed heterogeneity and μ_n describes unobserved heterogeneity in preferences toward travel characteristics.

If ε_{jn} in equation (1) were independently distributed according to identical extreme-value distributions, then equations (1) and (2) would constitute a conventional mixed-logit model where each choice probability can be expressed as a standard multinomial logit choice probability (conditional on β_n), integrated over the distribution of μ_n (which determines β_n).[8] Our model is more complicated because we specify the structure of ε_{jn} to account for certain special features of the data. One is the decision structure inherent in our choice alternatives. Another, which we describe later, is that we merge our data from several sources.

As noted, the decision structure involves three choice dimensions. Thus it is unlikely that the alternative-specific preferences ε_{jn} for the nine permitted alternatives are independent of each other. Rather, a natural approach is to specify random preferences for groups of alternatives.[9] We let ε_{jn} include four distinct preferences: for a transponder (T), for the express lane (X), for a two-person carpool ($H2$), and for a three-person carpool ($H3$). Thus

$$(3) \qquad \varepsilon_{jn} = \Delta_j^T v_n^T + \Delta_j^X v_n^X + \Delta_j^{H2} v_n^{H2} + \Delta_j^{H3} v_n^{H3} + \eta_{jn},$$

where Δ_j^T denotes a dummy variable equal to one if alternative j is one of those characterized by a transponder, and so forth. The four variables v_n^k are independent normal random variables, each with mean zero and a standard deviation σ^k to be estimated. (For parsimony, we impose $\sigma^{H2} = \sigma^{H3} \equiv \sigma^{HOV}$.) The remaining random terms, η_{jn} in equation (3), are assumed to be independent random variables (one for each alternative) with identical extreme-value distributions, just like in a logit model.

Naturally, one can expect to estimate the distribution of only a few of the many behavioral parameters contained in a model like this. We choose two key parameters, which means there are two components of μ_n in equation (2) with nonzero variances. One (μ_n^{Time}) is part of the coefficient of travel time, while

---

8. Small and Winston (1999) and Train (2003) contain expositions of the logit and mixed-logit models. The (normalized) extreme-value distribution for a random variable ε is defined by the probability $\text{Prob}[\varepsilon \leq x] = \exp(e^{-x})$.

9. For a description, see Brownstone and Train (1999). An alternative approach would be to use a nested-logit specification. The approach here is more flexible, typically better behaved numerically, and easier to implement given that we are using mixed logit.

the other (μ_n^{Rel}) is part of the coefficient of (un)reliability. Their standard deviations, to be estimated, are denoted σ^{Time} and σ^{Rel}.

To summarize the model's stochastic part, we specify six independent normal random terms (vs and μs) with five distinct unknown standard deviations (σs) to be estimated.

We define the value of travel time (VOT) and value of reliability (VOR) for individual n as the ratios of marginal utilities of travel time and reliability, respectively, to the marginal utility of money cost. That is,

$$(4) \qquad\qquad VOT_n = \frac{\beta_n^{Time}}{\beta_n^{Cost}},$$

$$(5) \qquad\qquad VOR_n = \frac{\beta_n^{Rel}}{\beta_n^{Cost}},$$

where in equation (1)

β_n^{Time}: the coefficient of travel time,
β_n^{Rel}: the coefficient of travel time reliability,
β_n^{Cost}: the coefficient of toll.

These values depend on observables $\mathbf{W}_n$ and random components $\boldsymbol{\mu}_n$ through equation (2).

Data Set and Econometric Issues

We combine survey data from three samples of people traveling between 4:00 a.m. and 10:00 a.m. on the California State Route 91 corridor westbound who have the option of using the express lanes. We collected data over a ten-month period in 1999 and 2000. The first survey was a telephone questionnaire generating 435 observations pertaining to actual travel on a particular day, conducted by researchers at California Polytechnic State University at San Luis Obispo (CalPoly) with our participation.[10] Thus it consists of revealed preference (RP) data.

The second and third samples are from a two-stage mail survey collected by us through the Brookings Institution. The initial stage collected RP data from seventy-nine respondents on actual trips taken during a week of travel, while a follow-up stage presented to each respondent eight stated preference

---

10. Sullivan and others (2000).

(SP) scenarios.[11] In each SP scenario, the respondent was asked to choose between two otherwise identical routes with specified hypothetical tolls, travel times, and probabilities of delay.[12] The SP sample contains seventy-eight respondents who generated 610 observations, and fifty-four of these people also answered the RP questions.[13]

By constructing a sample that contains both RP and SP observations, we can overcome the main drawbacks of each type of data. The use of RP data is often hindered by strong correlations among travel cost, time, and reliability, whereas SP data raise concerns about whether the behavior exhibited in hypothetical situations applies to actual choices. By specifying some parameters to be identical and others different in the utility functions generating RP and SP choices, we can improve the precision in estimating common parameters (due to low correlations designed into the SP questions) while allowing for expected behavioral differences in other parameters.

Table 1 presents some statistics on socioeconomic variables and trip distance. The Brookings RP sample appears to represent well the population characteristics of the SR91 catchment area, tracking census information for the two relevant counties except for household income—which, naturally, is higher for our respondents because most of them are commuters.[14] We estimate the average wage rate to be $23 an hour.[15] The CalPoly sample has higher household incomes and shorter trip distances than the Brookings samples, evidently being drawn from a smaller and more affluent geographical area. These sampling differences should not affect our parameter estimates because our model includes income and trip distance as explanatory variables.

---

11. The Brookings RP sample actually contains information for all commuting trips made within the survey week, which could be treated as separate observations. However, 87 percent of the respondents made the same choice every day and nearly all of the others varied on only one day. So we simplify, with little information loss, by creating a binary response variable equal to one if the respondent chose the express lanes for half or more of the days reported. We tried variants of this response variable with virtually no changes in results.

12. An illustrative scenario is presented in the paper's appendix.

13. Detailed descriptions of the samples are presented in Small, Winston, and Yan (2005b).

14. Our sample's median annual income is $46,250, whereas the average incomes in the two counties where our respondents lived were $36,189 and $39,729 in 1995, as estimated by the Population Research Unit of the California Department of Finance.

15. Data from the U.S. Bureau of Labor Statistics for 2000 record the mean hourly wage rate by occupation for residents of Riverside and San Bernardino Counties. We combine the bureau's occupational categories into six groups that match our survey question about occupation, and assign to each person in our sample the average Bureau of Labor Statistics wage rate for that person's occupational group. We then add 10 percent to reflect the higher wages likely to be attracting these people to jobs that are relatively far away.

Table 1. Socioeconomic Variables and Trip Distance

Variable	Value or fraction of sample		
	CalPoly-RP	*Brookings-RP*	*Brookings-SP*
Age (years):			
< 30	0.11	0.12	0.10
30–50	0.62	0.62	0.64
Household income ($000/year):			
< $60, 000	0.38	0.83	0.83
> $60,000	0.62	0.17	0.17
Female dummy	0.32	0.37	0.37
Mean actual trip distance (miles)	34.2	44.8	42.6
Number of respondents	435	79	78
Number of observations	435	369	610

Source: Based on data from the Brookings and CalPoly surveys and authors' calculations.
RP = Revealed preference data.
SP = Stated preference data.

Table 2 presents the choice shares of the nine alternatives associated with each RP sample. We observe a difference among carpooling propensities between the CalPoly and Brookings samples, with many fewer carpools in the latter. To better understand the difference, the CalPoly sample is disaggregated into four subsamples representing different ways of finding respondents.[16] The random subsample was obtained by telephone interviews drawn randomly from lists of telephone exchanges in the relevant area. The other three CalPoly subsamples came ultimately from license plates observed on the highway and are therefore choice-based (some were purposely carpool-enriched). Even in the CalPoly random subsample, however, the combined carpool shares are considerably higher (24 percent) than in the Brookings RP sample (6 percent), despite both being obtained from random telephone calls. The CalPoly random shares are much closer to the observed peak-period carpool shares on the SR91 roadway,[17] so we conclude that the Brookings sample undersampled people who carpool—possibly because the telephone screening questions to determine eligibility for the survey were originally designed to only find solo drivers and subsequently modified. Thus we use the CalPoly

16. Sullivan and others (2000).
17. Unfortunately, these are not measured at all precisely. Sullivan and others (2000) report the share of vehicles in a two-hour afternoon peak (eastbound direction) in 1999 to be 20.2 percent HOV2 and 3.7 percent HOV3. This would imply a share of commuters choosing to carpool of somewhat more than 24 percent, although how much more depends on how many of the passengers in carpools are also commuters. Also, because we model a four-hour morning peak period in the westbound direction, the comparison is not precise.

Table 2. Choice Shares of CalPoly and Brookings RP Samples
Percent

Alternative[a]	CalPoly sample				Brookings RP sample
	Random	New plates	Repeat	UCI	
NG1	41	28	17	11	51
TG1	16	26	33	39	23
TX1	19	15	16	22	20
NG2	7	9	3	0	0
TG2	3	8	16	6	2.5
TX2	8	5	7	22	1
NG3	3	3	0	0	0
TG3	1	3	3	0	0
TX3	2	3	5	0	2.5
All carpool	24	31	34	28	6
No. of observations	201	191	58	18	79

Source: Based on data from the Brookings and CalPoly surveys and authors' calculations.
RP = Revealed preference data.
UCI = University of California, Irvine.
a. Transponder acquisition: N = no, T = yes. Lane: G = general (free) lane, X = express lane.
Car occupancy: 1 = solo, 2 = HOV2, 3 = HOV3+.

random subsample as our measure of the population choice shares, and correct for choice-based sampling in our estimates by applying carpool-share weights to the other subsamples.[18]

We recognize that SR91 has a higher share of carpoolers than is the case for most other highways in the United States. Later in this paper we perform sensitivity analysis on the share of carpoolers to explore how our analysis applies to other U.S. metropolitan areas.

Specification and Estimation

We posit that motorists' joint choices are influenced by their socioeconomic characteristics and the characteristics of their journey, including the total trip distance and the toll, travel time, and (un)reliability of travel time on the portion of the journey where a lane choice exists.

The express lane toll for a given trip is the published toll for the time of day the motorist reported passing the sign that indicates the toll level. It is discounted by 50 percent if the trip was in a carpool of three or more. (We asked respondents, even in the SP survey, to indicate their vehicle occupancy for actual trips.)

18. Manski and Lerman (1977).

Our ability to measure individuals' preferences critically depends on capturing the different conditions they face when traveling at different times of day. Therefore we sought to measure those conditions carefully to construct variables for the RP portion of the analysis. We measured the reliability of service encountered by a traveler, as well as the travel time itself, by taking field measurements at many different times on eleven different days, corresponding approximately to the travel periods covered by our surveys. The field measurements consist of travel times clocked by students attending the University of California, Irvine, who drove the road repeatedly. Thus we were able to measure the median travel time observed across the eleven days, at any given time of day, as well as the entire distribution of travel times across those days, again as a function of the time of day. For our travel-time variable, whose coefficient is β^{Time} in equation (4), we use the median value. For our measure of unreliability of travel time, denoted *Rel* in equation (5), we use the difference between the 80th and 50th percentiles of the distribution of travel times across days. This measure captures the behavioral notion that people are more concerned with unexpected late arrivals than early arrivals. The measure also is less closely correlated with median travel time than a symmetric measure of dispersion such as the variance.[19]

The variables describing the individual include age, sex, household size, per capita income, total trip distance, and trip purpose (that is, a dummy for work trip). We explored other variables describing arrival-time flexibility, occupation, education, and workplace size, but found that they have little explanatory power and that omitting them did not materially influence the other parameter estimates.

The variables used in the SP analysis are defined, with one exception, identically to those in the RP data set, although the travel descriptors, of course, are generated differently, being specified in the survey questions instead of measured in the field. The one exception is reliability. We did not think we could explain percentiles of a probability distribution to survey respondents, so in the SP scenarios we described reliability as the frequency of being delayed ten minutes or more. We convert the responses into probabilities for purposes of analysis. The reliability variable therefore has different units and meaning in the RP and SP scenarios, so distinct RP and SP coefficients for it are estimated. However, it is the RP coefficients that we use to describe resulting values of reliability and to simulate policy scenarios.

19. Small, Winston, and Yan (2005b) discuss the procedures used to estimate these measures and to validate their accuracy.

A number of specification issues arise when we combine the RP and SP data sets. The RP analysis is described by equations (1), (2), and (3), to which we append superscript *RP* to distinguish those observations. The SP analysis, however, is different because we asked each respondent to express only a choice between the express or regular lanes, and we asked for this choice in eight different scenarios (each with different hypothetical values of travel variables). Because the SP choice is binary, it is convenient in the case of SP respondents to replace equation (1) by the utility *difference* between the express and regular lane. Thus in each choice scenario *t*, the respondent *n* chooses the express lane if, and only if

$$(6) \qquad U_{nt}^{SP} \equiv X_{nt}^{SP}\beta_n^{SP} + \varepsilon_{nt}^{SP} \geq 0,$$

with β_n^{SP} given by equation (2) with the addition of *SP* superscripts on each of the symbols there. Note that β_n^{SP}, representing the preferences of individual *n*, does not vary across the different choice scenarios *t* presented to that individual.

We account for three additional effects that may arise due to the nature of the SP sample and to combining it with the RP samples. First, we expect the random influence ε_{nt}^{SP} to exhibit a typical panel structure. That is, it contains one random term, which we denote ξ_n, common to all the choice scenarios considered by individual *n*; and another, denoted η_{nt}^{SP}, that is unique to each choice scenario. Second, in the fifty-four cases where the same individual answered both the RP and SP questions, we expect some correspondence between the unobserved influences on their actual behavior and their hypothetical responses. To capture this, we assume that part of the random utility is common between them. Specifically, we assume the SP error ε_{nt}^{SP}, expressing random preference for the express lane as revealed in SP responses, contains a term proportional to v_n^x from equation (3), representing random preference for travel in the express lane as revealed in observed (RP) behavior. Accounting for both of these effects results in the SP error in equation (6) given by:

$$(7) \qquad \varepsilon_{nt}^{SP} = \xi_n + \theta v_n^x + \eta_{nt}^{SP},$$

where

ξ_n: normally distributed with zero mean and variance normalized to one;
θ: a parameter to be estimated;
and η_{nt}^{SP} has a logistic distribution with standard deviation σ^{SP}.[20]

---

20. The logistic distribution describes the difference between two extreme-value variates, which is what we obtain because utility in equation (6) is the difference between the random utilities of express and regular lanes. Train (2003, p. 39) illustrates this point.

Finally, we follow standard practice in combining RP and SP data by allowing for differences between revealed and stated choices in the variance of random preferences. That is, the random factors affecting revealed choices may be larger or smaller than those affecting stated choices. For similar reasons, we allow for a difference between the two RP data sets in the variance of the random term in equation (1). The two data sets are Brookings RP (denoted BR) and CalPoly (denoted C). Thus the three standard deviations describing the three parts of our data (BR, C, and SP) are connected by two ratios that we estimate: $\tau^{BR} \equiv \sigma^{SP}/\sigma^{BR}$ and $\tau^C \equiv \sigma^{SP}/\sigma^C$. The ratios are described in our estimation results as *scale parameters*.[21]

We compute the log-likelihood function for our sample as the summation of logarithms of choice probabilities for RP observations (choice among nine alternatives) and for SP observations (binary choice), with the common error term v_n^x entering both RP and SP choices for those people who are members of both Brookings samples. As noted, each choice probability is expressed in the usual manner for mixed logit as an integral of a multinomial or binary logit probability, conditional on normal random variates, over the distribution of those variates. We obtain parameter estimates by maximizing this log-likelihood function using Monte Carlo simulation to compute the integrals.[22]

Identification

Every statistical model must make explicit or implicit identifying assumptions about which environmental factors are held constant as others are varied, thus enabling the analyst to isolate the parameters of interest. Our model's parameters are identified by assuming that the unobserved influences on transponder, vehicle occupancy, and lane choice do not vary systematically by time of day. If they did, they would be correlated with the cost, time, and reliability of travel and their presence would bias those coefficients. The validity of this assumption depends to a large extent on how well our observed variables capture taste variation across time of day. Fortunately, it appears that such variation is reflected in several of our variables. For example, a motorist's gender is correlated with the time of day of travel. Females constitute only 15 percent of those people traveling during the interval 4:00 a.m.–

21. As in the binary logit model, one of these standard deviations can be normalized, typically by setting it equal to $\pi/\sqrt{3}$ for mathematical convenience: Train (2003), pp. 44–46. We normalize σ^{SP} in this way.

22. This is the maximum simulated likelihood estimator developed by Lee (1992) and McFadden and Train (2000), and exposited by Train (2003, pp. 148–9).

5:00 a.m., but 39 percent of the 7:00 a.m.–8:00 a.m. group. Similarly, the proportion of respondents whose trips are work trips varies from 100 percent at the earliest time to 58 percent at the latest time.

In earlier work, we conducted a formal test of whether unobserved taste variation by time of day affects our estimates of cost and travel-time coefficients.[23] The test consisted of estimating models of lane choice that included five time-of-day dummy variables. The findings indicated that values of time and reliability were not affected very much by the inclusion of the dummy variables. We do not include the time-of-day dummies in the current model because in the previous work they reduced the precision of the estimates.

Estimation Results

Table 3 presents estimation results. We group the RP parameters as those for generic variables that influence all three choice dimensions (transponder, lane, and vehicle occupancy), and those that influence just one of those dimensions. We also group separately those parameters influencing only the SP lane choice and those having a common effect on RP and SP choices.[24] Most influences are statistically significant and have the expected signs. As indicated by the generic RP coefficients and the SP coefficients, motorists pay close attention to the toll, travel time, and reliability when choosing among the available alternatives.

Observed heterogeneity in preferences is indicated by interaction variables formed by multiplying a generic variable by a socioeconomic or distance variable.[25] For example, toll is multiplied by a dummy variable for income, and median travel time is multiplied by various functions of trip distance. The results show that, as expected, motorists with higher incomes are less responsive to the toll, a statistically significant effect for RP respondents. The deterrent effect of travel time varies with distance in an inverted U-pattern,

---

23. Small, Winston, and Yan (2005a).

24. We conducted an extensive exploration of alternative specifications and functional forms for the explanatory variables, including removing the equality constraints between certain RP and SP parameters reflected in the "combined estimates" in the table. The model presented here is robust to such variations and is not rejected by statistical tests against more general models.

25. That is, we multiply a component of variable vector $\mathbf{X}_{jn}$ in equation (1) by a component of variable vector $\mathbf{W}_n$ in equation (2), as required by substituting equation (2) into equation (1). The resulting coefficient is a component of parameter vector $\boldsymbol{\gamma}$ in equation (2).

Table 3. Estimation Results for Demand Model

Variable	Coefficient (standard error)[a]
RP coefficients	
Generic variables	
Toll (dollars)[b, c]	−2.4042 (0.3994)
Toll[b, c] × dummy for high household income (> $60,000)	1.3869 (0.3395)
Median travel time (min.)[b] × trip distance (units of 10 miles)	−0.5753 (0.1751)
Median travel time[b] × trip distance squared	0.1128 (0.0394)
Median travel time[b] × trip distance cubed	−0.0050 (0.0020)
Travel-time uncertainty (80th percentile minus the median) (minutes)[b]	−0.7489 (0.2668)
Transponder choice	
Transponder dummy × Brookings dummy	−2.0101 (0.7472)
Transponder dummy × CalPoly dummy	−3.6342 (0.7374)
Female dummy × age 30–50 dummy × transponder dummy	1.8535 (0.7979)
Commute dummy × transponder dummy	1.2502 (0.6967)
Standard deviation of transponder dummy (σ^T)	0.3276 (0.9422)
Lane choice	
Express lane dummy × Brookings dummy	0.2564 (1.1386)
Express lane dummy × CalPoly dummy	0.2264 (1.1691)
Standard deviation of express lane dummy ($\sigma^{X\text{-}RP}$)	3.7879 (0.8261)
Carpool choice	
Carpool dummy × Brookings dummy	−11.5192 (1.0339)
Carpool dummy × CalPoly dummy	−11.6719 (0.8883)
Female × age 30–50 × household size × carpool	1.4404 (0.3563)
HOV3 dummy × Brookings dummy	−9.2262 (0.9886)
HOV3 dummy × CalPoly dummy	−7.4263 (0.9909)
Common standard deviation of HOV dummies (σ^{HOV})	10.3225 (0.7837)
SP coefficients	
Express lane dummy	−3.0651 (1.1953)
Standard deviation of express lane dummy ($\sigma^{X\text{-}SP}$)	1.0530 (0.5237)
Toll (dollars)[b, c]	−1.4165 (0.3028)
Toll[b, c] × dummy for high household income (> $60,000)	−0.2492 (0.4808)
Travel time (minutes)[b] × long commute dummy (> 45 minutes)	−0.3538 (0.0812)
Travel time[b] × (1 − long commute dummy)	−0.3843 (0.0616)
Travel-time uncertainty[b]	−7.1139 (1.4507)
Combined coefficients	
Female dummy × express lane dummy	2.2434 (0.8384)
Age 30–50 dummy × express lane dummy	1.9277 (0.7955)
Household size (number of people) × express lane dummy	−0.7371 (0.2117)
Standard deviation of travel-time coefficient (σ^{Time})	0.3866 (0.0694)
Ratio of standard deviation to mean of coefficient of travel-time uncertainty ($\sigma^{Rel}/\gamma^{Rel}$)	1.3233 (0.3805)
Correlation parameter between RP and SP express lane choice (θ)	1.4808 (0.3209)
Parameters associated with scaling	
Scale parameter: CalPoly sample (τ^C)	0.4143 (0.0902)
Scale parameter: Brookings RP sample (τ^{BR})	0.6064 (0.2029)

Table 3. Estimation Results for Demand Model (*Continued*)

Summary statistic

Number of observations	1,124
Number of persons	538
Log-likelihood	1,059.63

Source: Based on data from the Brookings and CalPoly surveys and authors' calculations.

RP = Revealed preference data.

SP = Stated preference data.

a. Standard errors reported are the *sandwich* estimate of standard errors from Lee (1995). That is, each is the square root of the corresponding diagonal element in the matrix $\hat{V} = (-H)^{-1} P (-H)^{-1}$, where H is the Hessian of the simulated log-likelihood function and P is the outer product of its gradient vector (both calculated numerically). This estimate accounts for the simulation error in the likelihood function.

b. All cost, travel time, and unreliability variables are entered as the difference between values for the toll and free lanes. In the RP data, the cost for free lanes is zero, travel time for toll lanes is eight minutes, and unreliability for toll lanes is zero. In the SP data, cost, travel time, and unreliability are specified in the questions.

c. Value of cost for the toll lanes is the posted toll for a solo driver (for RP data) or the listed toll in the survey question (for SP), less 50 percent discount if car occupancy is three or more. For SP, car occupancy is determined from a question asking whether the respondent answered as a solo driver or as part of a carpool, and if the latter, what size carpool.

initially rising but then falling for trips greater than thirty-two miles. Following Calfee and Winston (1998), we conjecture that this pattern results from two opposing forces: the increasing scarcity of leisure time as commuting becomes longer and the self-selection of people with lower values of time into residences farther from work. For SP, we allow the coefficient on travel time to differ between people with long and short commutes, but we find the difference to be negligible.

We also find observed heterogeneity in alternative-specific preferences. The estimates listed under RP Coefficients in table 3 show that middle-aged females and all commuters are more inclined than other motorists to acquire a transponder. Middle-aged females with large families are more likely than other motorists to carpool, perhaps because they are more likely to make trips where family members ride together. Finally, as indicated by the combined coefficients, women, middle-aged motorists, and motorists in smaller households are more likely than others to choose the toll lanes, even after accounting for differences in transponder acquisition and car occupancy.[26]

Substantial unobserved heterogeneity in preferences over travel characteristics is indicated by the size and statistical significance of the estimated standard deviations σ^{Time} and σ^{Rel}. Similarly, there is unobserved heterogeneity

26. To better understand why women are more likely to use the toll lanes, we tried including an interaction of four variables: gender, age, household size, and either the express-lane dummy or the travel-time-uncertainty variable. This interaction sought to test whether working mothers with children might prefer the toll lanes or be more averse to unreliability due to tighter schedules. However, we could not find a measurable effect.

over absolute preferences for the express lanes ($\sigma^{X\text{-}RP}$) and for carpooling (σ^{HOV}). We tried also to estimate a random coefficient for the toll, but we were unable to obtain stable results. The standard deviations are estimated with good precision and are substantial in magnitude, ranging from roughly one-fourth of the corresponding mean coefficient to a multiple of it.[27] The scale and correlation parameters that describe the error structure are also estimated precisely and show, among other things, that the RP and SP responses from a single individual are strongly correlated.

We use our parameter estimates to compute properties of the distributions across individuals of motorists' implied value of time (VOT) and reliability (VOR).[28] In table 4 we provide summaries for all road users combined, and for users of the express lanes and free lanes separately. We use the Brookings RP sample for enumeration because it best represents the population, as argued above.[29] We characterize heterogeneity in VOT and VOR by the interquartile range (that is, the difference between the 75th and 25th percentile values) across individuals and across values of random parameters. This measure is relatively robust to the high upper tails typically found in distributions of ratios of random variables. The results are obtained by sampling across people in the enumeration sample and, for each, making repeated random draws from all estimated distributions.[30]

All of the 90 percent confidence intervals in the second column of table 4 are strictly positive, which indicates that all the reported estimates are statistically different from zero using a one-sided test at a 5 percent significance level. We find that the median value of time is $19.63 an hour, which is about 85 percent of the average wage rate and thus near the upper end of the range expected from previous work.[31] The median value of reliability is $20.76 an

---

27. The ratio of standard deviation to the mean coefficient is directly estimated for (un)reliability at 1.32. In the case of travel time, the estimated standard deviation of 0.39 may be compared with the SP coefficient of travel time of about −0.36 and with the derivative of utility with respect to RP median travel time, which is −0.76 at the mean trip distance of the Brookings RP sample.

28. These computations use the individual estimates for RP responses, which are derived according to equation (3) from the estimates of the mean coefficients from the section *RP Coefficients: Generic Variables* in table 3 and from the estimates of standard deviations from the section *Combined Coefficients*. Note that the latter estimates make use of both RP and SP responses.

29. There is no bias from choice-based sampling here because we use information only about respondents' characteristics, not their choices.

30. The same method is used, and described in greater detail, by Small, Winston, and Yan (2005a).

31. Small (1992, pp. 43–5).

Table 4. Implied Values of Time and Reliability for the Brookings RP Sample

Item	Median estimate	90 percent confidence interval [5th, 95th percentile]
Value of time (dollars/hour)[a]		
Median for:		
Entire sample	19.63	[8.75, 34.61]
Express lane users	25.51	[11.50, 39.99]
Free lane users	18.63	[7.76, 29.08]
Total heterogeneity[b] for:		
Entire sample	19.02	[12.57, 30.96]
Express lane users	29.30	[14.65, 55.97]
Free lane users	17.73	[11.37, 28.05]
Value of reliability (dollars/hour)[a]		
Median for:		
Entire sample	20.76	[8.37, 40.71]
Express lane users	23.78	[10.01, 48.29]
Free lane users	19.50	[5.73, 34.54]
Total heterogeneity[b] for:		
Entire sample	35.51	[14.95, 66.71]
Express lane users	44.70	[18.27, 84.24]
Free lane users	32.95	[13.70, 62.01]

Source: Based on data from the Brookings survey and authors' calculations.

RP = Revealed preference data.

a. Calculated from equations (4) and (5) using estimates of β_n^{Time}, β_n^{Rel}, and β_n^{Cost} applicable to RP responses (but note those estimates rely on both RP and SP data because they depend on σ^{Time} and σ^{Rel}).

b. Heterogeneity is expressed here as the interquartile range of the quantity in question across both individuals in the enumeration sample and random draws from the estimated distributions of the β's, in order to account for observed and unobserved heterogeneity, respectively.

hour.[32] Motorists also exhibit a wide range of preferences for speedy and reliable travel, as total heterogeneity in VOT and VOR is nearly equal to, or greater than, the corresponding median value. On average, express-lane users have higher values of travel time and reliability than do users of the free lanes, as expected, but wide and overlapping ranges exist within these two groups, resulting from the strong heterogeneity in preferences.

Simulating Highway Policies

We explore the policy implications of preference heterogeneity by developing a simulation model that uses our econometric results. It allows us to

---

32. Note that reliability is measured in hours because it is formed from percentiles of the distribution of travel time, which is measured in hours. Nevertheless, reliability, like travel time, is a property of the entire trip (more precisely, of the portion of the trip occurring on the section of the corridor we study).

examine current HOT and HOV policies and alternative pricing policies. We begin with a situation closely resembling the SR91 road-pricing experiment. Two ten-mile roadways, express and regular, are assumed to connect the same origin and destination and to have the same free-flow travel time of 8.0 minutes.[33] We model a four-hour peak period of 5:00 a.m.–9:00 a.m.

We find equilibria by iterating between the supply and demand sides of the model. The supply side is a standard static congestion model in which travel delays are proportional to the fourth power of the volume-capacity ratio.[34] Capacity is 2,000 vehicles an hour in each lane. Unreliability is assumed to be a constant fraction 0.3785 of travel delay (travel time minus free-flow travel time)—the fraction observed in our data on the free lanes averaged over 5:00 a.m.–9:00 a.m.

The demand side is obtained from the estimated demand model by sample enumeration, using the Brookings RP sample, which, as noted, is random and mostly representative of the population. The enumeration sample is assumed to represent a fixed population of size N potential commuters.

Our estimated demand model, of course, is conditional on travel in this corridor. However, we want to include the possibility of individuals altering their decision to travel in the corridor in response to policies we simulate, because other studies have shown that such responses can strongly affect the relative benefits of alternative pricing strategies.[35] Therefore we extend our estimated model by adding an outside choice representing nontravel (on the corridor).

The full procedure for this extension is described in the paper's appendix. Briefly, we postulate an outside or nontravel alternative labeled −1 (which could represent no trip, a trip outside the four-hour time period, or a trip on one of the other corridors that are some distance from the one we are modeling). Its utility is simply a constant $\bar{\delta}_{-1}$ plus a random term $\eta_{-1,n}$. The random terms for the other alternatives, that is, the terms η_{jn} in equation (3), are assumed to be more closely correlated with each other than with η_{-1}, just as in a nested logit model. A new parameter λ indicates the strength of this correlation. Choice probabilities (conditional on random parameters) are nested logit.[36]

33. This is the observed travel time on the section we study at 4:00 a.m., corresponding to a speed of seventy-five miles an hour.
34. U.S. Bureau of Public Roads (1964).
35. Verhoef, Nijkamp, and Rietveld (1996).
36. The choice probabilities are expressed in the appendix equations (A-2a-d).

Table 5. Initial Calibration of Expanded Demand Model

Item	Summer 2000 conditions		More congested conditions
	HOT-lane policy	No-toll policy	No-toll policy
Assumed toll[a]:			
Express lanes (dollars)	3.30	0	0
Free lanes (dollars)	0	0	0
Calibrated parameters:			
N	17,570	17,570	24,710
$\bar{\delta}_{-1}$	−12.65	−12.65	−23.41
Travel time (minutes):			
Express lanes	9.83	12.03	20
Free lanes	13.23	12.03	20
Arc elasticity of total corridor traffic volume with respect to full cost[b]	−0.40	−0.36	−0.36

Source: Authors' calculations.
a. HOV3+ pays half of the toll.
b. Based on 10 percent increase in time, unreliability, and cost for each travel option.

Calibrating the Expanded Demand Model

To use our model for simulation, we need to calibrate three parameters: the alternative-specific constant for the outside choice ($\bar{\delta}_{-1}$), the coefficient of the inclusive value of travel (λ), and the population size (N). Because we expect the travel alternatives to be much closer substitutes for each other than for nontravel, we choose λ as small as possible without causing numerical instability: namely, $\lambda = 0.2$. This choice does not seem to have much effect on the nature of the results. We calibrate the other two parameters ($\bar{\delta}_{-1}$ and N) to replicate observed traffic conditions during the morning peak on SR91 in the summer of 2000, which took place with an express-lane toll of $3.30 with 50 percent discount for HOV3. The key traffic conditions are a travel-time difference between the express and free lanes of 3.4 minutes (according to our field measurements), and nontravel share of 10 percent.[37] The parameters that achieve these results are shown in the first column of numbers in table 5, along with the resulting travel times and the implied elas-

37. The 10 percent figure is a plausible estimate based on the likelihood that a small portion of trips were forgone due to congestion, that an alternative route available for some travelers (SR241) had about an 8 to 9 percent share of the CalPoly sample, and that the share of public transit is less than 1 percent.

ticity of traffic volume with respect to the full cost of travel.[38] The middle column shows the travel times produced by simulating the base (no-toll) policy with those parameters: namely 12.03 minutes, indicating a speed of fifty miles an hour.

We recognize, however, that most areas considering new pricing or express-lane policies have far worse congestion than was observed on SR91 in 2000—which was only five years after a 50 percent increase in the road's capacity. We therefore raise population N enough to reduce average speed to thirty miles an hour under a no-toll scenario. In setting the parameters for this starting situation, we hold constant not $\overline{\delta}_{-1}$, but instead the total traffic elasticity under a no-toll situation, shown in the last row of table 5. That elasticity (−0.36) may be compared with the value of −0.58 estimated under the actual pricing scheme in effect on SR91 in 2000, based on the CalPoly data and using a model with no heterogeneity.[39]

The calibration exercise just described leads finally to the parameters shown in the last column of the table, which we use in our policy simulations. We perform sensitivity tests, described later, using different values of the elasticity of total traffic volume, including a value of zero.

Defining Policies

Based on our equilibrium model of supply and demand, we simulate results for several pricing and operational policies. For each, we calculate tolls, travel times, traffic volumes, revenue, changes in consumers' surplus, and total change in social welfare. In our base-case (or no-toll policy), the two roadways are not distinguished. We compare policy scenarios that have the same number of total lanes (six), and thus do not investigate whether the benefits of a particular policy would merit adding new lanes in order to implement it.

38. Full cost is toll plus the traveler's value of travel time and unreliability faced. We computed the full-cost elasticity by using our expanded demand model, with initial calibrated parameters just described, to simulate changes in total travel under a no-toll scenario and a scenario where travel time and reliability are both increased 10 percent for all alternatives. We also computed the implied money-price elasticity of express-lane travel, which is −1.12, for comparison to the value of the same quantity reported in Yan, Small, and Sullivan (2002), which is −0.7 to −0.8 but based on a model that did not account for preference heterogeneity. We believe the higher elasticity calculated here is realistic because preference heterogeneity creates a subset of people who are quite ready to shift into or out of the express lanes in response to tolls, even though they are not very likely to shift from travel to nontravel.

39. Yan, Small, and Sullivan (2002).

The change in consumer surplus for traveler n, relative to the base case, is determined by the log-sum rule for nested logit:[40]

$$(8) \qquad \Delta CS_n = \frac{1}{m_n} \Delta \ln \left[\exp(\overline{\delta}_{-1}) + \exp(\lambda I_n) \right],$$

where

Δ: indicates the difference between a given scenario and the base scenario;
I_n: inclusive value of the nine travel alternatives,
and m_n: individual's marginal utility of income, determined from the coefficient of the toll variable using Roy's identity.[41] The change in social welfare is the sum of expected changes in all individuals' consumer surplus and in toll revenues.

Besides the base policy (no toll), we first consider five other policies:
—HOV. A conventional carpool-lane policy in which the express lanes are open at no charge to carpools of two or more people.
—HOT. The express lanes are open both to carpools and to anyone willing to pay a toll.
—One-route toll. The express lanes are open to anyone willing to pay a toll, but with no discount for carpools.
—Two-route toll. All lanes are tolled, but with two different toll levels.
—Two-route HOT. Same as two-route toll except carpools can use either type of lane without charge.

For those policies requiring a toll, the toll is chosen to maximize social welfare subject to the constraints that define the policy. In the case of the HOT lane, the resulting optimal toll is smaller than would be charged under criteria typically used in current implementations.

The specific alternatives that are available for each policy are enumerated in table 6. Because their availability varies across policies, we must consider a feature of welfare analysis using discrete choice models, namely, adding more options increases welfare beyond any improvement in travel conditions that may actually result. This feature derives from the nature of a random utility model that assumes there are unobservable characteristics, captured

---

40. Choi and Moon (1997).
41. The equation for I_n is given as appendix equation (A-2c). We report all results on a per-trip basis, so Roy's identity equates m_n to minus the coefficient of the toll. Based on the results of table 3, $m_n = -(-2.4042 + 1.3869 * H_n)$, where H_n represents a traveler's value of the high household income dummy.

Table 6. Availability of Alternatives by Policy[a]

| | Alternative | | | Policy | | | |
| | | Description | | No | | HOT; | Two-route toll; |
Number	Mode	Transponder?	Lane	toll	HOV	one-route toll	two-route HOT
0	Solo	N	G	x	x	X	
1	Solo	T	G			X	x
2	Solo	T	X			X	x
3	HOV2	N	G	x	x	X	
4	HOV2	T	G			X	x
5a	HOV2	N	X		x		
5b	HOV2	T	X			X	x
6	HOV3	N	G	x	x	X	
7a	HOV3	T	G			X	x
7b	HOV3	N	X		x		
8	HOV3	T	X			X	x

Source: Authors' descriptions.

a. An x means that the alternative is available in that scenario; T indicates a transponder; N indicates none; G indicates the general lanes; X indicates the express lanes.

by ε_{jn} in equation (1), that differ among alternatives. We see from table 6 that some of our policies offer options with or without a transponder, while others offer express lanes as well as regular lanes. Our demand model was estimated in a situation including all nine possible alternatives described earlier, but when we simulate other policies, certain of these alternatives are eliminated from the choice set. This affects expected utility because the unobservable characteristics of eliminated alternatives are valued by some travelers. For example, some travelers in a HOT-lane environment value the day-to-day flexibility of lane choice that owning a transponder provides, whereas they do not have such flexibility in the no-toll or HOV policies.

Simulation Results

Table 7 shows simulation results. To facilitate understanding of the findings, we begin by presenting a detailed summary of the HOT-lane policy. The welfare-maximizing express toll for this policy is $9.23 a trip (first row). It produces a big reduction of travel times on the express lanes compared with the base policy (from 20.0 to 12.4 minutes), and a much smaller reduction on the general lanes (from 20.0 to 19.2 minutes). The next set of numbers gives the shares of selected combinations of alternatives (in which the shares for alter-

Table 7. Policy Simulation Results

Effect	No toll	HOV	HOT	One-route toll	Two-route toll	Two-route HOT	Limited two-route HOT
Toll on express lane (dollars)	0	0	9.23	8.69	10.14	6.33	9.65
Toll on general lane (dollars)	0	0	0	0	8.16	5.34	1.90
Travel times (minutes):							
Express lane	20.00	11.8	12.4	11.6	11.6	13.1	12.5
General lane	20.00	18.8	19.2	22.6	12.8	12.5	16.5
Aggregated choice shares (percent):							
No travel on corridor	7.4	3.3	3.4	6.4	8.5	3.0	3.3
Solo on express lane	24.8	0	2.6	8.9	8.0	7.6	1.7
Solo on general lane	49.6	52.0	52.5	54.5	27.9	25.0	46.3
HOV2 on express lane	5.1	32.6	30.0	15.4	16.3	23.1	31.7
HOV2 on general lane[a]	10.3	2.9	3.0	7.2	22.1	26.8	6.6
HOV3+ on express lane	0.9	8.8	8.1	6.7	8.5	6.9	8.9
HOV3+ on general lane[b]	1.9	0.6	0.4	0.9	8.8	7.6	1.4
All HOV3+	2.8	9.4	8.5	7.6	17.3	14.5	10.3
All HOV	18.2	44.8	41.5	30.2	55.7	64.5	48.6
Consumer surplus change (dollars/person)[c]:							
Average	0	2.11	2.01	0.50	−2.36	0.98	1.36
Distribution in population (percentile)							
75th	0	2.92	2.71	0.65	0.00	3.51	2.80
50th	0	0.77	0.62	−0.27	−2.68	0.52	0.33
25th	0	0.26	0.26	−0.98	−5.36	−1.91	−0.98
Toll revenue (dollars/person)[c]	0	0	0.24	1.64	5.35	1.81	1.05
Welfare change (dollars/person)[c]	0	2.11	2.25	2.14	2.99	2.79	2.41

Source: Authors' calculations.

a. In the HOT and one-route toll policies, this row combines shares for two alternatives, with and without a transponder: namely, alternatives 3 and 4 in table 6.

b. Same as note a, but combines alternatives 6 and 7a in table 6.

c. Consumer surplus and social welfare are measured relative to the no-toll scenario. These two and toll revenue are each divided by the total number of potential travelers N. Social welfare is the sum of consumer surplus plus revenue.

natives with and without a transponder are added together). Thus for example, 3.4 percent of the N potential travelers choose not to travel on this corridor; just 2.6 percent pay the toll in order to travel alone on the express lanes (alternative $TX1$); and 52.5 percent travel alone in the general lanes (alternatives $TG1$ and $NG1$).

The consumer-surplus change for this policy, relative to No toll, averages $2.01 a person—largely reflecting the reduced congestion caused by the shift to carpools (which is nearly as great as in the HOV policy, given that solo vehicles must pay a high express toll). The average, however, masks a wide dispersion in the gains to travelers, indicated by the percentiles shown next: the median traveler gets a 62-cent increase in consumer surplus, whereas the 75th percentile traveler gets a much larger $2.71 while the 25th percentile traveler gets only 26 cents. Finally, the toll revenue collected from the HOT lane is just 24 cents a person, reflecting the small percentage paying the high toll. Adding the average consumer surplus change of $2.01 to the average toll revenue of 24 cents gives the total welfare change per person, $2.25, shown in the last row of table 7.

We now compare the welfare properties of the policies. The introduction of HOV lanes improves efficiency by encouraging carpooling—more than doubling its share from the base case (table 7 row labeled *All HOV*). This policy significantly reduces travel time on the express lanes, but leaves the general lanes very congested (table 7, third and fourth rows). In all likelihood, the policy would be much less effective in a smaller metropolitan area. Dahlgren (1998) finds that HOV lanes are favorable (in terms of reducing total person delay) only when initial congestion is substantial (delays of thirty-five minutes or more) and when the initial modal share of carpools is sizable (20 percent or more). We explore the welfare properties of HOV lanes under these conditions when we perform sensitivity analysis.

Allowing solo motorists to use the express lane if they pay a toll (HOT) generates a small welfare improvement over the HOV policy by enabling a small share of travelers to switch lanes and drive faster. In the HOT-like policy without an HOV exemption (one-route toll), the general lane becomes even more congested and the welfare improvement over the initial HOV policy is negligible. The two-route toll and two-route HOT policies generate considerably more welfare gains, as expected. But they do so at the cost of imposing large consumer-surplus losses on many travelers: the distribution in the population shows that the two-route toll reduces consumer surplus for three-fourths of all travelers (because the 75th percentile traveler gains $0.00), while the two-route HOT reduces it for between one-fourth and one-half of them (because the 25th percentile gain is negative but the median gain is positive).

Table 8 provides more perspective on the policies' distributional effects by showing how consumer surplus varies between and within two different income groups. The dispersion within each group is quite large. For exam-

Table 8. Consumer Surplus Distribution by Income Group

Dollars per person	No toll	HOV	HOT	One-route toll	Two-route toll	Two-route HOT	Limited two-route HOT
High income (≥ $60,000) (percentile)							
75th	0	6.47	6.80	6.01	5.16	8.30	6.88
50th	0	1.68	1.61	1.27	0.92	4.48	2.47
25th	0	0.72	0.67	−0.92	−3.34	0.15	0.04
Low income (< $60,000) (percentile)							
75th	0	2.50	2.10	0.29	−0.55	2.47	2.00
50th	0	0.64	0.51	−0.37	−3.20	0.11	0.08
25th	0	0.22	0.22	−0.98	−5.60	−2.19	−1.04

Source: Authors' calculations.

ple, in the HOT policy the interquartile range is from 67 cents to $6.80 for the high-income group and from 22 cents to $2.10 for the low-income group. Note that these distributions show a great deal of overlap. For example, the one-quarter of the low-income group with the largest gains (that is, those above the 75th percentile) receive consumer surplus benefits of $2.10 or more, exceeding the gains of those at or below the median in the high-income group. As indicated previously, such findings reflect the considerable heterogeneity in VOT, VOR, and alternative-specific preferences that we found even controlling for income. Evidently there are many reasons besides income why some travelers strongly prefer one option over another.

Notwithstanding their sacrifice of economic efficiency, variants of HOV, HOT, and one-route pricing policies have attained a certain degree of public acceptance, suggesting that their distributional features are compelling enough to allow implementation. The first-best policy of tolling both lanes (two-route toll) produces a sizable gain in welfare over HOV and HOT policies, largely because it greatly reduces congestion on both lanes. However, it causes travelers to suffer high and disparate losses in consumer surplus, averaging $2.36 per trip and over $5.36 per trip for one-fourth of all travelers. Furthermore, the largest losses are associated with the lowest income groups, who tend to have the lowest values of time and reliability. These features obviously contribute to efficient pricing's lack of political appeal.

However, we find that policymakers can achieve most of the gains from first-best pricing, while partly addressing distributional concerns, by adding a carpool exemption to the two-route pricing policy (making it two-route

HOT).[42] The carpool share, already high in two-route pricing because of its financial incentives, increases even more, while congestion on both routes compares with the levels under two-route pricing. Remarkably, travelers, on average, obtain a substantial gain in consumer surplus (98 cents) from two-route HOT (compared with no toll); nevertheless, the policy is vulnerable to the concern that a substantial fraction of people incur sizable losses—those in the most disadvantaged quartile of users lose at least $1.91 per trip.

It is important to point out that if we assumed that travelers were homogeneous, our findings would change considerably, along the same lines as in other studies.[43] With homogeneous preferences, the relative welfare gain from the one-route toll, whose efficiency relies mainly on creating differential services, would drop significantly; HOT would become nearly identical in effect to HOV (because no additional benefits would result from separating users based on their preferences); and the one-route toll would be set much lower (because it cannot rely on attracting users just from the upper tail of the VOT and VOR distributions). In general, the reason that accounting for heterogeneity greatly affects policy comparisons is that diversity in users' preferences creates the opportunity to improve social welfare by providing differentiated services.

Toward a Better Policy Compromise

Our findings on the distribution of benefits and costs raise the question of whether it is possible to craft a policy that achieves an even better compromise between efficiency and political feasibility than the policies explored thus far. In particular, we seek a more efficient policy with the same attractive distributional features as the one-route toll. We choose one-route toll as a benchmark for political feasibility because at least two cases exist in North America where a policy resembling it has been successfully implemented. One case is SR91 itself. Although carpools did not all pay full fare on SR91, those with only two occupants did and those with three or more occupants paid half the fare during most of the time when the original private toll road

---

42. This policy, like others involving an express lane, incorporates the absolute preferences for the express lane from our demand model, which on average are slightly positive. For this reason, traffic is equilibrated when the express lane is slightly slower than the general lane, even though the express lane has a (moderately) higher price. While this may appear anomalous, it reflects other advantages of the express lanes on SR91, such as lack of trucks and intermediate entrances and exits, which we think would apply in many other express-lane applications.

43. Small and Yan (2001); Verhoef and Small (2004).

was in operation.[44] The other case is Highway 407 in the Toronto area. This is a publicly built highway (later sold to a private firm) that runs through the suburbs paralleling (a few miles away) a very congested east-west route through the city known as Queen Elizabeth Way. Projects such as these, and several others being actively considered, suggest that the public is willing to tolerate a toll road without HOV exceptions if a free alternative is available. In our simulation of the one-route toll, the free alternative exists in the form of a roadway immediately adjacent to the priced one, so this policy should be at least as acceptable as Highway 407.

We therefore quantify a benchmark for political viability as the 25th percentile of consumer-surplus change experienced by travelers under the one-route toll policy. Table 7 shows that this is −98 cents a trip. We then define an alternate version of two-route pricing that sets the two toll levels to maximize welfare, subject to the consumer surplus loss of the 25th percentile traveler not exceeding 98 cents a trip. The result is the limited two-route HOT policy shown in the last column in tables 7 and 8. It results in a sharply differentiated toll: for the express lane its magnitude ($9.65) compares with that in the two-route toll policy, but for the general lane it is only $1.90, much lower than either of the other two-route pricing policies. The policy achieves a general-lane speed of thirty-six miles per hour, intermediate between those of the no-toll and two-route policies. It also achieves greater efficiency than any of the policies that leave the general lanes unpriced.

Motorists in the limited two-route HOT policy achieve a consumer surplus gain, on average, of $1.36 compared with no tolls. This exceeds the gain achieved by any other two-route pricing policy. Furthermore, travelers are treated much more evenly than in the other two-route pricing policies, with the interquartile range only modestly greater than with HOT or HOV. Thus the limited two-route HOT policy succeeds in improving efficiency more than most other policies, while maintaining the attractive distributional characteristics comparable to policies that have been found to be politically feasible.

We stress that our policy simulations are based on an experiment concerning only a single ten-mile stretch of highway. Most significant congestion affects a

---

44. Although there were complaints about the high tolls and about charging HOV3+ vehicles, they do not appear to have undermined the stability of the arrangement, which had a strikingly high acceptance level in various polls. What did eventually undermine the private operation was an unrelated issue: the franchise allowed the private operator to veto any capacity improvements in the corridor, which it did through a lawsuit in a highly publicized dispute with the California Department of Transportation. As a result, the express-lane franchise was purchased in 2003 by a public agency, which has retained most of the toll policies of its private predecessor.

much broader region. If the distributional advantages of differentiated pricing enable it to be broadly adopted, its welfare gains will be greatly magnified.

Sensitivity Analysis for Simulation Results

The simulation results presented so far are based on a full-cost elasticity for total traffic of −0.36. Appendix tables A-2 and A-3 present simulation results where we assume the full-cost elasticity of total corridor traffic is −0.60 and zero, respectively. For the case of zero elasticity, the model has no outside option and so there is no parameter $\bar{\delta}_{-1}$ to calibrate. In the other case, the two parameters N and $\bar{\delta}_{-1}$ are simultaneously calibrated, as in the main results, to achieve the desired elasticity and travel-time differential with no toll. The results show that the welfare rankings of various policies, and the nature of their distributional impacts, do not depend on this assumed elasticity. We caution that specific numerical results are not necessarily comparable with different assumed elasticities because they imply different starting shares for HOV.

A more important area for sensitivity analysis, in our view, is varying the initial carpool share. As noted, many metropolitan areas have much smaller carpool shares than Los Angeles, a large city that has relatively long work trips. We therefore present an alternate simulation in which we change the parameters governing the alternative-specific utilities for HOV alternatives so as to produce HOV shares about half those of our primary scenario (table 7), under both the no-toll and HOV policies.[45] Results are shown in table 9. The policies do not perform as well as those in our main simulation, either in total welfare gain or in direct impact on consumers. For example, the median consumer-surplus change is uniformly negative. The smaller efficiency gains and less favorable distributional properties occur because the policies cannot induce as much carpool formation and therefore they achieve less relief from congestion. The HOV policy, especially, is much less effective—it produces a negative total welfare change and substantial consumer surplus losses both to the median and, especially, the 25th percentile traveler. This striking finding is consistent with policymakers' growing dissatisfaction with HOV lanes and growing interest in HOT lanes throughout the country.

---

45. We do this by adjusting the HOV dummy and its standard deviation. (The HOV3 dummy is adjusted proportionally to the HOV dummy.) The HOV share can be estimated approximately for about twenty existing corridors with HOV lanes in U.S. metropolitan areas from data in Pratt and others (2000, tables 2-2, 2-7, and 2-9). Almost all are between 15 and 30 percent, whose midpoint (22.5 percent) is almost exactly half the share predicted by our HOV policy simulation in table 7.

Table 9. Simulation Results with Low HOV Share[a]

Effect	No toll	HOV	HOT	One-route toll	Two-route toll	Two-route HOT	Limited two-route HOT
Toll on express lane							
(dollars)	0	0	8.03	8.20	11.10	9.47	8.35
Toll on general lane							
(dollars)	0	0	0	0	7.94	7.02	1.98
Travel times (minutes):							
Express lane	20.00	9.31	12.38	12.28	12.07	13.37	12.64
General lane	20.00	25.38	22.95	24.04	15.87	15.50	20.75
Aggregated choice shares (percent):							
No travel on corridor	7.49	13.31	7.84	9.26	18.37	13.23	9.08
Solo on express lane	27.88	0	14.66	17.75	16.80	15.57	14.59
Solo on general lane	55.77	64.09	61.43	61.55	48.38	47.43	58.47
HOV2 on express lane	2.47	16.71	11.84	5.90	6.70	12.70	12.58
HOV2 on general lane	4.94	1.12	1.21	3.22	5.89	6.26	1.72
HOV3 on express lane	0.48	4.61	2.77	1.85	2.41	3.29	3.17
HOV3 on general lane	0.97	0.16	0.25	0.47	1.45	1.52	0.39
All HOV3	1.45	4.77	3.02	2.32	3.86	4.81	3.56
All HOV	8.86	22.60	16.07	11.44	16.45	23.77	17.86
Consumer surplus change (dollars/person):							
Average	0	−0.50	0.41	−0.20	−4.22	−2.81	−0.67
Distribution in population (percentile)							
75th	0	0.30	0.68	0.28	−1.98	−0.16	0.00
50th	0	−1.12	−0.35	−0.69	−5.27	−3.86	−1.98
25th	0	−2.51	−1.14	−1.66	−7.01	−5.81	−2.51
Toll revenue							
(dollars/person)	0	0	1.18	1.75	6.44	4.82	2.38
Welfare change							
(dollars/person)	0	−0.50	1.59	1.55	2.22	2.01	1.71

Source: Authors' calculations.
a. See notes for table 7.

What about the limited two-route HOT policy? Can it outperform HOT? Although we found that it cannot meet its political acceptability, as indicated by HOT's 25th percentile consumer surplus loss, it can improve on HOT's efficiency if we define political acceptability relative to the 25th percentile consumer-surplus loss of HOV instead. Thus the possibility for an improved policy compromise exists for other metropolitan areas in the country, although we cannot be as sanguine about political feasibility as before.

Conclusion

Methodological advances in microeconometrics have enriched our understanding of consumer behavior by recognizing that consumers are not homogeneous. Applications have shown that accounting for heterogeneity is important when assessing policies in many domains, such as economic deregulation, job training, and poverty programs. We find that heterogeneity plays a similarly important role in policy toward highway transportation. Accounting for it creates the opportunity not only to introduce HOT lanes, as has been previously recognized, but to introduce more far-reaching pricing policies within the limits of distributional effects that appear to be politically acceptable in certain circumstances. We have been able to design a differentiated road-pricing scheme that fills in the gap between optimal but socially unpopular first-best pricing and pragmatic but less-efficient policies like carpool or HOT lanes.

Recent experiments have shown that policymakers are no longer unwilling to use the price mechanism to allocate scarce road capacity. The changing times give cause for optimism that more efficient policies, offering choices that appeal to diverse users, will become serious candidates for implementation.

APPENDIX

Stated Preference Survey Questionnaire

Eight hypothetical commuting scenarios were constructed for respondents who travel on California State Route 91. Respondents who indicated their actual commute was less (more) than forty-five minutes were given scenarios that involved trips ranging from twenty to forty (fifty to seventy) minutes. An illustrative scenario is presented in table A-1.

Extended Demand Model for Simulations

Let $\Omega = \{-1, 0, 1, \ldots, 8\}$ denote the choice set for a potential road user, where alternative -1 is the outside choice and alternatives $0-8$ represent the

Table A-1. Stated Preference Survey Questionnaire

Free lanes	Express lanes
Usual travel time: Twenty-five minutes	Usual travel time: Fifteen minutes
Toll: None	Toll: $3.75
Frequency of unexpected delays of ten minutes or more: One day in five	Frequency of unexpected delays of ten minutes or more: One day in twenty
Your choice (check one): Free lanes ☐	Toll lanes ☐

Source: Authors' descriptions.

different combinations of routes, transponder acquisition, and car occupancy defined previously. It is convenient to let $\widetilde{\Omega} = \{0, 1, \ldots, 8\}$ denote the subset of choices involving travel on the corridor.

The utility of individual n choosing alternative j is:

$$\text{(A-1a)} \qquad U_{-1n} = \overline{\delta}_{-1} + \eta_{-1n},$$

$$\text{(A-1b)} \qquad U_{nj} = X_j^{RP} \beta_n^{RP} + \varepsilon_{jn}^{RP}, j \geq 0,$$

with β_n^{RP} and ε_{jn}^{RP} as given by equations (2) and (3) in the text. Thus each traveler's utility for nontravel is divided into a mean $\overline{\delta}_{-1}$, which is constant for all commuters, and random deviation ε_{-1n}; whereas the utility for each alternative involving travel is the same as in the RP part of our estimated model, equations (1), (2), and (3) in the text. We henceforth omit the superscript *RP* for simplicity.

The random preferences for individual n therefore are represented by the vector $\boldsymbol{\Psi}_n = (\boldsymbol{\eta}_n, \boldsymbol{v}_n, \boldsymbol{\mu}_n)$, where $\boldsymbol{\eta}_n = (\eta_{-1n}, \eta_{0n}, \ldots, \eta_{8n})$, $\boldsymbol{v}_n = (v_n^T, v_n^X, v_n^{H2}, v_n^{H3})$, and $\boldsymbol{\mu}_n = (\mu_n^{Time}, \mu_n^{Rel})$. The density function of $\boldsymbol{\Psi}_n$ is specified as $\rho(\boldsymbol{\Psi}_n) = \rho_\eta(\boldsymbol{\eta}_n) \cdot \rho_{v\mu}(\boldsymbol{v}_n, \boldsymbol{\mu}_n)$. Here $\rho_{v\mu}(\cdot)$ is a product of independent normal random variables with standard deviations as estimated, while $\rho_n(\cdot)$ takes the nested-logit form in which the outside alternative -1 is one nest and the travel alternatives $\widetilde{\Omega}$ are another nest with similarity parameter λ. This specification captures the idea that the substitution pattern between any two travel choices may be different from that between nontravel and travel. The market share of alternative $j \in \widetilde{\Omega}$, within the submarket represented by people with characteristics of traveler n in our enumeration sample, is found by integrating the nested-logit probability formula, conditional on random parameters v_n and μ_n, over the distribution function of those random parameters:

$$(A\text{-}2a) \qquad S_{jn} = \int_{(v_n,\mu_n)} S_{jn}^{(v_n,\mu_n)} \cdot \rho_{v\mu}(\boldsymbol{v}_n,\boldsymbol{\mu}_n) d(\boldsymbol{v}_n,\boldsymbol{\mu}_n),$$

where

$$(A\text{-}2b) \qquad S_{jn}^{(v_n,\mu_n)} = \frac{\exp(X_{jn}\beta_n/\lambda)}{\exp(I_n)} \cdot \frac{\exp(\lambda I_n)}{\exp(\bar{\delta}_{-1}) + \exp(\lambda I_n)}$$

is the share conditional on values of the normal random variates, and

$$(A\text{-}2c) \qquad I_n = \ln \sum_{j=0}^{8} \exp(X_{jn}\beta_n/\lambda)$$

is the inclusive value of travel choices. The nontravel share is

$$(A\text{-}2d) \qquad S_{-1n} = \frac{\exp(\bar{\delta}_{-1})}{\exp(\bar{\delta}_{-1}) + \exp(\lambda I_n)}.$$

The total demand for an alternative j is therefore

$$(A\text{-}3) \qquad D_j = \sum_n w_n S_{jn},$$

where w_n is the number of people represented by motorist n. This number is just $w_n = N/79$, where N is the total population size, since our enumeration sample consists of seventy-nine equally weighted individuals. The traffic volume arising from those individuals who choose a travel alternative j involving occupancy O_j is $V_j \equiv D_j/O_j$.

Table A-2. Alternate Simulation Results: Elasticity = −0.60

Effect	No toll	HOV	HOT	One-route toll	Two-route toll	Two-route HOT
Toll on express lane (dollars)	0	0	8.41	8.53	9.41	6.02
Toll on general lane (dollars)	0	0	0	0	7.01	5.32
Travel times (minutes):						
Express lane	20.0	12.4	13.0	11.3	11.4	13.8
General lane	20.0	19.8	20.0	22.9	13.0	12.8
Aggregated choice shares (percent):						
Outside choice	16.5	9.8	10.8	15.9	19.7	9.8
Solo on express lane	22.2	0	2.8	7.4	7.2	7.9
Solo on general lane	44.3	47.9	48.0	48.9	26.7	21.9
HOV2 on express lane	4.8	30.8	27.9	14.1	14.1	20.4
HOV2 on general lane	9.6	2.7	3.0	6.9	18.8	26.7
HOV3 on express lane	0.9	8.5	6.9	5.9	7.2	6.0
HOV3 on general lane	1.7	0.4	0.6	0.9	6.3	7.3
All HOV3	2.6	8.9	7.5	6.8	13.5	13.3
All HOV	17.0	42.4	38.4	27.8	46.4	60.5
Consumer surplus change (dollars/person relative to No toll):						
Average	0	1.50	1.47	0.46	1.77	0.49
Distribution in population (percentile)						
75th	0	2.04	1.94	0.56	0.03	2.73
50th	0	0.10	0.03	−0.14	−1.76	0.08
25th	0	0.03	0.01	−0.87	−4.61	−1.94
Toll revenue (dollars/person)	0	0	0.24	1.40	4.24	1.63
Welfare change (dollars/person)	0	1.50	1.71	1.86	2.47	2.13
Consumer surplus distribution by income group (dollars/person)						
High income (≥ $60,000) (percentile)						
75th	0	5.04	5.04	5.16	4.85	6.67
50th	0	0.23	1.08	1.02	1.47	3.50
25th	0	0.08	0.02	−0.65	−2.28	0.18
Low income (< $60,000) (percentile)						
75th	0	1.75	1.42	0.20	−0.02	1.86
50th	0	0.09	0.02	−0.25	−2.26	0.00
25th	0	0.03	0.01	−0.89	−4.83	−2.28

Source: Authors' calculations.
Notes: See notes for table 7.

Table A-3. Alternate Simulation Results: Elasticity=0 (No Outside Choice)

Effect	No toll	HOV	HOT	One-route toll	Two-route toll	Two-route HOT
Toll on express lane (dollars)	0	0	8.47	8.64	10.46	6.17
Toll on general lane (dollars)	0	0	0	0	9.29	5.19
Travel times (minutes):						
Express lane	20.0	11.0	11.6	11.6	11.8	12.3
General lane	20.0	18.1	18.3	22.1	12.4	12.3
Aggregated choice shares (percent):						
Outside choice	0	0	0	0	0	0
Solo on express lane	26.6	0	3.5	10.4	9.7	8.8
Solo on general lane	53.2	54.3	54.5	57.6	26.6	26.6
HOV2 on express lane	5.6	31.7	28.7	15.2	16.4	21.7
HOV2 on general lane	11.3	4.2	4.5	8.5	26.4	28.1
HOV3 on express lane	1.1	8.9	7.9	7.0	8.9	6.6
HOV3 on general lane	2.2	0.8	0.9	1.3	11.9	8.2
All HOV3	3.3	9.8	8.8	8.3	20.9	14.9
All HOV	20.2	45.7	42.0	32.0	63.4	64.6
Consumer surplus change **($/person relative to No toll):**						
Average	0	2.94	3.09	1.17	−2.39	1.87
Distribution in population (percentile)						
75th	0	4.07	4.00	1.15	0.12	4.45
50th	0	1.47	1.64	0.14	−3.05	1.29
25th	0	0.56	0.91	−0.44	−5.78	−1.48
Toll revenue (dollars/person)	0	0	0.24	1.40	4.24	1.63
Welfare change (dollars/person)	0	1.50	1.71	1.86	2.47	2.13
Consumer surplus distribution **by income group** (dollars/person)						
High income (≥ $60,000) (percentile)						
75th	0	8.35	8.68	6.70	6.04	9.81
50th	0	3.06	4.02	1.79	1.49	5.30
25th	0	1.42	2.23	0.13	−3.10	0.93
Low income (< $60,000) (percentile)						
75th	0	3.38	3.04	0.71	−0.94	3.46
50th	0	1.22	1.40	0.01	−3.60	0.77
25th	0	0.49	0.82	−0.50	−6.08	−1.73

Source: Authors' calculations.
Notes: See notes for table 7.

Comments

Nathaniel Baum-Snow: Small, Winston, and Yan's paper provides valuable new insights on the potential social welfare gains associated with implementing various new urban highway lane pricing and carpooling options. The authors apply modern econometric techniques to estimate a partial equilibrium model of highway travel demand. Using the resulting estimates, the authors perform a detailed welfare analysis of different high-occupancy vehicle and toll lane policies. California State Route 91 (SR91) is an ideal case to evaluate. The road has few exits, considerable variation in congestion delays for different times of day, and variation across observations in the cost of the HOT lane. The structural approach lends itself well to the full welfare analysis of various policy alternatives performed at the paper's end. The authors choose their empirical specification to be flexible enough to inform us about distributional consequences of different HOV, toll lane, and HOT policies in addition to their mean effects. Finally, the authors deserve considerable credit for their data collection efforts. Without these unique data, this analysis would not have been possible. This paper should be of great use to urban transportation policymakers considering the implementation of highway congestion tolls and HOV lanes.

The authors cite a body of work documenting that road congestion delays have been rising rapidly since the early 1980s. At the same time, the fraction of the U.S. population commuting by car continues to increase, reaching 91 percent in 2000. Commuting by car has risen even in the face of large investments in public transit infrastructure. On the face of it, this may seem like a golden opportunity for carpool lanes. At very low cost, they have the potential to provide large congestion reductions, thereby increasing commuting speeds for many commuters. However, as seen in table 10, the fraction of auto commuters who carpool has been falling rapidly. In 1980 it stood at 20 percent, while by 2000 it had fallen to just 12 percent nationally. The decline in carpooling is seen for central city and suburban residents alike. It also holds

Table 10. Trends in Carpooling, 1980–2000[a]

Area			1980	1990	2000
United States	Central city	Fraction commute by car	0.75	0.75	0.62
		Car commuters who carpool	0.17	0.14	0.12
	Suburban	Fraction commute by car	0.90	0.92	0.92
		Car commuters who carpool	0.20	0.13	0.12
	All	Fraction commute by car	0.86	0.89	0.91
		Car commuters who carpool	0.20	0.14	0.12
Los Angeles CMSA		Fraction commute by car	0.88	0.89	0.90
		Car commuters who carpool	0.17	0.15	0.15

Source: Author's calculations using the 1980, 1990, and 2000 Census Public Use Microdata Samples (PUMS).
CMSA = Consolidated Metropolitan Statistical Area.
a. Sample includes all commuters in listed areas. Regions for which central city and suburban numbers are broken out vary over time.

in the Los Angeles Consolidated Metropolitan Statistical Area (CMSA), where the SR91 experiment took place, though to a lesser extent. In Los Angeles carpooling rates fell from 17 to 15 percent of drivers between 1980 and 2000. Over this period, the fraction of commuters using public transit declined by less in both absolute and percentage terms, despite considerable public investment in both transit and HOV lane infrastructure.

How can one explain steeply declining carpooling rates despite longer congestion delays and more drivers on the roads? A few clues are revealed by examining income levels and travel times. Table 11 presents average commuting times and total income levels (in 1999 dollars) of people who drive alone and people who carpool. It shows that carpoolers are considerably poorer than solo drivers and that their average commuting time is greater. This pattern holds in central cities and suburban areas, persists over time, and also holds for the Los Angeles CMSA. Two explanations may be important in accounting for these patterns. Poor people may have longer distance commutes and as a result may be more likely to find carpooling (and carpool lanes) to be useful. In addition, while carpooling reduces highway travel time where there are carpool lanes, it increases nonhighway travel time due to the need to circulate to pick up or drop off passengers. Population and employment decentralization can only have increased the fixed-time cost of carpooling. As such, the driving force behind more prevalent carpooling among the poor may be savings on pecuniary costs of car ownership and gasoline rather than time savings.

In the SR91 case, which involves longer than average commutes, about eight minutes is the maximum time savings available from carpooling under

Table 11. Income and Commuting Time of Solo Drivers and Carpoolers, 1980–2000[a]

Area	1980		1990		2000	
	Solo driver	*Carpooler*	*Solo driver*	*Carpooler*	*Solo driver*	*Carpooler*
United States						
Central cities						
Income	33,986	27,760	36,775	27,075	42,412	31,363
Minutes	20	24	21	25	26	30
Suburban area						
Income	36,551	31,925	40,129	31,133	47,830	33,740
Minutes	21	26	24	28	27	30
All						
Income	33,599	28,568	35,336	27,194	39,222	27,969
Minutes	20	25	21	26	23	27
Los Angeles CMSA						
Income	37,851	30,709	43,757	28,849	45,987	28,830
Minutes	23	27	25	28	27	29

Source: Author's calculations using the 1980, 1990, and 2000 Census Public Use Microdata Samples (PUMS).
CMSA = Consolidated Metropolitan Statistical Area.
a. Sample includes all those who reported commuting by car. Income reports total annual income adjusted to 1999 dollars, minutes are one-way commuting time.

any HOV or HOT lane scenario considered. Picking up and dropping off a carpooler, or even coordinating the departure of two people who live or work in the same location, can easily take this much time every trip. The suggestive evidence in tables 10 and 11 is consistent with the time cost of carpooling increasing faster as a function of the wage than the time cost of solo driving. This may reflect a large fixed-time cost associated with carpooling, implying that carpooling may only be attractive to the rich if they have very long commutes. Consistent with these observations, the authors estimate large negative marginal utilities of carpooling for the average SR91 commuter.

Given the bleak outlook for carpooling and dominant role of the car in commuting, it is natural to look for road pricing schemes that allow solo commuters to pay for the congestion externality they impose on others. Thus it is appropriate that the authors use a full congestion pricing scheme to estimate their model, and consider a broad set of policy alternatives.

The results presented in table 7 highlight a host of potential difficulties in selecting and implementing various toll policies. Since high-income people have the highest value of time and lowest value of money, they are the ones who will ultimately benefit the most from being able to pay for a faster commute. Full congestion pricing of the road leaves the poor with the costly options of paying a toll or using an alternate longer route, thereby making them worse off. With their lower value of time, the poor endeavor to trade off pecuniary costs for time. It is this same intuition that can explain much higher rates of bus usage among the poor than other groups. As the authors demonstrate in table 9, there has to be considerable flexibility to carpool in the population in order for a HOT lane scheme to generate welfare gains for all but those at the very top end of the income distribution. The HOT lane attracts those with a relatively low cost of carpooling who reduce congestion for everyone else, as well as solo drivers who have high values of time and reliability. In the authors' empirical model, those at the lower end of the income distribution only benefit from the congestion reduction due to carpooling; low-income commuters may be burdened with longer commutes if a HOT lane induces very few people to carpool as the free lane becomes more congested.

Given this friction between the interests of the rich and poor, what is the feasibility and efficacy of establishing HOT lanes or limited two-route HOT lanes in other areas? With current carpooling rates considerably less than the baseline of 18 percent in the SR91 case, one may find that implementing HOT lanes in other areas would have much more deleterious effects for the poor than seen in the SR91 case. Policymakers should thus be cautious in applying Small, Winston, and Yan's estimates to other situations. However, reestimation of the model with new stated preference data that include information on carpooling propensities for areas that are studying implementation of HOT lanes likely would be sufficient to perform the appropriate welfare analyses.

There are a few important considerations that fall beyond the scope of this paper. Congestion pricing of highways has the possibility of mitigating inefficient spatial dispersion in urban areas. Indeed, as noted by the authors, the negative externalities imposed by extra highway users not only manifest themselves as slower commute times for their commuting brethren, but also in inefficient land use patterns. Indeed, the general equilibrium consequences of improvements in the transportation infrastructure can be quite important, as seen in the influence highway construction had on suburbanization. The other general equilibrium response not considered by the authors but that may be important is commuting time-shifting. If poor individuals can adjust their commuting hours at low cost to avoid tolls, the authors may be underestimating the welfare benefits of road congestion tolls.

Overall, one learns a lot from Small, Winston, and Yan's work. It would be interesting to use their estimates, or new results using the same methodology estimated using data from a stated preference survey, to form predictions about lane choice and carpooling for projects coming on line in the next few years. Successful out-of-sample predictions for travel demand would lend further credence to the welfare analysis performed in this paper. With any luck, the methodology developed in this paper will be adopted by policymakers for evaluating potential road pricing schemes in the future.

José A. Gómez-Ibáñez: Small, Winston, and Yan set out to demonstrate, using traffic congestion as their example, that public policy can be improved by understanding how preferences vary among consumers. Local officials have long resisted the suggestion by many economists that the problem of urban traffic congestion can be significantly reduced by charging motorists tolls that depend on the level of congestion. Officials have been much more willing to build special high-occupancy vehicle (HOV) lanes to try to reduce congestion by encouraging the formation of carpools. In addition, some communities have converted their HOV lanes into high-occupancy toll (HOT) lanes, usually in response to criticism that the HOV lanes are underused while the general-purpose lanes remain very crowded. HOT lanes allow motorists who are driving alone (or who do not have enough passengers to qualify for HOV status) to use the exclusive lanes if they pay a toll. Only a few major urban areas (notably Singapore, in 1975, and London, in 2003) have been willing to toll all lanes, a practice that economists argue would establish strong incentives for motorists to form carpools, shift to mass transit, and travel in less-congested hours or to less-congested locations.

Small, Winston, and Yan cite research showing that HOV and HOT lanes can actually increase rather than reduce traffic congestion, particularly in circumstances where the lanes do not encourage the formation of many new carpools or the new carpools are formed primarily by former bus riders. The authors argue that HOV and HOT lanes are both inferior to congestion tolls on all lanes because the general-purpose lanes are left untolled and thus excessively congested. They contend that policymakers can fashion a politically acceptable policy that generates most of the benefits of congestion tolls by taking advantage of the variation in preferences for different commuting options. The basic idea is to offer a menu of options instead of a single policy, so that consumers can pick the option that reduces congestion at the least cost and inconvenience to them. The authors illustrate their argument by simulating alternative congestion-relief policies on a stretch of California State Route 91 (SR-91) that currently has four general-purpose and two HOV lanes.

Transportation planners and policymakers will not need much convincing about the importance of considering heterogeneous preferences. They have long understood, for example, that variations in preferences are the reason that several modes of transportation often serve the same territory or route. Trucks and railroads both can thrive on the same route because some shippers are more sensitive to travel time and reliability, while others are more sensitive to cost. Similarly, buses, trains, and automobiles often share the same commuter corridor because commuters differ in the value they place on travel time savings, their willingness to carpool, their need to run errands on the way to or from work, and other characteristics. Transportation planners commonly break down markets into different segments that vary not just by the origins and destinations of their trips but by their different preferences. Small, Winston, and Yan are encouraging planners to consider the implications of preference heterogeneity in a wider variety of applications.

Small, Winston, and Yan's simulations make it clear why economists have had such a difficult time convincing policymakers to impose congestion tolls. Congestion tolls on both the general-purpose and special lanes of SR-91 generate the largest estimated social welfare gain of any policy they simulate: $2.99 per commuter. But the average commuter actually loses $2.36 in consumer surplus from congestion tolling—only a handful of wealthy commuters who place a high value on time savings are better off. The reason that congestion pricing generates net benefits to society is that the government collects tolls averaging $5.35 per commuter. Who will benefit from the toll revenues depends on how the revenues are used. If they are used to cut taxes, then taxpayers benefit, and if they are used to expand government programs, then program users benefit. But the fear is that the benefits from toll revenues are likely to be spread so thinly over a large group of taxpayers and government program users that they will be hardly noticed, while the costs will be concentrated on commuters and very visible. Diffuse benefits and concentrated costs are a recipe for political resistance.

The most obvious solution to this dilemma is to attempt to return some of the toll revenues to commuters in a way that does not undermine the incentive properties of the tolls. For example, London made its congestion tolling scheme more popular by pledging to use the toll revenues to expand bus services.[1] Similarly, Hong Kong promised to use congestion toll revenues to reduce auto-

---

1. A more important factor in public acceptance of the London scheme was probably that 85 percent of the commuters working in the central area, where congestion tolls were applied, were already using public transit.

mobile registration fees and excise taxes. Hong Kong's proposal failed, in part, because motorists did not trust the government to keep its promises to cut auto taxes.

This paper's authors suggest a new strategy: taking advantage of the variation in consumer preferences for time savings and other attributes to set congestion tolls at levels that benefit, rather than harm, most motorists. The fact that there are two sets of lanes (special and general-purpose) allows Small, Winston, and Yan to offer two toll levels simultaneously: a high toll in the special lanes that delivers a substantial time savings and appeals to motorists who value time greatly, and a low toll in the general-purpose lanes level that delivers less time savings but is more attractive to motorists who place less value on travel time. In addition, carpools can travel free in the high toll lane. The authors tinker with the two toll levels until they find a pair of tolls that gives a net social gain of $2.41 per commuter, or 81 percent of the $2.99 maximum benefit that might be obtained. But with their tolls the average commuter gains a consumer's surplus of $1.36 instead of losing $2.36. Only roughly a third of commuters lose, and they typically lose only $1 per trip.[2]

While the authors' solution is very clever, they do not recognize that the designers of conventional HOT lanes have essentially anticipated their idea. Conventional HOT lanes also offer commuters three different options: untolled but slow travel in the general-purpose lanes (which appeals to those who do not value travel time savings highly); untolled and fast travel in the special-purpose lanes (which appeals to those who do not mind traveling in carpools); and tolled and fast travel in the special-purpose lanes (for those who highly value time savings and prefer not to carpool). As a result, the HOT lane policy generates a net social gain of $2.25 per commuter, or 75 percent of the $2.99 maximum possible and almost as much as the $2.41 generated by the authors' scheme. Equally important, the average commuter gains $2.01 instead of losing $2.36, and virtually all commuters are winners.[3] In short, the HOT lane scheme uses the same approach of providing a menu of options as the authors' proposal and, as a result, gains almost the same net social benefit and an even better outcome for commuters.

Small, Winston, and Yan might have made a stronger case for their particular proposal had they used a more representative highway than SR-91. This California road is ideally suited for HOV and HOT lanes because the commuters that use it travel very long distances. SR-91 crosses a barrier of hills

2. The authors report that the 25th percentile commuter loses 98 cents per trip.
3. The authors report that the 25th percentile commuter gains 26 cents per trip.

that separate job-rich Orange County and housing-rich Riverside County. As a result, the HOT lanes are ten miles long, without any intermediate entrances and exits, and the time savings for users is as much as ten to fifteen minutes a trip. Such an enormous time savings encourages more than 40 percent of commuters on SR-91 to carpool, a much higher percentage than found on roads with shorter HOV or HOT lanes. If the authors had used a more typical commuter highway as their example, their scheme of different toll rates on general- and special-purpose lanes might have outperformed the HOT lanes.[4]

The authors also may have overestimated the benefits of HOT lanes to the extent that they overestimated the preferences that commuters have for the intrinsic characteristics of certain options rather than the savings in cost, travel time, and travel reliability that those options offer. The authors acknowledge that consumer utility increases slightly in their model as the number of options increases, even if those options do not actually offer more variety. But it also appears that the intrinsic preferences for certain options, such as owning a transponder or traveling in the exclusive lanes, are estimated to be high as well. This may give HOT lanes an important advantage over congestion pricing in the model simply because HOT lanes offer commuters a wide variety of options. Unfortunately, the econometric techniques the authors must use to combine different surveys with different types of data are so complicated that it is difficult to tell whether the intrinsic preferences for options have been overstated.[5]

In sum, Small, Winston, and Yan's basic point is probably more important than their specific example of congestion pricing on SR-91 makes it seem. On a more typical highway, with shorter lanes and commutes, differential pricing on the special- and general-purpose lanes might have beaten HOT lanes. But the success of the HOT lanes on SR-91 supports, rather than refutes, their argument that offering more options improves public policy where preferences are heterogeneous. HOT lanes offer more variety than congestion pricing, so one should not be surprised that they do reasonably well.

4. The authors simulate a road with lower HOV shares but they do so by adjusting down the intrinsic preference for HOV rather than by changing the characteristics of the road that give it such a high HOV share.

5. In an earlier version of their paper, the authors reported how much of the estimated consumer surplus per commuter was due to increases in the number of alternatives, transponder and special lane preferences, and differences in toll, time, or reliability. Roughly half of the welfare gain for many options was due to increases in the number of alternatives and transponder and special lane preferences, while the remainder was due to differences in toll, time, or reliability.

References

Brownstone, David, and Kenneth Train. 1999. "Forecasting New Product Penetration with Flexible Substitution Patterns." *Journal of Econometrics* 89 (1–2): 109–29.

Calfee, John, and Clifford Winston. 1998. "The Value of Automobile Travel Time: Implications for Congestion Policy." *Journal of Public Economics* 69 (1): 83–102.

Calfee, John, Clifford Winston, and Randolph Stempski. 2001. "Econometric Issues in Estimating Consumer Preferences from Stated Preference Data: A Case Study of the Value of Automobile Travel Time." *Review of Economics and Statistics* 83 (4): 699–707.

Choi, Ki-Hong, and Choon-Geol Moon. 1997. "Generalized Extreme Value Model and Additively Separable Generator Function." *Journal of Econometrics* 76 (1–2): 129–40.

Dahlgren, Joy. 1998. "High Occupancy Vehicle Lanes: Not Always More Effective than General Purpose Lanes." *Transportation Research A* 32 (2): 99–114.

De Palma, André, and Robin Lindsey. 2004. "Congestion Pricing with Heterogeneous Travelers: A General-Equilibrium Welfare Analysis." *Networks and Spatial Economics* 4 (2): 135–60.

Hensher, David A. 2001. "The Valuation of Commuter Travel Time Savings for Car Drivers in New Zealand: Evaluating Alternative Model Specifications." *Transportation* 28 (2): 101–18.

Hess, Stephane, Michel Bierlaire, and John W. Polak. 2005. "Estimation of Value of Travel-Time Savings Using Mixed Logit Models." *Transportation Research A* 39 (2–3): 221–36.

Jiang, Meilan, and Takayuki Morikawa. 2004. "Theoretical Analysis on the Variation of Value of Travel Time Savings." *Transportation Research A* 38 (8): 551–71.

Lee, Lung-fei. 1992. "On Efficiency of Methods of Simulated Moments and Maximum Simulated Likelihood Estimation of Discrete Response Models." *Econometric Theory* 8: 518–52.

———. 1995. "Asymptotic Bias in Simulated Maximum Likelihood Estimation of Discrete Choice Models." *Econometric Theory* 11: 437–83.

Manski, Charles F., and Steven R. Lerman. 1977. "The Estimation of Choice Probabilities from Choice Based Samples." *Econometrica* 45 (8): 1977–88.

McFadden, Daniel, and Kenneth Train. 2000. "Mixed MNL Models for Discrete Response." *Journal of Applied Econometrics* 15 (5): 447–70.

Mohring, Herbert. 1999. "Congestion." In *Essays in Transportation Economics and Policy: A Handbook in Honor of John R. Meyer,* edited by J. Gómez-Ibáñez W. Tye, and C. Winston, pp. 181–222. Brookings.

Orski, C. Kenneth. 2001. "Carpool Lanes—An Idea Whose Time Has Come and Gone." *TR News* 214 (May–June): 24–28.

Poole, Robert W., Jr., and Ted Balaker. 2005. "Virtual Exclusive Busways: Improving Urban Transit While Relieving Congestion." Policy Study 337. Los Angeles: Reason Foundation.

Pratt, Richard H., and others. 2000. *Traveler Response to Transportation System Changes: Interim Handbook.* Transportation Cooperative Research Program (www4. nationalacademies.org/trb/crp.nsf/All+Projects/TCRP+B-12 [May 27, 2005]).

Santos, Georgina, ed. 2004. *Road Pricing: Theory and Evidence.* Oxford, United Kingdom: Elsevier Press.

Schrank, David, and Tim Lomax. 2005. *The 2005 Urban Mobility Report.* Texas Transportation Institute, Texas A&M University System, College Station, Texas.

Small, Kenneth A. 1992. *Urban Transportation Economics 51, Fundamentals of Pure and Applied Economics Series.* Chur, Switzerland: Harwood Academic Publishers.

Small, Kenneth A., and Clifford Winston. 1999. "The Demand for Transportation: Models and Applications." In *Essays in Transportation Policy and Economics: A Handbook in Honor of John R. Meyer,* edited by Gómez-Ibáñez, Tye, and Winston, pp. 11–55.

Small, Kenneth A., Clifford Winston, and Carol Evans. 1989. *Road Work: A New Highway Pricing and Investment Policy.* Brookings.

Small, Kenneth A., Clifford Winston, and Jia Yan. 2005a. "Uncovering the Distribution of Motorists' Preferences for Travel Time and Reliability." *Econometrica* 73 (4): 1367–82.

———. 2005b. Supplement to "Uncovering the Distribution of Motorists' Preferences for Travel Time and Reliability." *Econometrica Supplementary Material* 73 (4) (www.econometricsociety.org/suppmatlist.asp).

Small, Kenneth A., and Jia Yan. 2001. "The Value of 'Value Pricing' of Roads: Second-Best Pricing and Product Differentiation." *Journal of Urban Economics* 49 (2): 310–36.

Steimetz, Seiji S. C., and David Brownstone. 2005. "Estimating Commuters' 'Value of Time' with Noisy Data: A Multiple Imputation Approach." *Transportation Research B* 39 (10): 865–89.

Sullivan, Edward, and others. 2000. *Continuation Study to Evaluate the Impacts of the SR 91 Value-Priced Express Lanes: Final Report.* Department of Civil and Environmental Engineering, California Polytechnic State University at San Luis Obispo (December) (ceenve.ceng.calpoly.edu/sullivan/SR91).

Train, Kenneth E. 2003. *Discrete Choice Methods with Simulation.* Cambridge University Press.

U.S. Bureau of Public Roads. 1964. *Traffic Assignment Manual.* Washington.

Verhoef, Erik T., Peter Nijkamp, and Piet Rietveld. 1996. "Second-Best Congestion Pricing: The Case of an Untolled Alternative." *Journal of Urban Economics* 40 (3): 279–302.

Verhoef, Erik T., and Kenneth A. Small. 2004. "Product Differentiation on Roads: Constrained Congestion Pricing with Heterogeneous Users." *Journal of Transport Economics and Policy* 38 (1): 127–56.

Yan, Jia, Kenneth Small, and Edward Sullivan. 2002. "Choice Models of Route, Occupancy, and Time-of-Day with Value Priced Tolls." *Transportation Research Record* 1812: 69–77.

RICHARD J. MURNANE
JOHN B. WILLETT
KRISTEN L. BUB
KATHLEEN MCCARTNEY
Harvard Graduate School of Education

Understanding Trends in the Black-White Achievement Gaps during the First Years of School

THE GAPS BETWEEN THE average academic achievement of black and white children have been persistent features of American life. Until quite recently, obvious differences in the school resources provided to children of different races explained substantial portions of these achievement gaps. For example, in 1920 more than one-quarter of the racial gap in children's literacy rates could be explained by differences in easy-to-measure variables such as the school year length and per pupil expenditures.[1]

Given the history of blatant discrimination in the school resources provided to American children of different races, it is understandable why the U.S. Congress in the Civil Rights Act of 1964 ordered the commissioner of education to conduct a survey to document "the lack of availability of equal educational opportunities by reason of race, color, religion, or natural origin in public educational institutions at all levels. . . ."[2] In July 1966 the U.S. Office of Education published the survey results in a 737-page volume entitled *Equality of Educational Opportunity*. Better known as the Coleman Report, named after its lead author, the eminent sociologist James Coleman, this volume documented the substantial gaps between the average mathematics and reading

We thank Roland Fryer for providing the Stata code that he and Steven Levitt used in some of their work on the black-white achievement gap. We also thank Eric Hanushek and Rebecca Maynard for the thoughtful comments on the paper that they provided at the Brookings-Wharton conference.

1. Margo (1986).
2. Coleman and others (1966, p. iii).

achievement of black and white children. However, to the surprise of many educators and civil rights activists, the report found no clear-cut pattern showing that white children attended schools with substantially more of the school resources measured in the survey than did black children. Moreover, school-to-school variation in resources explained very little of the school-to-school variation in children's mathematics and reading achievement. As Harvard government professor Seymour Martin Lipset summarized the results in a conversation with Daniel Patrick Moynihan, "schools make no difference; families make the difference."[3]

The Coleman Report catalyzed the collection of new data that allowed researchers to challenge the report's findings. Many of the newer data sets provided information on school resources and on children's achievement at more than one point in time. These attributes have allowed researchers to demonstrate conclusively that students learn more in some classrooms and schools than in others. However, with a few exceptions noted below, the newer studies tended to replicate the Coleman Report findings that differences in conventional school resources, such as class size and teachers' educational attainments, do not explain much of the variation in student achievement nor do they explain much of the race-related achievement gaps.[4]

This background provides the context for two provocative papers recently published by Fryer and Levitt.[5] These economists documented a number of patterns in the relative academic achievement of young black and white children. Their work, which focuses particularly on differences by grade in the black-white test score gap in reading and mathematics, is based on analyses of data on the kindergarten cohort of the Early Childhood Longitudinal Study (ECLS-K), a nationally representative sample of more than 20,000 children who entered kindergarten in approximately 1,000 schools during 1998. Key findings of the two Fryer and Levitt papers include:

—at the beginning of kindergarten, the black-white achievement gap is approximately 0.40 standard deviations in reading and 0.60 standard deviations in mathematics;

—a parsimonious set of family background characteristics explains all of the black-white achievement gap in reading and more than 80 percent of the gap in mathematics;

---

3. Godfrey Hodgson, "Do Schools Make a Difference?" *Atlantic,* March 1973, p. 35.
4. For a summary of this evidence, see Hanushek (2003).
5. See Fryer and Levitt (2004 and 2005).

—the black-white achievement gap in both reading and mathematics increases by approximately 0.10 standard deviations during each of the first four years of elementary school (kindergarten through third grade);

—there are no important differences between black and white students in the average values of variables that are typically used to measure school quality (for example, average class size and educational attainments of teachers);

—the typical measures of school quality are not statistically significant predictors of students' reading or mathematics achievement. This suggests that reducing class size or requiring that teachers in schools serving large numbers of black students obtain more educational credentials is unlikely to close the black-white achievement gap.

Two aspects of the evidence presented by Fryer and Levitt are especially troubling. The first is that the black-white achievement gaps in both reading and mathematics are much larger at the end of third grade than at the beginning of kindergarten. This suggests (although it by no means proves) that schooling exacerbates inequalities rather than reduces them. The second is that the ECLS-K data appear to shed little light on why the black-white achievement gap becomes larger during the first four years of schooling. The lack of a clear explanation hinders efforts to design policies to alter these patterns.

The research described in this paper has two goals. The first is to examine the extent to which the results reported by Fryer and Levitt are sensitive to model specification. We focused particularly on the question of whether the evidence on the role of school quality is stronger when we fit models that take advantage of the longitudinal nature of the ECLS-K data set. The second goal is to examine whether the patterns that Fryer and Levitt documented in the ECLS-K data set are also present in a smaller but richer longitudinal data set collected with the support of the National Institute of Child Health and Human Development (NICHD). We focused on the question of whether the detailed information present in the NICHD data set on family and school experiences helps us explain the provocative patterns that Fryer and Levitt have documented.

We describe trends in the black-white achievement gap in mathematics and in English Language Arts (ELA). For three reasons we limit the discussion of school resources to their impact on students' mathematics achievement. First, a number of studies have shown that differences in school resources play a larger role in explaining gains in children's mathematics achievement than gains in reading achievement. Second, students' mathematics test scores predict post-graduation labor market earnings better than do reading scores. Finally, it enables us to keep the number of tables in the paper manageable.[6]

Our paper describes the NICHD data set and documents the steps we took to create an analysis sample from the ECLS-K data set that is comparable to the NICHD data set. We demonstrate that the sample distributions of critical variables common to the two data sets are similar, show that the trends in black-white achievement gaps in the two data sets are different in important respects, and suggest explanations for these differences. We also demonstrate that conventional school resources, defined as those that account for most of school expenditures, do not explain variation in students' mathematics achievement in either data set, and we show that less conventional measures of school quality, including the composition of the student body and how instructional time is spent, are important predictors of student achievement. These last findings suggest promising directions for future research on school-based interventions to close black-white achievement gaps.

NICHD Data Set

One data set we used in this study comes from phases I, II, and III of the National Institute of Child Heath and Human Development Study of Early Child Care and Youth Development (NICHD SECCYD). Families were recruited into the NICHD study via hospital visits to mothers shortly after the birth of a child in 1991. These hospitals were located in or near: Little Rock, Arkansas; Irvine, California; Lawrence, Kansas; Boston, Massachusetts; Morganton, North Carolina; Philadelphia and Pittsburgh, Pennsylvania; Charlottesville, Virginia; Seattle, Washington; and Madison, Wisconsin. Of the 8,986 women who gave birth during the sampling period, 5,151 met the eligibility requirements of the study and agreed to be contacted two weeks later.[7] Using a conditional random sampling method (see below), 2,352 families were subsequently phoned and 1,364 of the families that were called then participated in a home visit one month later for the purposes of data collection.[8]

---

6. For evidence on the first point see Murnane (1975); on the second point see Murnane, Willett, and Levy (1995).

7. Eligibility requirements include: mother healthy, at least age eighteen, and conversant in English; child healthy, singleton, and not adopted; family not planning to move, residing in a neighborhood that was not extremely unsafe, living within one hour of the research site, and not participating in another study.

8. For a detailed description of the recruitment plan, see NICHD Early Child Care Research Network (2001).

The conditional random sampling plan employed by the NICHD SECCYD was designed to include families from diverse ethnic groups, economic backgrounds, and geographic regions, with varying plans for maternal employment during the child's first year of life. The resulting sample is diverse, with 24 percent of the children being ethnic minority (13 percent African American, 6 percent Latino, and 5 percent Asian, Native American, or other ethnicities), 11 percent of mothers not completing high school, and 14 percent of the mothers being single parents. Mothers in the sample had an average of 14.4 years of education and the average family income-to-needs ratio was 3.6 times the poverty threshold.

NICHD Data Set Strengths

The NICHD data set has several important strengths. First, it contains rich descriptors of the child's family background measured longitudinally at all major assessment points, beginning when the target child was one month old and continuing through third grade. These variables include parental education, parental employment status, family income, household size, and an observational measure of mothers' parenting behavior. Second, children's skills in mathematics and ELA were assessed with a well-established instrument, beginning when the children were age fifty-four months (that is, just prior to kindergarten) and continuing through third grade. Student performance on these tests was reported on a scale constructed using Item Response Theory (IRT). Scores on this scale permit estimation of the determinants of skill growth over time. Third, the data set contains rich longitudinal information on each child's teachers and elementary school classrooms, including measures of the teachers' education and experience, the size and racial composition of the class, and indicators of the allocation of classroom time to different activities (derived from direct observations of the classrooms).[9]

NICHD Data Set Limitations

The NICHD data set also has three important limitations. First, its sample size of 1,364 is considerably smaller than that of the ECLS-K data set. Second, it is not completely representative of the population of all children in the United States. Specifically, the sampling strategy deliberately excluded infants who were twins; mothers who were not healthy, were under age eighteen, or

---

9. For a detailed description of the NICHD SECCYD, see NICHD Early Child Care Research Network (2001) or (http://secc.rti.org).

were not conversant in English; families that planned to move within the next year or give up the child for adoption; families that lived in a neighborhood considered unsafe for visits by the people collecting survey data. A consequence of these exclusion criteria is that the NICHD data set does not include adequate representation of U.S. children born into the most difficult family circumstances. Since black children are more likely than white children to be born into low-income families, estimates of black-white achievement gaps based on the NICHD data set may underestimate the gaps in the population of all U.S. children.

The NICHD data set's third limitation is that it provides no exogenous variation in school resources. This is problematic because resources are not equally distributed nor randomly assigned to students in American school systems. Instead, students with particular characteristics tend to receive different resources than students with other characteristics. For example, students of color tend to be assigned to relatively novice teachers.[10] In many systems, students with learning difficulties are assigned to small classes. A result of this nonrandom assignment of students to resources is that it is very difficult to differentiate the effects that school resources have on student achievement from selection effects.

It is important to note that this third limitation of the NICHD data set also pertains to the ECLS-K data set that Fryer and Levitt used in their analyses. For this reason caution is needed when interpreting relationships between school resources and student achievement in both data sets. However, the availability of longitudinal data on both school resources and student outcomes in the ECLS-K and NICHD data sets provides more opportunities to deal with selection effects than has been the case in prior studies based on less rich data sets. In particular, we can focus on the determinants of growth in student achievement rather than limiting ourselves to explaining the variation in achievement levels at one point in time. Also, the longitudinal data help in identifying selection mechanisms. Indeed, we will show that selection effects explain a counterintuitive pattern in the relationship between class size and student achievement in the ECLS-K data set.

The exclusion from the sample of Latino children whose mothers were not conversant in English makes the NICHD data set quite inappropriate for estimating trends in the achievement of Latino children. For that reason, we

---

10. See Clotfelter, Ladd, and Vigdor (2005).

do not discuss trends in Latino-white achievement gaps. However, we did retain Latino children in our analytic sample to make our analyses as comparable as possible to those of Fryer and Levitt.

Comparing the ECLS-K and NICHD Data Sets

In an effort to create comparable analytic samples of children from the ECLS-K and NICHD data sets, we applied to the ECLS-K data set five of the eight exclusion criteria that had been applied during the recruitment phase of the NICHD study.[11] Specifically, we excluded from the ECLS-K data set those families in which the mother was younger than age eighteen at the birth of the target child or was not conversant in English, those infants who were twins, those not healthy at birth, and those who were adopted. We also excluded from both the ECLS-K and NICHD analysis samples children whose race-ethnicity designation was something other than white, black, or Latino.[12] The resulting sample, which we refer to as the ECLS-K restricted sample, was approximately 14.5 percent smaller than the sample employed by Fryer and Levitt.

We then refitted, in the newly restricted ECLS-K data set, the regression models that Fryer and Levitt report fitting in the full ECLS-K data set. Our results were almost identical to those reported by Fryer and Levitt.[13] Next, we explored whether the Fryer and Levitt findings were sensitive to the decision to use ECLS-K sampling weights in fitting the regression models. We found that they were not. Finally, we created a series of balancing weights that we applied to individuals in the NICHD data set to match the sample demographically to the ECLS-K restricted (weighted) sample. First, we identified three strata—type of schooling (public versus private), region of the country (Northeast and Midwest versus South and West), and race-ethnicity (white, black, and other)—and obtained sample sizes within cells created by these strata in both data sets. We then created a ratio of children in the NICHD data set to

11. The ECLS-K data set lacked the data to apply three exclusion criteria: family neighborhood was deemed unsafe for research assistants to visit, family lived too far from study base, and family was planning on moving within a year.

12. We excluded from the analysis samples sixty-six children in the NICHD data set and 1,767 students in the ECLS-K data set whose racial-ethnic classification was something other than white, Latino, or black.

13. Copies of these analyses are available from the authors.

children in the ECLS-K data set within each cell. These estimates were used as balancing weights in the computation of all descriptive statistics.[14]

Table 1 presents descriptive statistics for the key outcome, family background, and school quality indicators in the restricted ECLS-K analytic sample and in our NICHD analytic sample. Overall, these statistics indicate that the ECLS-K and NICHD data sets are fairly well matched. The percentages of black children in the two samples are similar (14 percent in ECLS-K versus 13 percent in NICHD). However, the percentages of Latino children differ (21 percent ECLS-K versus 7 percent in NICHD). Univariate statistics describing selected family characteristics such as child gender and age at the start of kindergarten are also similar in the two samples. There are some minor differences in the distributions of some of the other family covariates. Specifically, the average birth weight of children in the ECLS-K data set is lower than that in the NICHD data set and the percentage of mothers who were teens at the birth of their first child as well as the percentage who reported being on public assistance are higher in the ECLS-K sample. These differences are not surprising given the criteria used in drawing the NICHD sample.

Measures

In the NICHD data set, time-invariant demographic information was collected via maternal report during home visits when the children were one month old. In addition, time-varying demographic information and information on children's mathematical and English Language Arts (ELA) skills were collected from mothers and children when the children were six, fifteen, twenty-four, thirty-six, and fifty-four months old, and again in the spring of the years when the children were attending first and third grades.[15] Similar information was collected from participants in the ECLS-K data set with one important difference: data collection for the ECLS-K cohort began at the beginning of kindergarten. Table 2 provides descriptive statistics by racial-ethnic group for

14. There are two reasons we examined how sensitive the results of fitting the Fryer and Levitt models with the restricted ECLS-K data set were to the decision of whether to use sampling weights. First, we are not confident about the effectiveness of our procedure for creating balancing weights to make the NICHD sample representative of the weighted restricted ECLS-K sample. Second, the software available to us for fitting models that take advantage of the longitudinal nature of the ECLS-K and NICHD data sets (STATA's XTREG procedures) does not permit estimation with sample weights.

15. For a detailed description of the NICHD SECCYD, see NICHD Early Child Care Research Network (2001) or (http://secc.rti.org).

Table 1. Means and Standard Deviations for Outcomes, Family Controls, and School Characteristics in the Restricted ECLS-K and NICHD Data Sets, Kindergarten through Third Grade

| | Descriptive statistics | |
| | ECLS-K | NICHD |
Indicator	Mean (SD)	Mean (SD)
Outcome variables		
Math—kindergarten/54 months	21.85 (8.90)	423.41 (20.55)
Math—first grade	55.31 (15.93)	469.96 (15.38)
Math—third grade	85.65 (17.68)	496.59 (13.36)
ELA—kindergarten/54 months	27.70 (9.78)	458.01 (13.93)
ELA—first grade	68.49 (20.26)	482.21 (11.92)
ELA—third grade	108.74 (19.82)	495.05 (11.38)
Race-ethnicity and gender indicators		
Black	.14 (.35)	.13 (.34)
Latino	.21 (.40)	.07 (.24)
White	.65 (.48)	.80 (.40)
Female	.485 (.500)	.479 (.500)
Personal characteristics and family background variables		
Age at kindergarten (months)	67.10 (4.38)	64.32 (3.44)
SES—kindergarten/54 months	.024 (.779)	−.083 (.685)
SES—first grade	.024 (.779)	−.121 (.742)
SES—third grade	.026 (.791)	−.028 (.692)
Children's books[a]—kindergarten/54 months	75.28 (60.13)	.754 (.431)
Children's books[a]—first grade	106.94 (143.78)	.754 (.431)
Children's books[a]—third grade	86.66 (175.24)	.964 (.186)
Birth weight (oz.)	104.84 (43.30)	123.34 (18.37)
Teen mother at first birth	.215 (.411)	.073 (.260)
Mother age 30+ at first birth	.159 (.366)	.393 (.489)
Assistance[b]	.429 (.495)	.097 (.296)
Early maternal sensitivity	n.a.	3.12 (.425)

(continued)

Table 1. Means and Standard Deviations for Outcomes, Family Controls, and School Characteristics in the Restricted ECLS-K and NICHD Data Sets, Kindergarten through Third Grade (*Continued*)

| | Descriptive statistics | |
| | ECLS-K | NICHD |
Indicator	Mean (SD)	Mean (SD)
Class size		
First grade	20.76	21.26
	(5.13)	(4.39)
Third grade	21.14	21.44
	(3.95)	(4.23)
Master's degree		
First grade	.524	.415
	(.500)	(.493)
Third grade	.423	.431
	(.494)	(.495)
First two years of teaching		
First grade	.074	.056
	(.262)	(.230)
Third grade	.055	.086
	(.228)	(.281)
25 percent or more students are black		
First grade	.239	.119
	(.335)	(.324)
Third grade	.102	.114
	(.303)	(.318)
25 percent or more students are Latino[c]		
First grade	.128	.021
	(.334)	(.144)
Third grade	.115	.032
	(.319)	(.177)
Percent students eligible for free lunch		
First grade	27.09	
	(27.64)	n.a.
Third grade	30.07	
	(27.87)	n.a.
Proportion of hour spent on math instruction		
First grade		8.31
	n.a.	(10.61)
Third grade		9.79
	n.a.	(4.39)

Source: Authors' calculations.

n.a. Not available.

SES = Socioeconomic status.

a. In the ECLS-K data set, the variable *children's books* was measured as the total number of children's books in the home; in the NICHD data set, *children's books* is a dichotomous variable indicating that there were ten or more books in the home.

b. In the ECLS-K data set, *assistance* was a dummy variable indicating whether the mother, child, or both received Special Supplemental Nutrition Program for Women, Infants, and Children (WIC) benefits. In the NICHD data set, *assistance* was a dummy variable indicating whether the family received public assistance, including Aid to Families with Dependent Children (AFDC). In the ECLS-K data set, student composition variables were collected at the school level; in the NICHD data set, student composition variables were collected at the classroom level.

c. In the ECLS-K data set, student composition variables were collected at the school level; in the NICHD data set, student composition variables were collected at the classroom level.

Table 2. Means and Standard Deviations by Race-Ethnic Group for Outcomes, Family Controls, and School Characteristics in the ECLS-K and NICHD Data Sets, Kindergarten through Third Grade

	ECLS-K		NICHD	
Indicator	*Black*	*White*	*Black*	*White*
Mathematics scores				
Kindergarten/54 months	18.19	23.88	404.89	427.96
	(6.38)	(9.11)	(22.09)	(17.00)
First grade	46.87	58.80	457.46	472.99
	(12.70)	(15.83)	(13.85)	(14.92)
Third grade	74.10	89.71	485.58	498.87
	(17.11)	(16.25)	(16.93)	(11.82)
ELA scores				
Kindergarten/54 months	25.02	28.84	447.97	460.99
	(7.84)	(10.07)	(10.50)	(13.82)
First grade	61.17	71.64	471.78	484.53
	(18.63)	(20.10)	(11.90)	(11.54)
Third grade	98.56	113.37	484.02	497.55
	(19.24)	(17.99)	(11.99)	(10.66)
Family background variables				
Female	.483	.483	.500	.478
	(.500)	(.500)	(.501)	(.50)
Age of entry into kindergarten (mos.)	66.89	67.37	64.79	64.23
	(4.44)	(4.36)	(4.11)	(3.30)
Family SES				
Early family SES (time-invariant)	n.a.	n.a.	−.490	−.008
			(.55)	(.76)
Kindergarten/54 months	−.322	.234	−.536	.061
	(.711)	(.734)	(.52)	(.68)
First grade	−.368	.234	−.543	.033
	(.663)	(.752)	(.64)	(.72)
Third grade	−.400	.237	−.343	.094
	(.708)	(.741)	(.481)	(.71)
Children's books[a]				
Kindergarten/54 months	39.23	93.85	.658	.765
	(38.14)	(59.83)	(.476)	(.42)
First grade	49.69	132.12	.658	.765
	(58.12)	(162.05)	(.476)	(.42)
Third grade	42.01	108.33	.879	.988
	(153.66)	(194.20)	(.328)	(.11)
Birth weight (oz.)	95.37	109.11	114.61	124.18
	(44.70)	(40.58)	(14.63)	(17.98)
Teen mother at first birth	.405	.150	.208	.051
	(.491)	(.357)	(.41)	(.22)
Mother age 30+ at first birth	.069	.201	.227	.454
	(.253)	(.401)	(.42)	(.50)
Assistance[b]	.735	.301	.376	.043
	(.442)	(.459)	(.49)	(.20)
Early maternal sensitivity	n.a.	n.a.	2.66	3.22
			(.497)	(.374)

(continued)

Table 2. Means and Standard Deviations by Race-Ethnic Group for Outcomes, Family Controls, and School Characteristics in the ECLS-K and NICHD Data Sets, Kindergarten through Third Grade (*Continued*)

Indicator	ECLS-K		NICHD	
	Black	*White*	*Black*	*White*
School quality variables				
Class size				
First grade	21.27	20.41	21.76	21.03
	(4.52)	(5.25)	(6.26)	(4.05)
Third grade	20.59	21.19	20.79	21.52
	(4.02)	(3.86)	(4.59)	(4.18)
Master's degree				
First grade	.571	.510	.440	.431
	(.496)	(.500)	(.498)	(.50)
Third grade	.388	.448	.407	.440
	(.488)	(.497)	(.493)	(.497)
First two years of teaching				
First grade	.098	.067	.043	.045
	(.298)	(.250)	(.20)	(.21)
Third grade	.065	.054	.123	.077
	(.246)	(.226)	(.33)	(.27)
25 percent or more students are black[c]				
First grade	.511	.068	.410	.076
	(.500)	(.252)	(.493)	(.265)
Third grade	.409	.051	.399	.073
	(.492)	(.220)	(.491)	(.260)
25 percent or more students are Latino[c]				
First grade	.079	.043	.017	.012
	(.270)	(.204)	(.131)	(.107)
Third grade	.069	.037	.012	.023
	(.253)	(.189)	(.107)	(.150)
Percent children in school eligible for free lunch				
First grade	50.81	19.64	—	—
	(33.28)	(20.83)		
Third grade	53.67	20.19	—	—
	(30.49)	(19.38)		
Math instruction				
First grade	n.a.	n.a.	10.04	8.05
			(13.43)	(10.33)
Third grade	n.a.	n.a.	9.66	9.81
			(4.30)	(4.29)

Source: Authors' calculations.
n.a. Not available.
SES = Socioeconomic status.
a. In the ECLS-K data set, the variable *children's books* was measured as the total number of children's books in the home; in the NICHD data set, *children's books* is a dichotomous variable indicating that there were ten or more books in the home.
b. In the ECLS-K data set, *assistance* was a dummy variable indicating whether the mother, child, or both received WIC benefits; in the NICHD data set, *assistance* was a dummy variable indicating whether the family received public assistance, including AFDC.
c. In the ECLS-K data set, student composition variables were collected at the school level; in the NICHD data set, student composition variables were collected at the classroom level.

mathematics and ELA scores at the beginning of kindergarten and end of first and third grades, as well as for family background variables and measures of school quality for both the ECLS-K and NICHD data sets.

Outcome Variables

At age fifty-four months, and at the end of first and third grades, children in the NICHD data set were administered subscales of the Revised Woodcock-Johnson Psycho-Educational Battery (WJ-R).[16] The WJ-R is a comprehensive set of individually administered tests designed to measure a broad range of cognitive abilities and achievement. The Tests of Achievement assess mastery of broad curricular areas such as reading, mathematics, written language, and general knowledge.[17] The Tests of Cognitive Ability measure factors such as long-term retrieval, short-term memory, processing speed, auditory and visual processing, comprehension, knowledge, and reasoning.[18] We used scores on the Applied Problems subscale of the Tests of Achievement as a measure of mathematics skills. We created a composite of each child's score on the Memory for Sentences and Picture Vocabulary subscales from the Tests of Cognitive Ability as a measure of their ELA skills. Since we analyze measures of children's mathematics and ELA skills obtained at different ages, we used vertically equated IRT-scaled scores as our measures of achievement.[19]

Among children in the NICHD data set, the black-white gap in average mathematics scores at age fifty-four months is about 23 points and the gap at the end of third grade is about 13 points (see table 2). Thus as measured in the age-equatable IRT score metric, the average math skill gap declined by 43 percent between the beginning of kindergarten and end of third grade. However, if we follow Fryer and Levitt's practice of measuring the achievement gap in terms of standard deviations in the score distribution at those particular ages, the size of the black-white mathematics achievement gap falls by only 9 percent, from 1.1 standard deviation at age fifty-four months to 1.0 standard deviation at the end of third grade. The reason, as shown in table 1, is that the standard deviation in the NICHD mathematics score distribution at the end of third grade is approximately one-third smaller than the standard deviation in the math score distribution at the beginning of kindergarten. Thus

16. Woodcock and Johnson (1989).
17. Woodcock and Mather (1989).
18. Woodcock and Mather (1989).
19. Rasch (1960).

the trend in the black-white mathematics achievement gap for members of the NICHD data set is very sensitive to the choice of a measurement metric.

The trend in the black-white ELA achievement gap for children in the NICHD data set is quite different from the trend in the mathematics skills gap. Expressed in IRT-scaled points, the gap is about 13 points at the beginning of kindergarten and at the end of third grade (see table 2). Thus in this metric, the size of the gap remains constant between the beginning of kindergarten and the end of third grade. However, this is not the case when the gap is measured using Fryer and Levitt's measurement convention. One reason is that the standard deviation of the NICHD ELA score distribution at the end of third grade is almost 20 percent smaller than the standard deviation in the ELA distribution at the beginning of kindergarten. Thus in Fryer and Levitt's metric, the black-white ELA achievement gap grows from one standard deviation at the beginning of kindergarten to approximately 1.20 standard deviations at the end of third grade.

We next examined the trend in the black-white mathematics skill gap in the ECLS-K data set. We found that it was also sensitive to the choice of measurement metric, although the pattern was quite different from that in the NICHD data set. Measured in the age-equatable IRT score metric, the black-white gap in mathematics scores increased from approximately 6 points at the beginning of kindergarten to approximately 16 points at the end of third grade (see table 2). Expressed as a percentage of the standard deviation at each age level, the black-white mathematics gap increased from 0.64 standard deviations at the beginning of kindergarten to 0.88 standard deviations at the end of third grade.

The trend in the black-white ELA skills gap is more similar to the trend in the math skills gap for the ECLS-K data set than for the NICHD data set. Expressed in the IRT score metric, the black-white ELA achievement gap grows from approximately 4 points at the beginning of kindergarten to 15 points at the end of third grade. Measured in Fryer and Levitt's metric, the gap increases from approximately 0.40 standard deviations to approximately 0.75 standard deviations.

A key part of the explanation for the difference between the two data sets in the black-white mathematics skill gap trend (and to a lesser extent the trend in the ELA gap) is that the tests are quite different. The tests used in the ECLS-K study focus on skills taught in the relevant grades in school. The Woodcock-Johnson tests used in the NICHD study are broad-based measures of skills.

Family Characteristics

Following procedures for the construction of a composite measure of family socioeconomic status (SES) laid out in the ECLS-K data codebooks, we created a time-varying measure of SES in the NICHD data set based on indicators of total family income as well as occupational prestige scores and education of each child's parents. For mothers who were not partnered, only maternal occupational prestige and education (as well as total family income) were included in the SES composite. We then created a time-invariant measure of the child's baseline SES by averaging the values of composite socioeconomic status at ages six months and fifteen months. We subtracted this baseline value from subsequent values of time-varying SES, and included these latter deviations as a time-varying measure of the child's SES in our later regression models along with the baseline measure itself.

One additional family variable we used in selected analyses was a measure of parenting behaviors, specifically maternal sensitivity. Sensitivity was assessed during a mother-child structured play interaction when children were six and fifteen months of age. Mother-child interactions were videotaped in semistructured fifteen-minute observations. Interaction activities included two tasks that were too difficult for the child to carry out independently and required the parent's instruction and assistance. The interaction was rated using seven-point global rating scales, which were designed to capture the mother's emotional and instrumental support for the child during collaborative interactions between mother and child. Our measure of maternal sensitivity is the simple average of the values at the two time periods of a composite of three subscales: supportive presence, respect for the child's autonomy, and hostility (reflected).[20] An attraction of this variable is that it provides a direct measure of the quality of stimulation and support very young children receive from their mothers. A limitation is that the variable may be endogenous in that babies' personalities and skills may elicit behaviors from their mothers. For this reason, we discuss in a separate section our exploration of the role this variable plays in predicting children's subsequent skill levels.

As indicated in table 2, the families of black children in the NICHD sample had fewer resources of a variety of types than did white children in this sample. The families of black children had lower socioeconomic status, were

---

20. For more information on the maternal sensitivity measure, see NICHD ECCRN (1999).

less likely to have at least ten books in the home, and were more likely to be on public assistance. Also, on average, black mothers scored more than one standard deviation lower on the maternal sensitivity measure than white mothers. The black-white differences in family background characteristics are even more stark for children in the ECLS-K sample than for those in the NICHD sample. The likely explanation is that the designers of the NICHD study excluded children who lived in neighborhoods too dangerous for interviewers to visit and black children are more likely than white children to live in such neighborhoods.

School Quality Indicators

In our analyses, we examined the impact on mathematics skills of three types of school quality indicators, each of which has been the subject of public policies aimed at improving school quality. The first are conventional resources, which are things that schools can alter relatively easily, including class size and whether teachers have a master's degree or more than two years of teaching experience. Given that the salaries of almost all teachers in U.S. public schools are based on salary schedules that reward highest degree attained and years of experience, it is not surprising that these conventional resource variables typically explain a large percentage of the variation in school expenditures per student.

There are relatively few differences in either data set in the average level of conventional resources provided to black and white children. As shown in table 2, average class sizes and the percentages of teachers who have master's degrees are about the same for black children as for white children. Thus to look for inequalities in school resources as an explanation for black-white achievement gaps one must look for differences in resources that are more subtle than class sizes and the educational attainments of teachers.

One exception to the general pattern that average levels of conventional resources are about the same for black children as for white children is the likelihood of being taught by a novice teacher. In both data sets, black children are more likely than white children to be taught by a novice teacher in some grades (see table 2). In the ECLS-K data set, this is the case when children are in first grade as well as third grade. In the NICHD data set, it is the case in third grade. This pattern, documented in many studies,[21] is disturbing because recent high-quality research has shown that novice teachers are less

---

21. See, for example, Boyd and others (2005); Clotfelter, Ladd, and Vigdor (2005).

effective than those with at least two years of experience in increasing students' achievement.[22] For this reason, we include among our measures of school resources a dichotomous variable that takes on a value of 1 if teachers are in their first two years of teaching (zero, otherwise).

The second set of school quality indicators are measures of the racial and ethnic composition of the student body in each student's school (in the ECLS-K data set) or class (in the NICHD data set). The ECLS-K data set only provides information on whether the percentage of black students and percentage of Latino students fell into particular numerical ranges, one of which was greater than 25. Preliminary analyses showed that the important distinction was whether the percentage of black students and the percentage of Latino students were greater than 25. For that reason we included dichotomous indicators for schools that fell in these categories. To keep the model specifications used in the two data sets as similar as possible, we adopted these same variable definitions for the NICHD data set.[23]

One reason racial composition measures are interesting is that reducing the racial segregation of American public schools has been a major public policy thrust over the last fifty years. Although analysts differ on the consequences of desegregation policies, several studies have found that children learn less in schools or classes in which a large percentage of the children are black or Latino.[24] A likely explanation is that race and ethnicity serve as indicators of poverty and schools serving high concentrations of children living in poverty find it especially difficult to create effective learning environments. To learn something about whether it is racial and ethnic composition *per se* that matters, or whether these variables serve only as proxies for concentrations of poverty, we fitted models using the ECLS-K data set in which we included more direct measures of the concentration of poverty, namely the percentage of children eligible for a free or reduced price lunch, as well as the racial-ethnic student body composition measures.

Not surprisingly, the racial composition of classmates is quite different for black children than for white children (table 2). In both data sets, at least 40 percent of the black children attended schools in which at least 25 percent

22. See, for example, Clotfelter, Ladd, and Vigdor (2006); Rivkin, Hanushek, and Kain (2005); Kane and Staiger (2005); Murnane and Phillips (1981); Rockoff (2004).

23. The results of preliminary data analyses with the continuous measures of the racial-ethnic composition in the NICHD data set were not substantively different from the results reported in the paper that are based on the dichotomous indicators of the racial-ethnic composition of the students in the class.

24. Hanushek and Rivkin (2006).

of their classmates were black, while only about 7 percent of white students attended schools in which at least 25 percent of the students were black. It was also the case that the percentage of children eligible for a free or reduced price lunch was much higher in schools attended by black children (about 50 percent) than the analogous percentage in schools attended by white children (about 20 percent) in the ECLS-K data set (these data were not available in the NICHD data set). These patterns reflect the segregated nature of housing patterns in the United States.

The third set of school quality indicators included in our analyses measures the amounts of time that teachers spent on mathematics instruction. These data, which are available only for the NICHD data set, come from classroom observations conducted by trained observers using the standardized Classroom Observation System (COS) in first and third grades.[25] During a three-hour observation cycle, trained viewers recorded data on child and teacher behaviors, activities, and setting quality. More specifically, during two forty-four-minute observation cycles, a time sampling method was used to record discrete codes describing the activities in one ten-minute period of thirty-second observe and thirty-second record intervals. As such, discrete behaviors were sampled for a total of thirty minutes across each of the two observation cycles, for a total of sixty minutes of observation. We created a summary score for the amount of time spent on mathematics instruction by first summing the number of observed behaviors of mathematics teaching across the thirty segments within an observation cycle and then by summing the total observed behaviors across the two cycles. The ensuing measure can be described as the average number of minutes per each hour of observation that the teacher was engaged in teaching mathematics.

The variable measuring amount of school time teachers spend teaching mathematics is interesting because prior studies have shown that the amount of instructional time matters.[26] If instructional time does affect student achievement, policies aimed at increasing the amount of time black children spend learning mathematics could contribute to closing black-white achievement gaps. However, there is a need for caution in interpreting the evidence on the relationship between instructional time and children's achievement in this study because instructional time may be endogenous. That is, teachers may devote more time to teaching mathematics, for example, if they find that

25. For more information on the COS, see NICHD Early Child Care Research Network (2002 and 2005).
26. See, for example, Carroll (1963).

children have trouble mastering critical mathematical skills. The estimate of the impact of instruction on achievement from single equation models may be downwardly biased as a result of this potential endogeneity.

As shown in table 2, primary school teachers of children in the NICHD data set allocate an average of eight to ten minutes of each instructional hour to teaching mathematics. There are no large, consistent differences between teachers of black children and those of white children in the allocation of time to mathematics instruction.

Statistical Analyses

We addressed our research questions by fitting random-effects and fixed-effects regression models separately within each data set. In each case, we began with a set of baseline models in which we investigated the relationship between the child's mathematics achievement and the child's age, race-ethnicity, and gender. A regression model typical of those we fitted is:

$$
\begin{aligned}
(1) \qquad Y_{ij} = {} & \beta_0 + \beta_1 t_{ij} + \beta_2 t_{ij}^2 + \beta_3 Black_i + \beta_4 Latino_i \\
& + \beta_5 \left(Black_i \times t_{ij} \right) + \beta_6 \left(Latino_i \times t_{ij} \right) \\
& + \beta_7 \left(Female_i \right) + \beta_8 \left(Female_i \times t_{ij} \right) \\
& + \beta_9 \left(Female_i \times t_{ij}^2 \right) + \left(\varepsilon_{ij} + u_i \right).
\end{aligned}
$$

In this hypothesized model, outcome Y_{ij} represents the ith child's IRT-scaled mathematics achievement on the jth occasion of measurement; predictor t_{ij} represents the child's age (measured in years and recentered on age of 4.5 years—that is, $t_{ij} = AGE_{ij} - 4.5$); $Black_i$ and $Latino_i$ are dichotomous time-invariant predictors representing the child's race-ethnicity; $Female_i$ is a dichotomous time-invariant indicator that the child is female; ε_{ij} is the usual child- and occasion-specific residual; and u_i represents the time-invariant random effect of the child.

In each data set, we found that the age-trajectories of children's mathematics achievement were consistently a quadratic function of their age. In addition, two-way interactions between ethnicity and linear age made statistically significant contributions to the prediction of mathematics achievement, as did two-way interactions between gender and both linear and quadratic age. Consequently, these terms are included here in our baseline model and in all subsequent hypothesized models below. In the ECLS-K data set, two-way interactions between race-ethnicity and quadratic age also made statistically significant contributions to the prediction of mathematics achievement. These interactions were included in the regression models fitted with the ECLS-K data set. It is the statistically significant presence of the non-linear impact of child age and the interactions between child race-ethnicity and age that permits the academic trajectories of children of different ethnicities to converge as they grow older, closing the achievement gaps. For each regression model fitted in both data sets, we conducted supplementary general linear hypothesis tests on the apparent gaps in average achievement between black and white children, at age 4.5 years and the end of third grade. Our fitted models and the results of these supplementary tests are reported below for each data set.

In follow-up analyses discussed later, we systematically refitted all hypothesized regression models in each data set, treating the child-specific random effects as fixed effects. In these additional models, all time-invariant effects—such as child ethnicity in the baseline models—drop from the regression model, but important interactions between ethnicity and child age are retained because they are time-varying. Where comparisons could be made, our principal findings did not differ between the random-effects and fixed-effects specifications of the hypothesized regression models. For that reason we provide only the fitted random effects models.[27]

After fitting the baseline regression models described above and conducting the supplementary tests, we added measures of SES to the random-effects model presented in equation (1).[28] Our purpose was to evaluate whether extant differences in children's achievement trajectories by race-ethnicity were, in fact, simply the effect of racial-ethnic differences in socioeconomic status. In these new hypothesized models, we tested for the presence of two-way interactions between the new measures of SES and the other predictors already present in the model, including child age and race-ethnicity. Where they proved important, these interactions were retained and their estimated effects are reported below. We also added to this model the set of time-invariant family background characteristics that Fryer and Levitt included in their models.

27. The results from fitting the models with fixed effects for students are available from the authors.

28. One difference between the regression models fitted in the two data sets is that the model fitted with NICHD data included measures of both time-invariant baseline and time-varying SES (the latter deviated from the baseline value, as described earlier).

Our next step was to add the measure of maternal sensitivity to the model that included family background variables. As explained above, this maternal sensitivity variable was only available in the NICHD data set. We did this to learn whether early parenting behaviors predicted children's mathematics scores several years later, even after accounting for conventional family background variables.

Finally, in each data set we added (sequentially) one of the three kinds of time-varying school quality indicators (described above) to the hypothesized regression models containing the effects of child age, race-ethnicity, socioeconomic status, and other family background variables. We first entered predictors representing conventional school resources. We then replaced these conventional measures of school resources with the measures of the classroom or school racial composition. Finally, we replaced these with measures of the amount of school time spent on mathematics instruction (in the NICHD data set only). In each case, we explored interactions between these new additions and the existing predictors in the model, conducted the supplementary general linear hypothesis tests (described above), and refitted the models treating the hypothesized random effects as fixed. Our findings follow.

Results

Table 3 provides the estimated regression coefficients from fitting the baseline model and the model that includes family background variables for both data sets. It also lists the results from a model fitted with the NICHD data set that includes the maternal sensitivity variable and its interactions with time. Random effects for children are specified in these models. Since the estimated coefficients on these control variables hardly change when the school resources variables are added to the model, we do not report these coefficients in subsequent models. The first panel in table 4 lists the coefficients on the three sets of school variables for the ECLS-K sample. The second panel in the table provides the analogous information for the NICHD sample.

Table 5 summarizes, for both the ECLS-K and NICHD data sets, the predicted sizes of the black-white mathematics and ELA skill gaps from random effects models that do not and that do include family background variables including socioeconomic status. The relevant entries in table 5 (−0.599 and 2.46) show the pattern that Fryer and Levitt emphasized, namely, that in the ECLS-K data set, there is no statistically significant black-white skill gap in mathematics and ELA at the beginning of kindergarten after taking into

Table 3. Results of Regressions Predicting Children's Math Scores Using the Restricted ECLS-K Data Set and the NICHD Data Set, with Random Effects for Individual Children

Variable	ECLS-K		NICHD		
	Baseline	All family background controls	Baseline	All family background controls	Early maternal sensitivity
Age	26.20****	26.34****	24.84****	25.12****	36.79****
Age^2	−2.06****	−2.09****	−1.80****	−1.85****	−3.49****
Age at entry to kindergarten	.444****	.487****	−5.55****	−6.38****	−6.66****
Black	−5.57****	−.599	−20.31****	−12.77****	−8.65****
Latino	−6.23****	−1.83****	−11.39****	−7.95****	−6.26****
Black × age	−4.46****	−4.30****	1.91****	1.07****	.554
Latino × age	−2.22****	−2.08****	1.53****	1.10***	.916**
Black × age^2	.458****	.434****	—	—	
Latino × age^2	.280****	.246****	—	—	
Female	.118	.108	4.64****	4.38****	3.60****
Female × age	−1.03****	−1.09****	−4.27****	−4.16****	−3.93****
Female × age^2	.060*	.078**	.663****	.655****	.615****

Early SES (time-invariant)	n.a.			5.16****	3.47****
Early SES × age	n.a.			-1.18****	-.791****
SES (time-varying)	3.46*****			2.51****	2.07****
Children's books	.003*****			7.12**	4.60
Birth weight (oz.)	.017*****			.043**	.034
Teen mother at first birth	-2.18*****			-3.26*	-2.12
Mother age 30+ at first birth	1.92*****			2.04**	1.36*
Assistance	-3.65*****			-5.14****	-2.83**
Early maternal sensitivity					12.88*****
Early maternal sensitivity × age					-3.70****
Early maternal sensitivity × age^2					.524*****
Variance components					
σ^2_U	111.94	87.98	139.95	115.56	110.46
σ^2_e	72.93	72.59	97.61	95.65	93.70

Source: Authors' calculations.

n.a. Not available.

SES = Socioeconomic status.

****$p < 0.001$, ***$p < 0.01$, **$p < 0.05$, *$p < 0.10$.

Table 4. Results of Regressions Predicting Children's Math Scores Using the Restricted ECLS-K Data Set and the NICHD Data Set, with Random Effects for Individual Children

ECLS-K data set	Conventional school resources	Racial-ethnic composition of student body	Racial-ethnic composition and percent students in poverty
Control variables[a]	✓	✓	✓
Class size	.065***		
Master's degree	−.025		
First two years of teaching	−.350		
25 percent or more students are black		−.741**	−.011
25 percent or more students are Latino		−.705**	.004
Percent students eligible free lunch			−.030****
Variance components			
σ^2_U	85.56	88.74	88.55
σ^2_e	69.72	71.06	70.73

NICHD data set	Conventional school resources	Racial-ethnic composition of student body	Math instruction
Control variables[a]	✓	✓	✓
Class size	−.004		
Master's degree	−.256		
First two years of teaching	−.074		
25 percent or more students are black		−1.22	
25 percent or more students are Latino		−2.65	
Math instruction			.053*
Variance components			
σ^2_U	114.70	114.70	115.99
σ^2_e	95.65	95.84	95.65

Source: Authors' calculations.

****$p < 0.001$, ***$p < 0.01$, **$p < 0.05$, *$p < 0.10$.

a. The control variables include all of the child and family covariates listed in columns 2 and 4 of table 3. In addition, we controlled for whether or not the child was held back in kindergarten, first, and third grade, as well as the interaction between held back in kindergarten and age.

account the effects of differences in observed family background characteristics. The relevant entries in table 5 (−12.77 and −7.68) show that the patterns are quite different in the NICHD data set. Even after taking into account the effects of observed family background characteristics, there are substantial black-white skill gaps in mathematics and ELA at the beginning of kindergarten for children in the NICHD data set. The likely explanation is that the Woodcock-Johnson tests measure a broader range of skills than do the tests administered to the ECLS-K sample.

As shown in table 5, the trend in the fitted black-white mathematics and ELA skill gaps for children in the ECLS-K data set are as reported by Fryer

Table 5. Predicted Black-White Gap in Math and ELA Scores at the Beginning of Kindergarten and End of Third Grade in the Restricted ECLS-K and NICHD Data Sets

	ECLS-K		NICHD	
Score	*Beginning of kindergarten*	*End of third grade*	*Beginning of kindergarten*	*End of third grade*
Mathematics				
No controls	−5.58****	−15.72****	−20.31****	−12.00****
Family covariates	−.599	−10.47****	−12.77****	−8.12****
Family covariates plus maternal sensitivity	n.a.	n.a.	−8.65****	−6.24****
ELA				
No controls	−3.77****	−15.58****	−12.75****	−12.97****
Family covariates	2.46****	−13.38****	−7.68****	−9.63****
Family covariates plus maternal sensitivity	n.a.	n.a.	−5.17****	−6.93****

Source: Authors' calculations.
n.a. Not available.
****$p < 0.001$, ***$p < 0.01$, **$p < 0.05$, *$p < 0.10$.

and Levitt: they grow markedly between the beginning of kindergarten and end of third grade. This is true both in models that control for family background and those that do not. In contrast, the trend in the fitted black-white mathematics skill gap for the NICHD data set, as measured by IRT-scaled scores on Woodcock-Johnson tests, declines by 40 percent between the beginning of kindergarten and end of third grade and the ELA skill gap remains stable in size (see table 5). Again, the likely explanation for the striking difference in trends is that the Woodcock-Johnson tests measure somewhat different skills than do the tests administered to the ECLS-K sample. It is also important to keep in mind that trends in the size of the black-white achievement gap depend on the measurement metric. We report here trends in test score points on the vertically equatable IRT test scale metric. The patterns are somewhat different when the gaps are measured in terms of standard deviation of the test score distribution measured at that particular age—the metric Fryer and Levitt used.

Maternal Sensitivity

As explained above, the maternal sensitivity variable that we constructed for the NICHD data set provides a direct measure of the quality of stimulation and support very young children receive from their mothers. The variable has the potential to shed light on the importance of children's early at-home experiences in determining later school success.

We recognize that there may be problems of endogeneity with the measure of mother's parenting behavior. That is, we have no way of knowing whether sensitive mothers produce higher-performing children or whether higher-performing children evoke sensitive responses from their mothers. By including sensitivity measures from a very early age (an average of the scores taken when children were six and fifteen months old), we attempted to reduce the endogeneity, though we cannot be sure that we have eliminated it.

To explore whether the maternal sensitivity variable predicts subsequent math skills for children in the NICHD data set, we added the measure of maternal sensitivity and its linear and quadratic interactions with time to the model that included conventional family background variables. The results are reported in the far right column of table 3.

Children whose mothers scored highly on the measure of maternal sensitivity performed much better on subsequent tests of mathematical skills than did children whose mothers had lower scores on this measure. Since black mothers, on average, scored more than one standard deviation lower on the maternal sensitivity measure than did white mothers, it follows that controlling for this variable reduces the predicted size of the black-white gap in mathematics skills. As indicated in table 5, net of the impact of conventional family background characteristics, the predicted black-white mathematics score gap at the beginning of kindergarten is 12.77 IRT-scale points. In the model that also controls for maternal sensitivity, the predicted black-white mathematics skill gap is 8.65 points. In other words, differences in early parenting behaviors explain approximately one-third of the black-white gap in mathematics skills at the beginning of kindergarten that remains after taking conventional family background characteristics into account. The impact of early maternal sensitivity on mathematics skills declines somewhat with age. However, as shown in table 5, differences in early parenting account for almost one-quarter of the black-white mathematics skills gap at the end of third grade that remains after taking conventional family background variables into account.

Differences in early parenting behaviors are equally important in explaining that part of the black-white gap in ELA skills that remains after taking conventional family background characteristics into account. As shown in table 5, differences in early parenting behaviors explain approximately one-third of the remaining ELA gap at the beginning of kindergarten and slightly more than one-quarter of the remaining ELA gap at the end of third grade.

The results on the role of early parenting behavior in predicting children's subsequent mathematics and ELA skills have two implications. First, they support the argument of child psychologists that children's experiences during their first years of life have lasting impacts. Second, the results show that measures of children's mathematics and ELA skills measured at the beginning of kindergarten and at the end of first grade do not capture the full influence of early childhood experiences. As Todd and Wolpin (2003) explained, this pattern illustrates the difficulty of developing models that accurately estimate the impact of home and school influences on children's achievement.

Conventional School Resources

As shown in table 4, there was no evidence from either data set that teachers with a master's degree are more effective in enhancing students' mathematics skills than are teachers without this degree. This pattern is consistent with the results of the vast majority of prior studies. It also makes sense because the requirement imposed by many states that teachers acquire a master's degree within their first few years of teaching has created incentives for the creation of a large number of relatively undemanding, low-quality master's degree programs.

We also do not find any statistically significant evidence in either data set that novice teachers are less effective than those with at least two years of experience (see table 4). Differences in the design of both the ECLS-K and the NICHD data sets are the likely explanation for why our results differ from those of several recent studies that do show that individual teachers become more effective as they gain experience. Neither the ECLS-K nor the NICHD studies follow teachers over time. For that reason our estimates compare the performances at one point in time of teachers who have different levels of experience. Selective attrition of the most-effective teachers from the classroom would lead us to underestimate the extent to which teachers improve their performance over their first several years in the classroom.[29]

A surprising pattern is that class size is positively associated with student achievement in the ECLS-K data set (see table 4). We believe that the explanation for this counterintuitive finding is the process by which students are assigned to classes. We found strong statistically significant negative relationships between class size for students in grade t and their reading and math scores in year t-2. In other words, schools tended to place struggling students in smaller classes. Even with the benefits of the smaller classes, these students made less progress than the more-skilled students in larger classes. This

---

29. For a discussion of this issue and evidence of the impact of research design on results, see Murnane and Phillips (1981).

illustrates the difficulty of isolating productivity effects of school resources in settings in which there is nonrandom assignment of students to resource levels.

Student Body Composition

Estimates based on the ECLS-K data set show that students in schools in which more than 25 percent of the student body consists of black or Latino students learn less mathematics than students in schools with a lower percentage of students of color. The coefficients in the regression models fitted with the smaller NICHD data set show the same pattern although they are not statistically significantly different from zero.

An interesting question is whether the racial-ethnic composition of the student body affects student learning or whether these easily observed variables stand in for less commonly observed variables measuring the percentage of students living in poverty and coming to school with especially great learning needs. To examine this question, we fitted a regression model in the ECLS-K data set that included the percentage of students eligible for free or reduced-price lunch as well as the two indicators of the racial-ethnic mix of the student body. The results are reported in the far right column of the top panel in table 4. The coefficients on the racial-ethnic mix of the student body are not statistically significantly different from zero in this model, but the percentage of students living in poverty is a strong, statistically significant negative predictor of student achievement. This supports the position that the important characteristic of the student body is the percentage of students living in poverty. Schools serving high concentrations of students from poor families face especially large challenges, ones that relatively few schools have been able to consistently master.

Instructional Time

In the NICHD data set we found that the more classroom time teachers devote to teaching mathematics, the more mathematics student learn during the school year. A causal interpretation of the coefficient implies that an increase of ten minutes of math instruction during each hour of the school day (equivalent to an increase of fifty minutes per day in a five-hour school day) would result in an increase in 0.58 points in each student's math score at the end of the school year.[30] Over four years of school (from the beginning

30. As we explain earlier in this paper, the presence of selection effects may have led us to underestimate the impact of instructional time on achievement. The logic is that teachers whose children are having difficulty with mathematics may devote more time to teaching it.

of kindergarten to the end of third grade) the predicted increase would be 2.32 points, approximately 20 percent of the black-white gap in math skills at the end of the third grade. Another way of expressing the magnitude of the effect is that closing the 12 point black-white achievement gap in math achievement at the end of third grade (approximately 0.90 standard deviations) would require that black students receive four to five hours more math instruction per day over the first four years of school than white students receive. We interpret our results as indicating that providing more instruction is a possible policy approach for closing the black-white achievement gap. However, it is also important to invest in improving the quality of instruction so that the payoff to each hour of instruction is larger.

Discussion

The results of our examination of black-white mathematics and ELA achievement gaps in the ECLS-K and NICHD data sets shed light on several aspects of Fryer and Levitt's provocative findings. Perhaps most important, their finding that a relatively small set of background characteristics explains almost all of the gaps in mathematics and ELA skills at the beginning of kindergarten appears to stem from the narrow focus of the tests in the ECLS-K data set. In the NICHD data set, substantial black-white gaps in mathematics and ELA skills are present at the beginning of kindergarten even after accounting for virtually the same set of family background characteristics that Fryer and Levitt used in their studies. Moreover, studies using other data sets also report large black-white skill gaps at the beginning of kindergarten.[31]

We also show that the substantial growth in the black-white mathematics and ELA skill gaps over the period from the beginning of kindergarten that Fryer and Levitt present in the ECLS-K data set are not present in the NICHD data set. Measured in IRT-scaled points, the black-white skill gap in mathematics for children in the NICHD data set declines markedly during the first four years of school. The gap in ELA skills does grow, but at a much slower rate than in the ECLS-K data set. We also show that trends in the gap are sensitive to the choice of measurement metric.

We find that a measure of parenting skills constructed from observational data when the child was six and fifteen months old is a strong predictor of children's mathematics and ELA skills during the first years of school. Differences

31. Rouse, Brooks-Gunn, and McLanahan (2005).

in the observed measure of parenting skills account for more than one-quarter of the black-white skill gap that is present among children with the same conventional family background characteristics.

Turning to school resources, the one difference in the distribution of conventional school resources is that black children are much more likely to be taught by novice teachers than are white children. This pattern, which is present in both data sets, is disturbing because a number of recent studies with strong designs show that teachers are much less effective in their first two years of teaching than they are after acquiring at least two years of experience.

We find no evidence supporting the argument that across-the-board cuts in class size are an effective strategy for improving school quality. In interpreting this evidence, it is important to keep in mind that the class sizes in our data set average twenty-one to twenty-three students. Thus our evidence sheds no light on the role of class size in influencing student achievement in classes with thirty-five or forty-five students.

We also find no evidence that requiring teachers to earn master's degrees is an effective strategy for improving school quality. As explained above, a likely explanation is that the master's degree requirement stimulated the creation of many low-quality master's degree programs.

Our evidence based on the NICHD data set is that the amount of time teachers devote to mathematics instruction influences how much mathematics children learn. This suggests the importance of focusing school policy on strategies to improve the quantity (and quality) of instruction children receive in school. Designing public policies to increase the quantity and quality of instruction children receive at school is more difficult than designing policies to reduce class size or to mandate that all teachers earn additional educational credentials. Evidence from schools that have produced student achievement gains by increasing the quality and quantity of instruction shows that schools can play an important role in increasing the achievement of black students.[32] However, going to scale with instructional improvements remains an enormous challenge in the schools most of the nation's black children attend.

A final pattern is that student body composition matters, and the percentage of students living in poverty is a better indicator of the challenges schools face in enhancing student achievement than is the racial-ethnic composition of the student body. Altering the housing patterns that produce schools segregated by race and income is a challenge the United States has never been

---

32. See Levy and Murnane (2004, chap. 8).

willing to embrace. Closing the black-white achievement gap when schools remain segregated by race and income is extraordinarily difficult. To succeed, schools that serve concentrations of poor children must be staffed with skilled, experienced teachers who have learned to work together to provide large amounts of consistent, coordinated, high-quality instruction. Closing the gap is the greatest educational challenge facing the United States today.

Comments

Eric Hanushek: This is a high-quality paper of the type that I have come to expect from these researchers. More importantly, they have turned their attention to a set of intellectual issues that have quite large policy importance. Murnane and his colleagues have picked up on Fryer and Levitt's very provocative analyses, which could be interpreted as suggesting that schools contribute to a growing racial gap in achievement. Murnane and others' analysis in this paper suggests that Fryer and Levitt's data and analysis are in question.

The most important Fryer and Levitt findings (in simplest terms) are that schools appear to contribute to a widening black-white achievement gap, but obvious school policies show little hope for improving the situation. Given the continued policy concerns about the distribution of a student outcomes, these findings that take the focus to the earliest school experiences lead to a new round of questions about what options are available.

Fryer and Levitt's unique study, however, needs some corroboration before policy is based on it. Specifically, much of the evidence is indirect—that differences in school achievement can be explained by neither measured differences between family background characteristics nor school factors, even though preschool differences can be explained by these factors. Further, the results could depend on the measures and samples of a new effort to study achievement—the Early Childhood Longitudinal Study (ECLS-K). This new education sample may in itself have some peculiarities.

This background motivates the study by Murnane and others. They have a simple but important research plan. First, they introduce a new and highly detailed data set from the National Institute of Child Health and Human Development (NICHD) in order to study the sensitivity of the results to the ECLS-K sample. Second, they investigate the sensitivity of the results to various aspects of the model specification.

This activity is extraordinarily valuable. There are many examples of alleged facts that come from one study or one sample proving to be much

128

less than facts when they are overturned by another study. This situation is especially problematic when policies are swirling around as they are in the area of the racial achievement gap and there is the possibility of making premature policy judgments. The authors of this paper show the merits of careful and imaginative replication. Their findings put a different twist on the racial gap. First, while they confirm the finding that black students enter school less prepared than whites, they find that the early achievement gap looks larger and less explicable than that portrayed by Fryer and Levitt. But second, they find that the gap shrinks with time in school, as opposed to expanding. Third, in the category of old results, they confirm that measured attributes of teachers and schools have little to do with either achievement or the racial gap (a Fryer and Levitt finding). Black and white students face roughly the same measured characteristics of schools, but they are not important in explaining achievement.

Murnane and his colleagues at the same time fail to confirm two common findings in previous work. They do not find that having a rookie teacher is a particular detriment, even though black students tend to get new teachers a disproportionate amount of the time. Further, these authors do not see that the more-segregated schools that black students are likely to attend are a particular disadvantage *per se* (although their measure of racial composition is quite imprecise). Instead, they find that racial composition is simply an imperfect proxy for the aggregate composition of student family income—that is, it is student socioeconomic status and not race.

Finally, the authors do find support for the idea that time on task has a positive effect. To people outside of education research, this seems like something that does not need to be explained. Nonetheless, this seemingly trivial finding has been difficult to document in a convincing way, and even here has some uncertainty surrounding it because Murnane and his colleagues have trouble sorting out the underlying causal mechanism.

Their work leaves a number of puzzles and suggestive ideas. They show quite convincingly that the differences in the samples do not appear to be the cause of the differing results. They do a very careful job of matching samples, and the overall conflict of results remains. So what lies behind the differences? They are led to concentrating on possible differences in test measurement, although it seems like more analysis is needed in this area. While this is plausible, there seem to be many questions on that, and there is no direct evidence.

They do point out clearly that there are alternative test metrics that can be used and that the choice can affect the results. Specifically, it is possible, and common, to translate everything into standard deviation units of performance (effect sizes), but one can also use the Item Response Theory scaling that puts different levels on the same scale. In the authors' work, the choice can change the conclusions in noticeable ways. Yet the choice is rather arbitrary without any external valuation of educational outcomes. Indeed, while the authors here do not linger on this, the topic of measurement scales for student performance is one that will undoubtedly receive increased attention over time.

The analyses of specific resources and factors affecting performance, while confirming much of the past work on specific resource effects, would seem to need more work. The authors have a small sample that lacks much detail on schools and teachers. In addition, they have trouble telling a compelling story that they have identified causal influences. Because of these limitations, this portion of their study presents the most uncertainty (and probably cannot be resolved with their data).

Perhaps the biggest question revolves around the differences between models of math gaps and English Language Arts (ELA) gaps. Specifically, the authors' ability to explain preschool gaps and the pattern of these gaps in school differs significantly across tests. Essentially, in their new data, the math gap significantly declines with schooling, but the ELA gap is constant or somewhat increasing. While it is possible to tell stories about why these different subject areas might respond differently to parental and school inputs, they all seem to require a lot more analysis.

There are two relatively new and intriguing findings. First, Murnane and his colleagues find powerful and continuing effects of early parenting behavior. This work is starting to dig further into what actually takes place in the family, and it is a welcome line of inquiry. Too much research stops at just finding that family income is correlated with student outcomes and fails to tell us anything about that relationship.

Second, the authors underscore the importance of time on task for determining achievement. This finding hopefully will spur more work in the area. It comes up in many of today's policy debates. For example, recent questions about federal accountability (for instance, No Child Left Behind) have centered on the idea that accountability in a few areas may lead to changes in the emphasis of schools. In particular, schools desiring to improve math and reading performance might spend more time on these subjects. The findings of this paper indicate that this might be an effective strategy by schools. Of course, part of the discussion lingers on whether or not this is a good idea, because spending more time on math implies spending less time on some other things, given an overall time budget. These extended ideas about the pluses and minuses of more time unfortunately go beyond what Murnane and his colleagues can analyze within their data.

Rebecca Maynard: Murnane and others have undertaken a very careful exploration of the size and character of early differences in math and reading achievement of young children, with a particular focus on differences in the average achievement levels of blacks and whites. This research is important for several reasons. First, as a group, black children (as well as children from most other minority race or ethnic groups) consistently underperform academically relative to white children. Second, the differences in math and reading achievement between black and white children are sufficiently large to matter in terms of the economic and social prospects children face when they reach adulthood. The empirical evidence is quite clear that raising the academic performance of black children is critical for reducing disparities in earnings. Third, whatever worked to reduce achievement differences in the years following the release of the Coleman Report no longer worked by the 1980s.

This paper is a small but very important contribution to understanding the causes of the residual differences in achievement and for identifying promising policy or practice changes that could increase the academic success of black children without compromising that of white children. Three highlights from the paper by Murnane and others follow.

First, this study underscores the importance of identifying appropriate measures of the skills that are important for children of various ages. There is no common currency for measuring academic achievement and, indeed, the currency used affects quite substantially the conclusions that follow. The achievement test itself matters in so far as different tests measure different skills. Yet there is no obvious basis for preferring one test to another. For example, before one can make real meaning out of the fact that the results for reading and math are more similar for the Early Childhood Longitudinal Study (ECLS-K) study sample than for the National Institute of Child Health and Human Development (NICHD) study sample, one should understand how well the achievement tests used in each study measure outcomes that are important for subsequent learning and lifelong success.

It also is important to better understand the interpretation of the metrics for judging achievement. Indeed, as pointed out by Murnane and his colleagues, standardized means provide a quite different picture of changes in black-white achievement gaps over the early grades than do scale results based on Item Response Theory. Standardized mean differences, for example, tell something about where the mean performance of one group of children stands relative to the overall distribution of performance levels. They tell nothing about performance differences relative to any particular standard of achievement. Moreover, standardized mean differences are highly sensitive to changes in the distribution of scores over time. Raw scores pose different issues. For instance, while they order children in terms of their overall performance, they do not incorporate judgments about whether equal size gains are more valuable at one end of the distribution than another.

A second contribution of this study relates to its findings on the value of increased instructional time. It seems clear from the study results that increased instructional time alone could make an important, but quite modest, contribution to closing the achievement gap. Murnane and others project that four or five hours of math instruction a day over the first four years of school would be required to eliminate the black-white achievement gap in mathematics. This, of course, assumes that the marginal relationship between math instructional time and achievement based on the current range of practice could be extended to a quite different profile of the use of class time, where almost the full school day would be devoted to math instruction or the number of hours in the school day would be extended substantially. Possibly, if increased instructional time were paired with more effective curricula and with better use of the before- and after-school hours, large gains in performance could be achieved. Murnane and others were not able to assess the benefits of such strategies with their data sets. However, there is an emerging literature—which is being enhanced through a number of ongoing randomized controlled trials initiated by the Institute for Education Sciences, U.S. Department of Education—that will provide evidence on the potential benefits of such strategies.

The study's third contribution relates to the clear reminder that schools play a very important role in promoting social justice and economic opportunity, but schools are not the sole solution to social and economic inequities. Much of what matters for the health and well-being of children occurs outside of the school setting—in the home or neighborhood. Murnane and others found evidence that parenting matters. This is important because there is evidence that policy interventions (for example, some home-visiting programs) can improve parenting. Furthermore, it might be possible to improve parenting through strategies involving media campaigns, community education programs, or parenting education classes for high-school students.

Murnane and others also note, but do not pursue, the fact that poverty, not race, seems to be the more important determinant of academic achievement. Therefore both housing and employment as well as training policies are potentially more important than education policies for reducing the achievement gap. Historically, however, policies in these areas have not been designed with any attention to their implications for educational outcomes for children.

This paper suggests three areas for further research. One area relates to understanding better what leads to low achievement, possibly through closer examination of so-called *defiant* children. For example, what is special about low-income, black children who succeed and what is special about those non-poor, white children who fail?

A second area for further study relates to who is having children and how a parent influences a child's achievement. More than 400,000 children are born to teenagers annually and one-third of all children (including a large majority of those born to teens) are born to single mothers. Both teen and single parenting affect the family and neighborhood contexts in which children are reared in ways that increase substantially their risk of poor academic and social outcomes. Quite possibly, finding ways to reduce teen and single parenthood would do as much to improve the achievement of black children relative to white children as would changes in education policies or practices.

The third area for further study relates to the implications for students' achievement of various school-based strategies being promoted through the No Child Left Behind policy to raise performance of students at the bottom—for example, supplemental and compensatory services as well as accountability policies. Understanding what is working, for whom, and under what conditions to raise the performance of blacks and other low-achieving groups and knowing the profile of those children still left behind would be valuable input to future policy decisions.

The usefulness of research in all three of these areas would be enhanced if there were agreement on the essential skills children should master and how to measure achievement of them. Hopefully, this study by Murnane and others will stimulate further work on this fundamental issue.

References

Boyd, David, and others. 2005. "Explaining the Short Careers of High-Achieving Teachers in Schools with Low-Performing Students." *American Economic Review* 95 (2): 166–71.

Carroll, John B. 1963. "A Model of School Learning." *Teachers College Record* 64: 723–33.

Clotfelter, Charles T., Helen F. Ladd, and Jacob L. Vigdor. 2005. "Who Teaches Whom? Race and the Distribution of Novice Teachers." *Economics of Education Review* 24: 377–92.

———. 2006. "Teacher-Student Matching and the Assessment of Teacher Effectiveness." Working Paper 11936. Cambridge, Mass.: National Bureau of Economic Research (January).

Coleman, James S., and others. 1966. *Equality of Educational Opportunity.* Office of Education, National Center for Educational Statistics. Washington.

Fryer, Ronald G., and Steven D. Levitt. 2004. "Understanding the Black-White Test Score Gap in the First Two Years of School." *Review of Economics and Statistics* 86 (2): 447–64.

———. 2005. "The Black-White Test Score Gap through Third Grade." Working Paper 11049. Cambridge, Mass.: National Bureau of Economic Research (January).

Hanushek, Eric A. 2003. "The Failure of Input-Based Schooling Policies." *Economic Journal* 113 (February): F64–F98.

Hanushek, Eric A., and Steven G. Rivkin. 2006. "The Evolution of the Black-White Achievement Gap in Elementary and Middle Schools." Paper presented at the American Economic Association Annual Meetings, Boston, Massachusetts, January 6–8.

Kane, Thomas J., and Douglas O. Staiger. 2005. "Identifying Effective Teachers with Imperfect Information." Working Paper. Harvard Graduate School of Education (April).

Levy, Frank, and Richard J. Murnane. 2004. *The New Division of Labor: How Computers are Creating the Next Job Market.* Princeton University Press.

Margo, Robert A. 1986. "Educational Achievement in Segregated School Systems: The Effects of 'Separate-but-Equal.' " *American Economic Review* 76 (4): 794–801.

Murnane, Richard J. 1975. *The Impact of School Resources on the Learning of Inner City Children.* Cambridge, Mass.: Ballinger.

Murnane, Richard J., and Barbara R. Phillips. 1981. "Learning by Doing, Vintage, and Selection: Three Pieces of the Puzzle Relating Teaching Experience and Teaching Performance." *Economics of Education Review* 1 (4): 453–65.

Murnane, Richard J., John B. Willett, and Frank Levy. 1995. "The Growing Importance of Cognitive Skills in Wage Determination." *Review of Economics and Statistics* 78 (2): 251–66.

NICHD Early Child Care Research Network. 1999. "Child Care and Mother-Child Interaction in the First Three Years of Life." *Developmental Psychology* 35: 1399–413.

———. 2001. "Nonmaternal Care and Family Factors in Early Development: An Overview of the NICHD Study of Early Child Care." *Applied Developmental Psychology* 22 (5): 457–92.

———. 2002. "The Relation of Global First-Grade Classroom Environment to Structural Classroom Features and Teacher and Student Behaviors." *Elementary School Journal* 102 (5): 367–87.

———. 2005. "A Day in Third Grade: A Large-Scale Study of Teacher Quality and Teacher and Student Behavior." *Elementary School Journal* 105 (3): 305–23.

Rasch, Georg. 1960. *Probabilistic Models for Some Intelligence and Attainment Tests.* Copenhagen: Danish Institute for Educational Research.

Rivkin, Steven G., Eric A. Hanushek, and John F. Kain. 2005. "Teachers, Schools, and Academic Achievement." *Econometrica* 73 (2): 417–58.

Rockoff, Jonah E. 2004. "The Impact of Individual Teachers on Student Achievement: Evidence from Panel Data." *American Economic Review* 94 (2): 247–52.

Rouse, Cecilia Elena, Jeanne Brooks-Gunn, and Sara McLanahan, eds. 2005. *The Future of Children: School Readiness: Closing Racial and Ethnic Gaps.* Brookings and Woodrow Wilson School of Public and International Affairs, Princeton University.

Todd, Petra E., and Kenneth I. Wolpin. 2003. "On the Specification and Estimation of the Production Function for Cognitive Achievement." *Economic Journal* 113.

Woodcock, Richard, and M. Bunner Johnson. 1989. *Woodcock-Johnson Psycho-Educational Battery, Revised.* Allen, Texas: DLM Teaching Resources.

Woodcock, Richard, and N. Mather. 1989. "W-J-R Tests of Achievement: Examiner's Manual." In *Woodcock-Johnson Psycho-Educational Battery, Revised.* Edited by Richard Woodcock and M. Bunner Johnson. Allen, Texas: DLM Teaching Resources.

KRISTIN TURNEY
University of Pennsylvania

SUSAN CLAMPET-LUNDQUIST
St. Joseph's University

KATHRYN EDIN
University of Pennsylvania

JEFFREY R. KLING
Brookings Institution and National Bureau of Economic Research

GREG J. DUNCAN
Northwestern University

Neighborhood Effects on Barriers to Employment: Results from a Randomized Housing Mobility Experiment in Baltimore

MOVING THE POOR OUT of inner-city neighborhoods of concentrated poverty (where jobs are scarce), and into low-poverty suburban neighborhoods (where jobs may be more plentiful) has been suggested by Wilson's (1987) theory of social isolation and Kain's (1968) theory of spatial mismatch to lead to greater

Primary support for this research was provided by grants from the Russell Sage Foundation and William T. Grant Foundation. Additional support was provided by the U.S. Department of Housing and Urban Development (HUD); Princeton Industrial Relations Section; Bendheim-Thomas Center for Research on Child Wellbeing; Princeton Center for Health and Wellbeing; Institute for Policy Research at Northwestern University; National Institute of Child Health and Development and National Institute of Mental Health (R01-HD40404 and R01-HD40444); National Science Foundation (9876337 and 0091854); MacArthur Foundation; Robert Wood Johnson Foundation; Smith Richardson Foundation; and Spencer Foundation. The authors are grateful to Todd Richardson and Mark Shroder of HUD; Eric Beecroft, Judie Feins, Barbara Goodson, Robin Jacob, Stephen Kennedy, Larry Orr, and Rhiannon Patterson of Abt Associates; our collaborators Jeanne Brooks-Gunn, Lawrence Katz, Tama Leventhal, Jeffrey Liebman, Jens Ludwig, and Lisa Sanbonmatsu; and our project staff including Karen Burke, Stefanie DeLuca, Alessandra Del Conte Dickovick, Heather Hill, Katie Hunt, Rebecca Kissane, Roi Lusk, Mikaela Luttrell-Rowland, Rechelle Paranal, Jennifer Pashup, Joanna Reed, Annette Rogers, Emily Snell, and Anita Zuberi.

137

employment and earnings. Between 1994 and 1997, the U.S. Department of Housing and Urban Development (HUD) launched the Moving to Opportunity for Fair Housing Demonstration Program (MTO) in an attempt to examine the effects of housing mobility on various factors including economic self-sufficiency. The MTO demonstration gave families living in distressed public housing in Baltimore, Boston, Chicago, Los Angeles, and New York the opportunity to relocate to private market housing in low-poverty suburban and city neighborhoods. MTO applicants were randomly assigned to one of three groups: an experimental group, with members receiving a voucher to be used in a census tract with a poverty rate of less than 10 percent; a Section 8 group,[1] with members receiving a voucher to move anywhere; or a control group. In 2002 all participating families, regardless of their MTO start date, were surveyed. Pooling data from all five cities, a recent study finds no significant effects on employment or earnings of adults in the experimental group, suggesting that receiving a voucher to move to a low-poverty neighborhood does not increase the economic self-sufficiency of poor families.[2]

In this paper we use data from an embedded in-depth qualitative study of MTO families in Baltimore to explore the social processes that might underlie these results. We present survey data from Baltimore that estimate the effect of the MTO vouchers on employment and earnings of adults, compared with the results from all five MTO cities. The difference in employment rates for the experimental and control groups is positive and of moderately large magnitude in Baltimore (larger than in the five cities combined), but statistically insignificant. The experimental group in Baltimore had lower average earnings than the control group. The lack of a large positive effect on employment and earnings is puzzling. In 2003 and 2004 we conducted in-depth interviews with a random sample drawn from all the Baltimore MTO families. Although the qualitative sample is relatively small, the in-depth nature of the data allows us to derive hypotheses that can be used to guide further qualitative work and the next round of survey work with the MTO population, scheduled for 2007.

We find that though experimentals and controls have similar rates of employment and earnings, both at the time of the survey (2002) and qualitative interview (2003–04), the nature of respondents' relationship to the labor force does differ by program group, at least in the qualitative sample. Additionally, we identify three barriers to employment that are common across program groups. Using these data, we generate hypotheses about why the MTO

---

1. Housing Choice Vouchers are commonly referred to as *Section 8* vouchers.
2. Kling, Liebman, and Katz (2007).

intervention may not have as strong an effect on the employment or earnings of Baltimore participants as originally projected.

First, many of the MTO experimentals had significant human capital barriers—including lack of adequate education and work experience, as well as mental and physical health problems—before moving to a low-poverty neighborhood. The MTO demonstration was not designed to address these deficits. In addition, employed respondents in both groups are heavily concentrated in retail and health care jobs. To get and keep jobs, many of these respondents relied heavily on a particular job search strategy—informal referrals from weak social ties (work contacts, acquaintances, or casual associates) who already held entry-level jobs in these sectors. Though experimentals were more likely to have employed neighbors, few of their neighbors held jobs in these sectors and therefore were not providing such referrals. Controls have fewer employed neighbors overall, but they were more likely to come across these useful weak ties in the course of their daily routines. Finally, the configuration of the Baltimore metropolitan area's public transportation routes in relationship to the locations of most jobs, in particular hospitals and nursing homes, posed special transportation challenges for experimentals as they searched for employment or tried to retain their jobs.

Background

Existing empirical studies that try to explain the employment problems of the urban poor usually focus on the influence of individual-level factors such as human capital or structural factors such as social isolation and the geographic accessibility of jobs. We look at how hypotheses and empirical support surrounding these three themes—human capital, social isolation, and spatial mismatch—are used to explain barriers to employment.

There is a strong positive connection between individual human capital and socioeconomic outcomes such as employment status and earnings.[3] Many argue that the unemployment problems of the poor are due to a mismatch between their education and skills and the demands of a changing economy.[4] For example, about 75 percent of entry-level jobs now require a high-school diploma, references, and general work experience.[5] Human capital barriers

3. Becker (1975).
4. See Handel (2003) for a review of the literature. See also Kasarda (1985); Holzer and Danziger (1998).
5. Holzer (1996).

are most detrimental to employment when they appear in conjunction with other additional barriers to employment. For example, welfare recipients with a combination of educational deficits and mental and physical health problems have worse employment outcomes than individuals who only lack education or who only have health problems.[6]

The social isolation of those poor who live in high-poverty inner-city neighborhoods may contribute to their employment difficulties. One seminal study defines social isolation as "the lack of contact or of sustained interactions with individuals and institutions that represent mainstream society."[7] This theory implies that individuals' actions are shaped by the actions of those who live around them. The neighborhood creates a normative climate that defines acceptable and unacceptable behaviors. Neighborhoods with high employment rates have a certain rhythm to daily life that may be beneficial to all residents. On a more practical level, employed neighbors can pass along job information to the unemployed. Additionally, communities with high employment rates will have more resources to invest in institutions that benefit all residents.[8] Conversely, those living in neighborhoods with low employment rates may be isolated from a normative climate that promotes work, job information and referrals, and community resources.[9]

Another relevant line of research is in how most workers acquire their jobs. The majority of Americans find employment through social ties rather than help wanted advertisements or other formal methods.[10] Neighborhood poverty may interact with how effective local social ties are in obtaining a well-paying job. In a study using the Atlanta Multi-City Study of Urban Inequality (MCSUI) data, researchers find that, controlling for individual-level characteristics, increases in neighborhood poverty lower the odds of having a social tie who has steady employment.[11] Even the few job contacts within these poor neighborhoods may not prove to be helpful in terms of social mobility. Another analysis with the same data finds that for African Americans, using a neighborhood job contact depresses annual income by $3,214, whereas there is no effect for whites.[12] Similarly, African American residents of poor and racially

6. Danziger (2000).
7. Wilson (1987, p. 60).
8. Wilson (1996).
9. See also Massey and Denton (1993).
10. Granovetter (1974); Lin, Ensel, and Vaughn (1981); Lin and Dumin (1986); Fernandez and Weinberg (1997); Reingold (1998); Stoloff, Glanville, and Bienenstock (1999); Kleit (2001); Chapple (2002); Mouw (2002).
11. Tigges, Brown, and Greene (1998).
12. Green, Tigges, and Browne (1995).

segregated neighborhoods who use social ties to find their jobs usually work with predominantly African American coworkers.[13] This racial composition within the job, in turn, has a negative effect on their annual earnings.

Granovetter (1973) argues that the most successful job searches are those that use weak ties (casual acquaintances), not strong ties (close friends or immediate family members). Residents of high-poverty inner-city neighborhoods are less likely to have access to the kind of social ties most effective for a job search, that is, extensive, varied, spatially dispersed, nonkin ties.[14] Perhaps because of this, some analyses find that low-income workers tend to rely on strong (rather than weak) ties when seeking employment.[15] One study of scattered-site public housing tenants in Maryland found that respondents used strong network ties when looking for jobs rather than neighbors, even though many of their neighbors were employed and had considerably more economic means than their close friends and family.[16] Mendenhall (2005) examined the neighborhood networks of a sample of twenty-five Gautreaux housing assistance participants, African American women who were given the opportunity to move out of Chicago's public housing and segregated neighborhoods. Mendenhall found that among adult suburban movers, female neighbors in the higher-resource communities served as a valuable source of job networks for the least-educated women. But for women with somewhat higher levels of education, such as those certified for clerical work, their suburban neighbors were less helpful in the job search process.[17]

Another structural explanation for labor market disparities between inner-city and suburban job seekers is Kain's (1968) spatial mismatch hypothesis, which argues that the spatial location of jobs vis-à-vis inner-city workers may account for their low employment rates. According to this line of reasoning, the suburbanization of jobs, when combined with increasing residential segregation by class, has exacerbated the employment problems of the urban poor. Similarly, Wilson (1987 and 1996) argues that the decline of manufacturing jobs has left inner-city neighborhoods bereft of employers, while the rise of service sector employment has occurred mainly in the suburbs. Thus

13. Elliott (1999).

14. Granovetter (1995); Reingold (1998); Green, Tigges, and Diaz (1999); Elliott (2000).

15. Elliott (1999); Kleit (2001).

16. Kleit (2001, 2002).

17. Although early studies of Gautreaux found that the adult suburban movers experienced a modest gain in employment compared to those who stayed in the city (Popkin, Rosenbaum, and Meaden 1993), a recent analysis of a more representative sample, using administrative data, does not find a city versus suburb difference in the proportion of calendar quarters with positive earnings (Mendenhall, DeLuca, and Duncan, forthcoming).

many urban residents have the education or experience to fill these jobs but not the means to get to them. Research has shown that urban residents also suffer from a lack of information about suburban job openings and experience greater levels of hiring discrimination in the suburbs than in the city.[18]

Methods

This paper uses quantitative and qualitative data collected from individuals who signed up to participate in the MTO demonstration in Baltimore. We are in the unique position of having experimental data from a large quantitative sample of all Baltimore individuals who signed up for the mobility program by 1997 ($N = 636$), and a smaller, stratified, random qualitative sample ($N = 124$). The methodological problem of self-selection plagues most studies of neighborhood effects, as individuals have a certain amount of choice in deciding what neighborhood they live in and how long they remain in that neighborhood.[19] Individual-level factors, within structural constraints of housing availability and financial resources, influence these decisions. The randomized design of MTO allows us to isolate the effect of neighborhood context on individual outcomes, since it encouraged otherwise similar groups of individuals to live in different types of neighborhoods.

We first use the quantitative data to estimate the effect of the MTO treatment on employment and earnings outcomes in Baltimore. We then use the qualitative data and methods of analytic induction to examine the processes by which these outcomes occur and generate hypotheses about the relationship between residential mobility and employment.

Quantitative Methods

The quantitative data for this paper come from a 2002 survey designed to test the effects of moving from public housing and some of the nation's poorest neighborhoods to low-poverty neighborhoods. These data contain information on individuals at two points in time, at baseline and in 2002.

When public housing residents enrolled in the MTO program between 1994 and 1997, the head of the household completed a baseline survey. Although

18. Kain (1968, 1992); Wilson (1987, 1996); Holzer (1996); Ihlanfeldt and Sjoquist (1998).
19. Tienda (1991); Brooks-Gunn, Duncan, and Aber (1997).

data exist for MTO participants in all five cities, this analysis primarily focuses on Baltimore respondents.[20] Of the Baltimore MTO participants, 97 percent of household heads are African American and 99 percent are female. These Baltimore families had high rates of unemployment, low educational attainment, and were likely to be receiving governmental cash assistance; 74 percent of respondents were unemployed at baseline, 43 percent did not have a high-school diploma or General Equivalency Diploma (GED), and 80 percent received cash welfare payments.

In addition to the baseline survey, respondents participated in a survey four to seven years after families were randomly assigned to one of the three groups. Data were collected from January to September 2002 and the sample includes all families randomly assigned through December 31, 1997. The overall response rate was 89.6 percent across the five cities.[21] In Baltimore, the response rate was 89.3 percent.[22] Fieldworkers conducted in-person surveys with adults, and the sample includes 2.6 members per family, including 1.6 children. The interviews took place primarily in the respondents' homes, using Computer-Assisted Personal Interviewing (CAPI) on laptop computers.

The experimental design of MTO allows us to draw conclusions about the effect of a low-poverty housing mobility policy on individuals, beyond individual and family-level characteristics. In this paper we look at the effects of living in a low-poverty neighborhood on employment and earnings outcomes by comparing average outcomes of adults assigned to the experimental and control groups. Because we have data from two points in time, and because of the experimental nature of the study, we are able to make inferences about causal mechanisms. This intent-to-treat (ITT) coefficient in our regression analyses estimates the causal effect of offering families the services—including the voucher to move to a low-poverty neighborhood, housing counseling, and budget counseling—made available through the experimental treatment. Although

20. The appendix shows how Baltimore participants compare with all MTO participants at baseline.

21. During fieldwork, a three-in-ten subsample of hard-to-locate families was taken in order to focus resources on difficult-to-find cases. Observations from the subsample receive greater weight in the analyses. Accounting for the fact that subsample observations are used to represent observations that were not in the subsample, we calculate an effective response rate (ERR) based on the phase one response rate (R1) and the subsample response rate (R2). ERR = R1 + (1-R1)*R2.

22. See Orr and others (2003) for a detailed description of the data collection and analysis of the survey data.

only 58 percent of Baltimore experimental group members used the voucher to make a low-poverty move (compared to 47 percent of experimental group members in the five cities combined), all still received some form of treatment if they attended the counseling sessions.

We calculate this ITT effect using ordinary least squares (OLS) regression with a set of covariates (X) representing prerandom assignment baseline characteristics.[23] All of the models are computed using sample weights.[24] Although all three groups (experimental, Section 8, and control) are in the data, we omit adults in the Section 8 group from our analyses.[25] This leaves us with a sampling universe of 3,039 across all five cities and of 449 in Baltimore.

We use regression analyses to estimate the control mean of seven employment and earnings outcome variables. We first look at these seven outcomes across all five MTO sites, and then use the same models to analyze Baltimore outcomes. Let Y be the outcome of interest and Z be membership in the experimental group. Equation (1) shows a simple regression model used to estimate the control means (β_{10}) and the ITT differences between the experimental and control groups (β_{11}):

(1) $$Y_i = \beta_{10} + Z_i\beta_{11} + \varepsilon_{1i}.$$

In order to increase precision of the estimates and control for any small sample differences in baseline covariates (X), the primary quantitative analyses in this paper use regression-adjusted ITT effects, as estimated using equation (2):

(2) $$Y_i = \beta_{20} + Z_i\beta_{21} + X_i\beta_{22} + \varepsilon_{2i}.$$

---

23. Means of these covariates can be found in the appendix.

24. These weights have three components, and they are described in detail in Orr and others (2003, appendix B). Three-in-ten subsample members receive greater weight since they represent individuals who were not contacted during this subsampling phase. For child and youth outcomes, youth from larger families receive greater weight. Since two children were randomly sampled from each household, they represent a larger fraction of the population. Finally, weights are used to take into account a change in the ratio of individuals randomly assigned to treatment groups.

25. For this reason, our coefficients are different than the results reported in Orr and others' (2003) analysis. We compare experimentals to controls, and Orr and others estimate experimental and Section 8 effects simultaneously.

Qualitative Methods

The qualitative data consist of transcripts and field notes from in-depth, semistructured interviews with a stratified random subsample of families who volunteered to participate in the MTO experiment. We sampled among all three program groups and evenly among three household types: (1) households with children ages 8–13 years only, (2) households with children ages 8–13 years and 14–19 years, and (3) households with children ages 14–19 years only. Of the 149 families sampled in Baltimore, we interviewed 124 adult respondents in the experimental, Section 8, and control groups (for an 83 percent response rate).[26] Reasons for nonresponse include inability to locate the respondent, death of the respondent, and respondent refusal.

The in-depth interviews with adult respondents took place between July 2003 and June 2004. Intensive locating and tracking efforts were followed by interviews usually lasting from two to five hours. The respondents were asked questions about their neighborhood, social status, employment, focal child (ages 8–13 years), focal youth (ages 14–19 years), and physical and mental health. Interviewers were instructed to ask specific questions, although the wording and timing of the questions often varied so that the interview felt like a conversation. Adult respondents were paid from $50 to $85 for their time, depending on whether we asked them about one or two children. These interviews were tape recorded, transcribed, coded thematically, and entered into a database by theme. Subsequent coding and analysis allowed us to take an inductive approach that is traditional in qualitative work, exploring the relationship between neighborhood characteristics and employment and earnings across the program groups. The extensive effort and cost required to obtain and process each interview limited the total number of families we could interview for this study.

Not all households assigned to the experimental group used the MTO voucher to make a move.[27] Among the fifty-one Baltimore respondents in the qualitative sample assigned to the experimental group, 62 percent used their voucher to move to a low-poverty neighborhood. Of these thirty-three *compliers* (the terminology used to describe respondents who moved with their MTO

26. We also interviewed a stratified random subsample of sixty-four families in Chicago, but this paper focuses solely on Baltimore families.

27. MTO participants had a limited period (typically 120 days) to use the voucher, and sometimes reported difficulty finding a unit in a low-poverty neighborhood or finding a landlord who would accept Section 8 housing.

voucher), only four were living at their placement address at the time of the qualitative interview. The rest had moved to different units, often in different neighborhoods.

We focus our qualitative analysis on the experimental compliers and a set of control group respondents who likely would have moved through the MTO demonstration had they been assigned to the experimental group. We use a matching procedure to determine those controls that likely would have moved through the program. We select nineteen likely control noncompliers to be the counterparts of the eighteen experimental noncompliers, with the reasoning that there should be the same fraction of adults in the control group who would not have complied as there is in the experimental group.[28] We select 100,000 random samples of nineteen from all Baltimore controls and then compare the average values of the eighteen experimental noncompliers to these nineteen controls on fourteen demographic, neighborhood, and employment variables.[29] Each of the 100,000 samples is given a similarity score and the most similar of the 100,000 constitute the nineteen likely control noncompliers. Similarity is defined as the sum of the difference in means for each variable divided by the control group standard deviation for that variable—essentially, the sum of the difference between groups in the average z-scores for the fourteen variables. Each variable receives equal weight in the calculation. Based on this matching procedure, we select a group of control noncompliers that are similar, on average, to the experimental noncompliers (as shown in appendix table A-2). For our qualitative analysis, we exclude the experimental noncompliers and control noncompliers. We use data from the experimental compliers—those who moved to a low-poverty neighborhood through the MTO program—and their likely control complier counterparts to explore the relationship between neighborhood mobility and employment in Baltimore.[30] For simplicity, we refer to experimental compliers as *experimentals* and likely control compliers as *controls* when discussing our qualitative sample.

Although the sample sizes are small, these qualitative data are very useful for exploring the processes by which neighborhoods may affect employment

---

28. We attempted to interview sixty-two Baltimore adults in both the experimental and control groups. We completed fifty-one interviews with experimental group participants (including eighteen of the twenty-two noncompliers) and fifty-three interviews with control group participants.

29. See the appendix for a description of the variables.

30. This paper does not look at adults assigned to the Section 8 group, although these families are included in the qualitative sample.

and earnings outcomes in a manner that cannot be captured by survey data. Interviewers systematically asked respondents about both human and social capital, so it is possible to look at how these factors interact with employment and earnings outcomes in the context of a housing mobility program. Examples of interview questions include, "Tell me the whole story about how you got [this/your last] job," and "Tell me about the events that led you to leave your last job." The matching of the experimental noncompliers with the likely control noncompliers allows us to take full advantage of the study design; those who used the MTO voucher are different than those who did not move, and lumping all of the experimental and control respondents together would not allow us to separate out these differences.[31]

Quantitative Results

We use data from the Interim Survey to look at the types of neighborhoods in which the MTO participants are living. We then examine employment and earnings outcomes for Baltimore respondents, and find that the MTO intervention did not have a significant effect on the economic self-sufficiency of these individuals.

Neighborhood Characteristics

Table 1 shows descriptive neighborhood information for the five-city survey sample and Baltimore survey sample. We define neighborhood by the census tract the individual lived in at each point in time and use data from the 2000 Census. We look at neighborhood socioeconomic disadvantage in the following four ways: poverty rate, percent of residents with college diplomas, percent employed among the civilian population, and percent African American. The percentage of African American residents does not directly estimate neighborhood quality, but serves as an indicator of racial residential segregation, which perpetuates the notion of the African American underclass and has implications for economic well-being.[32]

---

31. Although our qualitative sample comes from a random sample of MTO participants in Baltimore, our small sample size prohibits these results from being representative of all Baltimore respondents or generalizable to the entire MTO population.

32. Massey and Denton (1993).

Table 1. Neighborhood Characteristics for Five-City and Baltimore Surveys, 2002[a]

| | Five cities[b] | | Baltimore | |
| | Control group | | Control group | |
Characteristic	*mean*	*E – C*	*mean*	*E – C*
Household income below	.392	−.085*	.355	−.066*
poverty line in tract		(.008)		(.018)
College degree in tract	.142	.043	.123	.048*
among those over age 25		(.005)		(.013)
Employed in tract	.410	.054*	.411	.063*
		(.005)		(.014)
African Americans in tract	.562	−.014	.840	−.049*
		(.010)		(.028)

Source: Authors' calculations based on U.S. Department of Housing and Urban Development's Interim Survey data on the Moving to Opportunity program.
E – C = experimental − control (intent-to-treat) difference.
*$p < 0.05$.
a. Estimates are based on equation (2) in main text. Sample size is 2,501 for five cities and 376 for Baltimore.
b. Five cities include Baltimore, Boston, Chicago, Los Angeles, and New York.

Across nearly all measures of neighborhood quality in Baltimore, experimentals were living in higher-quality neighborhoods than their control-group counterparts at the time of the 2002 survey (four to seven years after random assignment). These neighborhoods are a substantial improvement to the poor-quality neighborhoods that respondents were living in at baseline, where about half of the residents were living below the poverty line.

Employment Results

We use quantitative data from the 2002 survey to predict employment and earnings outcomes for Baltimore respondents. For these models, we use the full experimental and control sample so the coefficients are valid estimates of the MTO treatment. Consistent with previous employment and earnings findings on the MTO intervention,[33] we look at seven employment and earnings outcomes: currently employed; employed with health insurance; employed full time (thirty-five or more hours a week); weekly earnings above poverty; annual earnings in 2001; weekly earnings at main job; and employed at job greater than one year.

The dependent variable in each of our models is one of these seven employment or earnings outcomes. The independent variable is a dummy variable

33. Kling, Liebman, and Katz (2007).

Table 2. OLS Regression Models for Employment and Earnings Outcomes[a]

Outcome	Five cities[b]			Baltimore		
	Sample size	Control group mean	E – C	Sample size	Control group mean	E – C
Currently employed	2,525	.520	.016 (.021)	379	.577	.061 (.050)
Employed with health insurance	2,499	.293	.024 (.019)	373	.390	.080 (.054)
Employed full-time (35 or more hours)	2,501	.389	.001 (.021)	372	.481	.012 (.054)
Weekly earnings above poverty	2,386	.321	–.006 (.020)	351	.386	.033 (.055)
Annual earnings in 2001	2,386	8,839	130 (448)	353	10,047	–142 (1059)
Weekly earnings at main job	2,386	178	0 (9)	351	192	15 (23)
Employed at job greater than one year	2,496	.359	.031 (.021)	374	.401	.085 (.053)

Source: Authors' calculations based on U.S. Department of Housing and Urban Development's Interim Survey data on the Moving to Opportunity program.

E – C = experimental – control (intent-to-treat) difference.

a. Estimates are based on equation (2) in main text, using covariates described in the appendix. Robust standard errors shown in parentheses. All data weighted to adjust for sampling design.

b. Five cities include Baltimore, Boston, Chicago, Los Angeles, and New York.

for experimental group status (with control group status as the reference category), and we include thirty-eight covariates for baseline adult characteristics. These covariates allow us to account for any slight differences between the experimental and control groups at baseline and add precision to our models. We first look at the effect of the MTO treatment among all participants, and then restrict our models to Baltimore respondents. Table 2 displays our results.

These results are consistent with previous quantitative analyses that find the MTO intervention did not have any significant effect on the employment or earnings of participants.[34] In Baltimore, on which we base our qualitative sample, those assigned to the experimental group do not have employment and earnings outcomes that are statistically different from their control group counterparts. However, the treatment may have had a bigger impact in Baltimore than across all five cities. Compared to the control group, for example, the employment rate rose 6.1 percentage points in the experimental group.

34. Kling, Liebman, and Katz (2007).

Additionally, the number of respondents holding jobs with health insurance rose 8.0 percentage points, and the number holding their job for greater than one year rose 8.5 percentage points. Although the results in Baltimore are statistically insignificant, the magnitudes suggest some economically meaningful differences between the experimental and control groups. On other measures such as average earnings, however, there was no evidence of a meaningful difference.

Qualitative Results

The effects on adult economic self-sufficiency outcomes were not large or significant, which raises various questions. Do these results provide evidence that a housing mobility intervention does not greatly affect employment and earnings? Or is there a more complex story underlying these results—a story about how a very disadvantaged group of Americans who have spent years, perhaps an entire lifetime, in some of the nation's most distressed public housing projects, go about seeking, obtaining, and maintaining jobs? We turn to in-depth interviews with a random subsample of experimental and control group members in Baltimore to develop a set of hypotheses about some of the social processes that might be at work. Keep in mind that when we refer to experimentals in this section, we are referring to compliers, those who actually used their MTO voucher. When we refer to controls, we mean the matched set of control-likely compliers.

Profile of Baltimore Qualitative Respondents

Table 3 compares the demographic characteristics of experimentals and controls in the qualitative study, and the groups are fairly similar across these measures. Though there are differences in educational attainment, these are not statistically significant.[35] All respondents are women, most live with dependent children, and all but one are African American.[36] At the time of the qualitative interview, the respondents were, on average, about thirty-eight years old (ages ranged from twenty-six to fifty-seven). Twenty-eight percent of experimentals and 47 percent of controls had neither finished high school nor obtained a GED. On the other end of the spectrum, only 5 percent had gradu-

35. Although our overall number of cases is relatively small, we present percentages throughout the paper to preserve a sense of proportion.
36. One respondent identifies as multiracial.

Table 3. Descriptive Characteristics of Baltimore Qualitative Respondents[a]

	Compliers	
Characteristic	*Experimental*	*Control*
Demographic		
Female	1.00	1.00
African American	0.970	1.00
Age	38.39	37.53
Education		
High-school dropout	0.281	0.471
High-school diploma/GED	0.594	0.529
College degree	0.094	0.000
Number of children	2.82	3.09
Number of people in household	3.42	4.47
Housing		
Lived in public housing as child	0.476	0.480
Current housing		
Public housing	0.091	0.212
Subsidized housing	0.576	0.424
Unsubsidized private housing	0.152	0.182
Homeowner	0.121	0.182
Other	0.000	0.030
Poverty rate < 10 percent	0.242	0.059
Poverty rate 10 to 20 percent	0.333	0.294
Poverty rate > 40 percent	0.242	0.294
Employment and public assistance receipt		
Employment status		
Full time	0.455	0.324
Part time	0.212	0.235
Unemployed	0.333	0.441
Receives Temporary Assistance for Needy Families (TANF)	0.094	0.242
Receives food stamps	0.406	0.393
Receives medical assistance	0.563	0.576
N (sample size)	33	34

Source: Authors' calculations based on qualitative interview data from the Moving to Opportunity program.

a. Experimental compliers used an experimental voucher to move to a low-poverty area. Control compliers are control group members not selected as likely noncompliers on the basis of matching average characteristics of experimental noncompliers, as described in the text.

ated from a two- or four-year college program, obtaining an associate's or bachelor's degree, or are licensed practical nurses or registered nurses.

Approximately half each of experimentals and controls said they lived in public housing as a child. Of course, all were living in Baltimore public housing when they enrolled in the MTO program. Although the MTO demonstration did not provide the controls with a voucher to move, the residential mobility of both groups after random assignment is high. By the time we conducted the in-depth interviews in 2003, six to nine years after random assignment, the majority of experimentals had moved from their low-poverty, MTO placement neighborhoods. This was possible because the MTO voucher reverted to a standard Housing Choice Voucher (Section 8 voucher)—that is, it lost its geographic restrictions—after one year of use in the placement neighborhood. Similarly, as a result of the widespread demolition of Baltimore public housing, most controls were not living at their baseline address by 2003 either. Indeed, those whose units had been demolished were offered the option of a standard Housing Choice Voucher.

At baseline, both experimentals and controls were living on the east and west sides of the center of Baltimore—neighborhoods characterized by very high rates of poverty, unemployment, and labor force detachment, as well as a host of other neighborhood distress indicators. Subsequently, the experimentals who took up the MTO offer and moved were dispersed to the outskirts of Baltimore City, the inner suburbs in Baltimore County, and several more distant suburbs. Most experimentals moved to neighborhoods that, while low in poverty, were still predominantly African American or mixed in their racial composition.

Over time, the experimentals moved somewhat closer toward the center of Baltimore City, though few moved back to their baseline neighborhoods. Meanwhile, controls usually moved to and remained within the city, often in quite close proximity to their origin neighborhoods. Despite high rates of residential mobility in both groups, the experimentals are still more likely than controls to be living in neighborhoods with poverty rates 20 percent and under (about 58 versus 35 percent), somewhat more likely than controls to live in subsidized private housing (about 58 versus 42 percent), and less likely to be living in public housing (about 9 versus 21 percent) than controls.

Labor Market Context

Experimentals and controls exhibit many similarities in their employment status and job quality, and nearly all respondents say they value work and that having a job is an important goal, in part because they believe it boosts self-worth. But the unemployed controls have less consistent work histories and have been unemployed longer than their unemployed experimental counterparts, who typically have been cycling between employment and unemployment.

Among experimentals, about 46 percent are employed full time, another 21 percent are employed part time, and 33 percent are unemployed by 2003. In the six to nine years since these respondents signed up for MTO, their overall employment rate has increased dramatically. Two-thirds are currently working, as opposed to only 15 percent at baseline. This is presumably due, in part, to the more stringent work requirements mandated by welfare reform, implemented in Maryland in 1996.[37] The increase in employment is also presumably due to a booming economy (unemployment in Baltimore County dropped from 5.3 percent in 1995 to 3.7 percent in 2000),[38] and other factors that substantially boosted the work rates of low-income single mothers across the country.[39] Respondents' children also got older, reducing the potential costs of working (for example, child care) and enabling them to balance work and parenting more easily. The changes that resulted in increased employment for low-income women in general set an extraordinarily high bar for individuals assigned to the experimental group to show a significant difference from a control group experiencing the same trends. The experimental participants also had to negotiate neighborhood environments that were very different than those they had been used to, and they had to compete with other similarly skilled individuals to find a job.

However, many former welfare recipients who have left welfare for employment have been funneled into particular types of jobs, namely jobs in health care or retail establishments. These patterns are readily evident in our data, as half of the employed experimentals are working in health care either as nursing assistants, medical billing clerks, or as housekeepers, prep cooks, and other nonhealth care jobs within hospitals. Cheryl,[40] for example, a 29-year-old mother of four, works full-time as a prep cook for a Baltimore hospital, and Quresha, a 40-year-old mother of three, works full-time as a housekeeper at a hospital in a Baltimore suburb. Overall, just more than half of those working in health care work in these pink-collar jobs in hospitals. Nearly four in ten experimentals (37 percent) work in other service sector jobs, either in retail establishments, as janitors, in food service, or as child care workers. A few (18 percent) work as administrative assistants or in other office jobs, in blue-collar jobs (9 percent), or in the informal economy (9 percent).

Six of the eleven unemployed experimentals are only temporarily unemployed. These six women have steady work histories and are actively

37. National Health Policy Forum, George Washington University, "Welfare Reform in Maryland: Flexibility in Action" (www.nhpf.org/pdfs_sv/SV_MD02.pdf [April 25, 2002]).

38. U.S. Bureau of Labor Statistics, "Labor Force Data by County, 1995 Annual Averages" (ftp://ftp.bls.gov/pub/special.requests/la/laucnty95.txt); and "Labor Force Data by County, 2000 Annual Averages" (ftp://ftp.bls.gov/pub/special.requests/la/laucnty00.txt [accessed April 25, 2006]).

39. Meyer and Rosenbaum (2000).

40. We use pseudonyms throughout the paper to protect the confidentiality of the respondents.

searching for jobs, and some even have jobs lined up. The MTO survey, conducted four to seven years after random assignment and two years before our qualitative interviews, did not attempt to measure the nature of unemployment. Sadie, for example, lost her job as a housekeeper at a hotel one month before the interview. She was terminated from her job because she needed to take a week off to devote all of her energy to getting her son, Kevin, age seventeen, out of jail. He spent a month in jail on a robbery charge, only to be released after the police conceded it was a case of mistaken identity. Sadie, who has a steady work history, spent six months as a custodian at her son's school before working at the hotel (she was fired from the school job because she needed to deal with another child's asthma), tended bar for four years, and worked as a cashier at a convenience store. Now that Sadie's son is out of jail, the 41-year-old mother of three is again actively seeking work, looking daily in the want ads, and has an interview lined up for a job at a warehouse. LaShonda, a 40-year-old mother of two, has worked as a unionized welder for the past two years, and was laid off from her welding job two months ago. This job paid LaShonda $17 an hour and included health and retirement benefits. When she worked overtime, she made $25.50 an hour. She collects unemployment now, but anticipates working again soon.

In contrast to the experimentals, only one of the unemployed controls can be considered temporarily unemployed. Overall, unemployed controls have less consistent work histories—it has been several years since most of them have last worked—and most do not have concrete plans for future employment. This stands in stark contrast to the employment aspirations of the experimentals.

In our qualitative subsample, a somewhat smaller proportion of controls are currently working, compared to experimentals (about 56 versus 67 percent). Although half of employed experimentals are working in hospitals or health care jobs, only a few (16 percent) controls hold similar jobs. Mercedes, age thirty-three, is the only control employed as a nursing assistant, a job she has held for four years. Two other respondents, 37-year-old Sharon and 40-year-old Jane, work as customer service representatives at hospitals in Baltimore. More than four in ten (42 percent) employed controls work in service sector jobs outside of the health care sector as custodians, housekeepers, or in retail. Nearly a third (32 percent) do secretarial work, a few (16 percent) work blue-collar jobs (as meter maids or low-level municipal employees) and one respondent is self-employed, making gift baskets out of her home.

The fact that experimentals are more likely to be employed in health care jobs may give them an important advantage over the controls over time, as health care jobs are more likely to have medical benefits and career ladders than jobs in other sectors. In addition, the demand for such workers should increase significantly in the future; one analysis projected an increase of 36 percent between 2000 and 2010.[41] Tisha, a 32-year-old woman employed full-time as a medical billing team leader at a local hospital, says, "When you get into the medical field, it's nonstop growth there. You know, it's just nonstop [opportunity]. So I just feel like I'm just gonna take this and go all the way as far as I can until I just get burned out." On the other hand, though, many entry-level health care jobs are physically demanding and have high rates of turnover, posing additional barriers for those individuals in the profession.

Human Capital Barriers to Employment

Experimentals and controls have similar barriers to employment, such as low educational attainment and poor mental and physical health, which may in part result from years of exposure to concentrated poverty neighborhoods. These barriers were not explicitly addressed through the MTO demonstration. While many experimentals and controls were able to overcome such limitations, these barriers still pose difficulties.

At the time of the qualitative interview, a substantial minority (28 percent) of experimentals have neither graduated nor earned a GED, though some (9 percent) have a two- or four-year college degree. A handful of experimentals told us that MTO not only encouraged them to move out of their neighborhood, but also to further their education because their experiences were broadened. Lisa, a 38-year-old mother of three employed in a federal government office, attributes completing her bachelor's degree at Coppin State University, located in the Baltimore suburbs, to MTO. "That is how I took advantage of the [Moving to Opportunity] program. Where most people took advantage of it as far as maybe, well, it was still a better environment, but I wanted a full package. I wanted a better environment, a better education," says Lisa, who has plans to go back to school to earn her master's degree. Peaches, a 34-year-old experimental, began taking classes at Baltimore City Community College just before moving through the program, but completed her associate's degree after moving and was motivated to do so by her MTO move. "You know, it just opened up a whole another world for me. And, it was like a big change and I was like 'wow.' I was missing out on this whole experience, you know."

41. Harmuth (2002).

In addition to having more traditionally reported educational certifications such as GEDs or high-school diplomas, about 30 percent of experimentals have graduated from other short-term programs offering credentials for occupations such as home health aides or pharmacy technicians. Many of these respondents have three or four different certificates of this kind. Certificates that credential respondents for health care jobs are the most common, which probably explains in part why such a large proportion of experimentals work in such jobs.

One way housing mobility programs may benefit participants is from contact with new, employed neighbors who will offer job information and referrals. But the educational credentials of many respondents limit the usefulness of drawing upon these resources from those in their new environments. Experimentals rarely activate neighborhood social networks to search for jobs, as we discuss in more detail below. But this is partly due to the large differences between their own human capital and the education and skills of their new neighbors. Many respondents, especially those still living in very low-poverty neighborhoods at the time of the qualitative interview, say their neighbors all work in white-collar or professional jobs. Keona, a 30-year-old woman living in a low-poverty neighborhood, says that all of her neighbors have office jobs rather than the kind of work she seeks. "Office. I can see the way they dress. I can tell it's for an office. Not for a factory, you don't see, not even in nursing. . . . You know how you see more briefcases, suits." Terry, who also lives in a low-poverty neighborhood, says that many of her neighbors are lawyers or other highly educated professionals. Tina, a 32-year-old woman still residing in a low-poverty neighborhood, says her neighbors mostly work as doctors, police officers, and at the naval academy.[42] Although it is unlikely that all of the experimentals' neighbors are doctors or lawyers, some of them probably are working in these occupations. More important, the fact that experimentals perceive their neighbors to be working in these jobs means that since they lack these credentials themselves, they usually do not even attempt to approach neighbors for job information or referrals. Even if they tried, it is unclear whether these ties would generate more or higher quality jobs than they are already getting through other means.

In addition to low education, experimentals also report a number of physical and mental health conditions that militate against finding work and staying

---

42. Experimentals not living in low-poverty neighborhoods talk about their neighbors' being employed, for example, as custodians, corrections officers, teacher's aides, and informal and formal child care providers.

employed. Living in high-poverty, economically depressed neighborhoods has a negative effect on one's health,[43] and as indicated earlier in this paper, past MTO research has shown significant physical and mental health gains for those who moved through MTO relative to controls.[44] In fact all five of the unemployed experimentals who are not cycling in and out of the labor market report debilitating physical or mental health barriers.

Roneesha, a 44-year-old mother of two and grandmother of two, is one example. Although Roneesha is HIV-positive, she managed to remain stably employed for many years until she began to suffer from panic attacks on the job. She had worked at her most recent job—a data entry position paying $11.49 with full benefits—for seventeen years, but left the job after being hospitalized after her first panic attack. She explains, "I couldn't get myself together for nothing, then I was really panicking out and I started shaking and rocking and shaking and rocking and so then finally recognized it was a panic attack and not no heart attack or nothing." In addition to suffering from HIV and panic attacks, Roneesha suffers from diabetes and depression.

Thirty-nine-year-old Rochelle and 32-year-old Sonya both suffer from serious mental health problems as well. Rochelle, who had a nervous break-down several years ago and receives disability payments for her depression, says she has never had a job and has no plans to search for one. Because of her mental health problems, interviewers had a difficult time constructing an employment profile for Sonya. Our fieldworker wrote after the interview, "The respondent has clearly some pretty serious mental illness issues . . . there were lots of stream of consciousness associations to strange objects to coat hangers and rattles." Obviously, these conditions would not only influ-ence respondents' ability to sustain employment but their capacity to forge and maintain social connections as well—connections they might have relied on to secure a job.

Experimentals and controls had a similar mix of educational credentials at baseline, and there is no statistically significant educational attainment dif-ference between the two groups at the time of the qualitative interview. In addition, about one-third of respondents in both groups have completed at least one short-term training program that certifies them for a job, usually low-level health care jobs.

43. Ross and Mirowsky (2001); Boardman and others (2001).
44. Kling, Liebman, and Katz (2007).

Like their experimental counterparts, unemployed controls demonstrate an acute awareness of the importance of education and experience for employment and pay. Rachel, a 37-year-old unemployed control who has worked in the past as a nursing assistant and an addictions counselor, says that these jobs now require a certificate or degree, and her lack of either is the reason for her lengthy recent spell of unemployment. "Everybody wants you to have a degree now, you know, and before it wasn't a big issue. I could get a job in addictions just like that. And now they want you to have a degree." Rachel, who dropped out of high school and never received a GED, is currently enrolled in a program in which she can earn her high-school diploma, and she believes this credential will help her find a job. Missy, a 36-year-old unemployed mother of three, says that her lack of work experience is holding her back. "Some of 'em, I have the experience, but I don't have the working experience [in recent] years, I don't have that kind," says Missy, whose last job as a housekeeper was five years ago. She says she tried to enroll in a training program recently but was not allowed to participate because of a conviction for marijuana possession.

Experimentals and controls also have similar physical and mental health barriers that sometimes prohibit them from getting a job or staying employed. Depression is the most common problem. Kenya, a 30-year-old mother of two who has been unemployed most of her adult life, has trouble sleeping through the night because of stress related to her cousin's fatal drug overdose. As a result, she falls asleep unexpectedly throughout the day. When we interviewed her, in fact, she fell asleep several times and we had to wake her. Kenya, a control, points to other sources of stress as well. "What stresses me out? My children's fathers, they ain't no good. Life itself stresses me out. The trials and tribulations that I've been through. Stresses me out thinking about it." Wendy, a 35-year-old mother of five who has been unemployed for two years, has severe arthritis, which prohibits her from jobs requiring her to stand all day on her feet or do physical labor. "Each job I just couldn't work; it was my legs swelling up," says Wendy. "Cramping, aching. . . . It just get me, oh God, my hands too."

As indicated above, analyses of the MTO 2002 survey, occurring four to seven years after random assignment, found mental health gains for experimentals relative to controls.[45] These results are encouraging, and suggest that moving to a low-poverty neighborhood can reduce psychological distress and depression. Among those in the qualitative sample, however, there are no

---

45. Kling, Liebman, and Katz (2007).

noticeable differences in respondents' reports of depression, stress, or other mental health problems as they relate to employment, though we did not use formal measures of depression and stress.

Social Connections and Residential Mobility

We now turn to the processes by which respondents search for jobs. In particular, we examine the extent that neighbors versus other members of respondents' social networks (close family, friends, and acquaintances) influence the job search process. Experimentals and controls find employment through similar channels and, when activating social networks to find a job, mostly rely on a particular type of weak tie, acquaintances who have similar jobs to those they seek and similar job credentials. Usually, these are not one's immediate neighbors. For experimentals, too few neighbors have such qualifications, and for controls, too few neighbors have jobs at all. Rather, both rely on casual encounters with acquaintances they have met on the job, in training, or in other venues over the years.

The employed experimentals used three job search strategies: formal methods, agency-based methods, and social networks.[46] When we asked these respondents how they got their current job, only a small number (14 percent) used formal methods, such as help wanted ads and direct application, to find their current job. Nearly a third (32 percent) used a temporary agency or local social service agency to find their job. Yet more than two-thirds (68 percent) relied on social networks (some respondents used more than one method, so these numbers total more than 100 percent). Of those who used social connections, about four in ten used a friend, though rarely a close friend. Other referral sources include current or past coworkers or other casual associates from school, church, or elsewhere. Only rarely did family members play this role.

Thus consistent with Granovetter (1974 and 1995), but not all prior research, the majority of experimentals who found their current job through social connections used a weak tie, not a strong tie. For example, 46-year-old Jacqueline found her part-time job as a crossing guard through a friend's father. "I used

---

46. Formal methods of job search include the following specific strategies: direct application, newspaper search, Internet search, Yellow Pages search, and responding to a flier. Agency-based methods of job search include using a social service agency, going through a temporary employment agency, participating in a job training program, and attending a career fair.

to check back and forth down at civil service . . . and I also know someone that used to work with the city, and she helped me. Matter of fact, her father, he used to work [down there], and he knew someone. Sometimes you have to know somebody to get a job."

Yet none of the experimentals say they found their current job through a neighbor. "A lot of neighbors, they don't, they don't tell you too much about a job," says 37-year-old Renee. Though neighbors did not play a direct role in job searches, several respondents describe how a neighbor's example or encouraging words have motivated them when searching for a job. Amy, who spends weekends and some evenings as an evangelist traveling from church to church in the Baltimore area, says her neighbors have encouraged her to be persistent in her job search. Sheila, a 38-year-old nursing assistant still living in her MTO placement neighborhood, says she often talks to her neighbors about her job search, but these conversations and the tips they have shared have never led to employment.

Though no current jobs flowed through neighbor referrals, one experimental did find a past job through a neighbor and another says a neighbor helped her secure a job at a grocery store. This respondent, Cookie, is thirty-nine years old and lives in a low-poverty neighborhood. "As a matter of fact, one day I went to the store and after [my neighbor] had told me about [a job opening in the store she owned], I said, no, I don't want to do it. . . . Then I got to the store—as a matter of fact I went there to get something. We was planting the flowers out in the back and I was all dirty. Went up there and I just happened to see Gail and I said, you know, let me fill out an application. And talked to her right there and she was like, 'Well, don't you wanna start next week?' I was like, 'All right, OK, I can do that.' So I start next week." These are the exceptions, however. "I don't really do a lot of interacting with my neighbors other than just speaking, you know, just small conversation," says Joyce, a 41-year-old mother of two. Roneesha says, "No, 'cause like I say, I don't associate with [my neighbors]. Not a lot."

Although many experimentals have not forged close ties with neighbors, most have noted their neighbors' employment status and have some notion of what kind of work they do. Further, most eagerly point to the benefits of living in a community where most residents work as opposed to those where workers are few. Experimentals are proud that their neighbors are working. Tina brags that mostly everyone in her low-poverty neighborhood has a job where they wear uniforms, such as police officers. "You rarely catch anybody in their regular civilian clothes," says this 32-year-old woman who is employed full time as a hospital laundry aide.

Neighbors who are working, many experimentals say, "take care of themselves" and do not "get into others' business." Peaches, who lives in a low-poverty neighborhood and is employed as a hospital help desk technician, tells us, "It makes a big difference when you have people focused on a goal or focused on something positive. It changes the whole environment where you live at. Because you know they are going somewhere. They are doing something positive with their life." Unemployed residents, on the other hand, are not viewed as beneficial to the community. Lisa, the respondent employed at a Social Security office who has been living in her current neighborhood for five years, says, "[When people don't have jobs], it brings the community down. What if you are a working person, and you have all this noise and you have to get some sleep and everybody in the neighborhood is just having a party, having a good time?"

There are no striking differences in the job search strategies of experimentals and controls. The two groups report using formal and agency-based methods to find their current job in relatively similar proportions. Among both groups, respondents who used social networks to secure a job are much more likely to report using a weak tie as opposed to a strong tie; 60 percent of experimentals and 79 percent of controls report using a casual acquaintance with similar skills and credentials for job referrals. Controls, however, find it easier to use these connections, because sheer proximity brings them into contact with such individuals more often. The low-poverty move limits access to individuals working in occupations similar to the ones the respondents usually seek. Getting a job not only requires that respondents have the required educational credential or relevant work experience, but that they learn of a given job opening promptly. Here, respondents believe, informal channels work best because such jobs fill rapidly, and by the time the job is listed in the newspaper or through other formal means it is generally too late to apply.

The controls mirror the experimentals in that none of them report getting information about their current job through an actual neighbor, but for a different reason than experimentals. For the controls, too few of their immediate neighbors are working. Baltimore survey results also show no effect of the MTO program on the probability of using a neighbor to find a current job. However, due to their residential location, controls' daily routines do bring them into contact with others who can provide the relevant information. Experimentals have to work harder in order to make these· sorts of contacts. They try to make up for this deficit by attempting to draw on their close ties—family members and close friends who may still live in or near their origin neighborhoods. However, since such ties are redundant (the parties know many of the same people), they are rarely effective in linking individuals to social networks outside of their own.[47]

Controls have more ability to use social connections to find work. Their neighbors are less likely to be employed overall, but they are more likely to have neighbors employed in occupations similar to their own. More importantly, because of their residential locations, they are more likely to make contact with acquaintances who work in such jobs in the course of their daily routines. Unlike the experimentals, none of the controls say their neighbors work in white-collar or professional jobs. Instead, they say their neighbors work in health care jobs, such as nursing assistants, in service sector jobs at retail establishments, and in blue-collar jobs, such as security jobs or guards at correctional facilities.

When we examine what controls say about their neighbors' employment (or lack of employment), we find they echo themes of the experimentals. The controls speak positively about the benefits of having neighbors who work, as employed neighbors do not have time to meddle in others' business and foster a desire to work. "If it's more working people, then you know it's less trouble. Everybody is focused on what their agenda is for the next day or whatever," says 37-year-old Cathy, who is employed in the informal labor market. Tammy, a 37-year-old woman employed part-time as a custodian, says that having employed neighbors motivates her. "If I don't work, and most people do, that's going to encourage me to work. And if it's the other way around, I may not be able to keep up with working," she says. Controls often lament the fact that many of their neighbors do not work. Only half live in neighborhoods where they perceive that most people work, and about a quarter (26 percent) say almost none of their neighbors are workers. Yet the perceived gains to experimentals of having working neighbors seems to have been diminished by more limited access to ties best able to provide useful job referrals.

Space and Residential Mobility

Next, we look at how moving to a low-poverty neighborhood changes the spatial dynamics of these families' lives. Experimentals are still living geographically farther from their baseline neighborhoods than controls are by the time we interview them, six to nine years after random assignment. Not only does this place them farther from the social ties that are so crucial to getting a job in their field, in this city at least, it places them farther from (not closer to) many of the jobs for which their education and skills qualify them. Both experimentals and controls say transportation is a problem when

47. Granovetter (1973).

it comes to getting and keeping a job, but transportation problems are often exacerbated by a low-poverty move. While many experimentals are able to overcome these barriers eventually, and do secure employment at a reasonable distance from their homes, the barriers impede attempts to get jobs or search for better jobs.

As noted earlier, experimentals perceive many benefits of living in low-poverty neighborhoods, such as stronger community norms supportive of work. But housing mobility also comes with a cost for some families. When the experimentals used their voucher to move to a low-poverty neighborhood, most moved to neighborhoods a substantial distance from their public housing developments, on average 8.46 miles from their baseline address, although there was significant variation in the distances that families moved (ranging from 2.49 to 20.30 miles). After living in their low-poverty neighborhood for the required year or longer, many experimentals chose to move on to neighborhoods in the inner suburbs or the city's outskirts. At the time of the qualitative interview, experimentals are living, on average, 5.82 miles from their baseline public housing units. Unless they are lucky enough to live close to a job, public transportation routes often demand that workers take multiple bus routes to get to their jobs. Furthermore, most of the jobs they actually hold are in the city, not the suburbs.

As noted earlier, half of all employed experimentals are working in either health care jobs or in other hospital jobs, and the majority of these positions are in the city. Since such a large proportion of respondents are employed in health care occupations, we mapped the location of all hospitals and nursing homes in the metropolitan area (Baltimore City and Baltimore County) (see figure 1). Although we do not capture all possible health care jobs in the Baltimore area, we were able to gain address information for these larger health care employers. While there are twenty-two hospitals and fifty-seven nursing homes in Baltimore City, there are only eleven hospitals and fifty-one nursing homes in the geographically larger area of Baltimore County.

Ironically, then, many of the health care jobs for which many MTO participants are qualified are actually closer to where respondents were living at baseline than the neighborhoods they moved to through the program. This is not consistent with notions of spatial mismatch, which partly attributes the unemployment of urban residents and the persistence of urban poverty to the out-migration of jobs to the suburbs.[48] A substantial number

48. Kain (1968, 1992); Wilson (1987, 1996); Holzer (1996); Ihlanfeldt and Sjoquist (1998).

Figure 1. Hospitals and Nursing Homes in Baltimore City and County, 2005

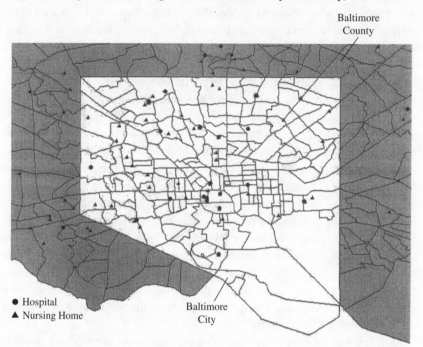

Source: Baltimore City and County hospitals' locations: University of Maryland Consumer Resources web page and Baltimore City Planning Office. Baltimore City and County nursing homes: www.zapconnect.com.

of experimentals nonetheless have managed to secure health care jobs, and are more likely to have done so than controls despite an equal level of credentialing. However, this is in part because once the voucher became a standard Housing Choice Voucher, many moved closer to the city, where so many of these jobs are located.

Not only did experimentals' initial move place them farther from job referral networks, network ties provide two other crucial benefits for some—the child care and transportation that often enable single mothers to work. In the course of our interviews, we asked respondents to name their three closest friends and provide other descriptive information about them. Only 30 percent of experimentals say they have a friend in their neighborhood. In fact, many explicitly say they are not friends with their neighbors. Of the eight experimentals still living in a very low-poverty neighborhood, all but one fail to name a single close friend or family member in their neighborhood. This finding is consistent with Clampet-Lundquist's (2004) examination of social ties among Philadelphia public housing tenants who moved through the HOPE VI initiative.[49]

While 37 percent of experimentals own a car, only one experimental still living in a very low-poverty neighborhood does so. Car ownership is clearly important for employment among this group, as half of employed experimentals but only one unemployed experimental (the unionized welder who is only temporarily laid off), has a car. Of course, respondents who work may be more likely to own cars because they can afford them. However, having to rely on public transportation, which many deem unreliable, is commonly named as a barrier to finding work or sustaining employment, especially in the suburbs where buses run less frequently. Cheryl, the respondent employed full-time at a hospital in Baltimore, says she had to quit a previous job because she did not have reliable transportation to work. Cheryl, who does not own a car, says that "something was going on with the [Maryland Transit Administration] buses" and that she could not get to her job working in a medical records office. Terry, a 33-year-old experimental, discusses how transportation issues often result in her being late to her job as a school nurse at an elementary school in Baltimore. "The bus driver, she was late one day and then the next day she didn't come at all. I be out there looking for another bus to catch. I am at the point where I am ready to buy a car," she says, but gets depressed because she cannot afford car insurance.

Although not having a car presents a barrier to employment for some respondents, others demonstrate incredible perseverance in navigating the metropolitan area's public transportation system. Roneesha, the respondent whose current health conditions prohibit her from working, has had a steady employment history despite never owning a car. She discusses her long commute to her administrative assistant job when still living in her MTO placement neighborhood. Roneesha says that she did not have to be at work until 8:00 a.m., but had to leave her house at 5:30 a.m. for her two bus, hour-long commute because of the irregular and often unreliable bus schedule.

Tina's case is an exception to the transportation problems faced by respondents living in low-poverty neighborhoods. This 32-year-old respondent has a four-minute walk to her job as a laundry aide at a convalescent center in

49. HOPE VI, administered through HUD, is a public housing redevelopment program that frequently relocates tenants in the process of redevelopment. Clampet-Lundquist (2004) found that in the short term families who moved through the program stay to themselves because they did not care to make new friends and they wanted to avoid potential conflict with neighbors.

Anne Arundel County. Tina has lived at her placement address for eight years and has gotten by without a car, but says that transportation poses a problem in other aspects of her life. She talks about how she used her social connections to help navigate the new neighborhood. "When I first came out here, I was lost about everything. I used to catch a cab back to Baltimore before I knew the bus line was only down the road from me. As far as finding stores, [my neighbor who] I didn't know . . . someone that lived above me . . . took me to the stores out here. [My] transportation is basically the bus or [rides from] friends that I have met out here."

Transportation problems were also a motivation for some experimentals to move on from their MTO placement neighborhoods to somewhat more disadvantaged neighborhoods on the outskirts of the city, where buses and trains ran more frequently. Tisha, for example, did not have a car when she moved through the MTO program to a Baltimore County suburb. "I had to get back into the city where more buses run on a frequent basis than in the County. . . . If you miss the [bus], if you missed it, go back home, sit down at the table, whatever. 'Cause the next bus comes an hour and a half to two hours later. So that was ridiculous and there was a lot of stress and when I moved back to the city, I told my sister, I said, 'I feel so good. And much as I hate the bus I was never so happy to be back in the city where I could catch the bus to get anywhere I needed to go.' "

It is important to note, though, that transportation concerns also weigh heavily on lives of the controls. Nearly half of controls own cars (53 percent of employed controls and 40 percent of unemployed controls), but many of these vehicles are unreliable. Kenya, who is currently unemployed, describes how she used to miss work or be late because of her unreliable car: "I wouldn't go in. I'd call [my boss] and tell him, 'I can't make it. I don't have a car.' Or I'd borrow my friend's car every now and then." Nevertheless, among the qualitative respondents, the employed controls have shorter commute times than the experimentals, regardless of whether they drive or take public transportation to work. Additionally, since the controls are living closer to the center of the city, where buses and trains are more frequent, they have fewer complaints about access to public transportation.

Due to the widespread demolition of public housing in Baltimore, most of the controls have moved from their baseline addresses, too. Yet most are still living significantly closer to their baseline neighborhoods than the experimentals (3.11 miles versus 5.82 miles).[50] This seemingly small difference in

50. One control, who moved to North Carolina, is excluded from this analysis.

distance is still important, especially because before MTO, many respondents in both groups had been living in their baseline neighborhoods for a significant portion of their lives, sometimes their entire lives, and had virtually no exposure to a low-poverty neighborhood. Moving away from what is familiar can bring a host of challenges such as navigating new public transportation routes, finding child care and after-school programs, and locating an accessible coin-operated laundry, grocery store, or health clinic. Additionally, though all who moved from their baseline unit described suffering some severing of social ties, the disruption was much more severe among experimentals. Even six to nine years after random assignment, both experimentals and controls still talk fondly of the neighbors they had in their public housing projects, and lament about the amount of time it takes to build new neighborhood connections. The greater proximity of controls to their baseline neighborhoods is perhaps part of the reason why only 30 percent of experimentals mention having a close friend or family member in their neighborhood while nearly half (47 percent) of controls report a close neighborhood social connection.

In sum, the experimentals talk repeatedly about how they benefited from living in their low-poverty neighborhoods. But these neighborhoods posed unique challenges to them—they had to navigate transportation concerns and develop new social networks—that could create difficulty when searching for and maintaining employment.

Discussion and Conclusion

Previous analyses of the 2002 survey, conducted four to seven years after random assignment, find virtually no significant effects on employment or earnings of adults who moved to low-poverty neighborhoods through the MTO program.[51] Given past theory and research, the lack of a larger effect of the MTO program on employment warrants further examination.

Our analysis of in-depth interview data from a random subsample of Baltimore MTO experimentals and controls explores the job search strategies and other social processes that may underlie the survey results. First, we find important differences in the labor market attachment of those experimentals and controls who are currently unemployed. The unemployed experimentals are cycling in and out of jobs with low wages and high turnover, and report considerable job stress. However, while their work experiences have been

---

51. Kling, Liebman, and Katz (2007).

far from ideal, they express a strong commitment to ongoing labor force participation. In contrast, more of the unemployed controls are permanently detached from the labor force, and fewer have been recently employed or are currently seeking employment.

Experimentals and controls have similar barriers to employment, such as low educational attainment and poor mental and physical health. These barriers, most of which predate their participation in MTO, may be a result of years of exposure to neighborhoods that are among the most distressed in the nation. Furthermore, these barriers were not explicitly addressed by MTO. Even many low-wage service sector jobs now require employees to possess a high-school diploma or GED. And those employers who do not require this credential will presumably choose a high-school graduate over someone without such credentials. Similarly, respondents who are battling depression or other mental and physical health problems have a more difficult time sustaining employment—and forming and maintaining social connections that can lead to employment—than healthy respondents.

Additionally, the move to their low-poverty neighborhood may have decreased experimentals' access to a particular type of social tie that has proved particularly effective in the job search process for the employed respondents in both program groups, namely acquaintances with similar skills and credentials who work in jobs similar to those the respondent is seeking. In respondents' views, such jobs typically fill quickly, often before they are posted in the newspaper or by other formal means. Thus insider tips about upcoming or recent openings are crucial to successfully securing a job. Ironically, though experimentals are more likely to have working neighbors, take pride in that fact, and sometimes credit the presence of these neighbors for providing them the motivation to get and keep jobs, no experimental was referred to her current job through a neighbor. Meanwhile, experimentals' residential locations may have decreased the probability of a chance encounter with these crucial social ties. Controls had fewer employed neighbors and rarely got job information and referrals from neighbors either, but their residential locations led to more of these chance encounters in the course of their daily routines. Since the majority of respondents in both groups tend to rely on social ties to find jobs, MTO may have simultaneously increased the motivation to work while inadvertently making the process of job search more difficult.

Transportation poses an additional challenge to MTO participants. Many experimentals are employed in the expanding health care sector, which bodes well for their future employment, as there is an increasing demand for health care workers. But in the Baltimore metropolitan area, these jobs are more likely to be located in the city or on the city-suburban fringe than in the suburbs. Suburban residents who rely on public transportation must often commute to the city center first, and then on to their job. Suburban buses also run less frequently, increasing commute time. Though most experimentals eventually find work that does not involve an onerous commute, in the qualitative sample at least, this is often because they have rejected jobs that are too difficult to get to or because they have made a subsequent move in order to be closer to their job or to more reliable public transportation.

The respondents in our qualitative sample were randomly chosen from the entire MTO population in Baltimore, but our sample size is small. Thus we cannot generalize these results to all MTO participants. Nor do we intend to make causal claims of any kind. Rather, we deploy these data to develop hypotheses about the array of complex social processes that may underlie the MTO survey results. Basing our hypothesis development directly upon the experiences of MTO families has helped identify which of many potential theories are most grounded in the particular context in which the families live. We hope that these results will help guide questionnaire design in future waves of the MTO survey and future quantitative analyses of housing mobility programs.

APPENDIX

Table A-1. Means of Covariates Used in Regression Analyses

Covariates (at baseline)	Five cities[a]		Baltimore	
	Experimental	Control	Experimental	Control
Male	0.01	0.02	0.01	0.02
Black	0.67	0.66	0.98	0.99
Other nonwhite race	0.26	0.27	0.02	0.01
Hispanic	0.29	0.29	0.02	0.02
Age 19–29	0.36	0.37	0.33	0.38
Age 30–39	0.42	0.41	0.48	0.43
Age 40–49	0.15	0.16	0.13	0.14
GED	0.18	0.21	0.14	0.17
High-school diploma	0.41	0.38	0.45	0.39
Enrolled in school	0.16	0.16	0.14	0.17
Never married	0.62	0.62	0.73	0.74
Under age 18 at birth of first child	0.25	0.24	0.27	0.27
No teen children in household	0.59	0.62	0.62	0.67
Employed	0.29	0.25	0.22	0.30

continued on next page

Table A-1. Means of Covariates Used in Regression Analyses (*continued*)

	Five cities[a]		Baltimore	
Covariates (at baseline)	Experimental	Control	Experimental	Control
Received AFDC/TANF	0.74	0.75	0.78	0.79
Had car that runs	0.17	0.15	0.05	0.03
Any household member disabled	0.16	0.16	0.12	0.08
Core family size = 2	0.23	0.20	0.26	0.28
Core family size = 3	0.30	0.32	0.36	0.35
Core family size = 4	0.23	0.22	0.21	0.23
Previously applied for Section 8	0.41	0.45	0.52	0.58
Moved 3+ times in past five years	0.08	0.11	0.10	0.13
Lived in neighborhood 5+ years	0.61	0.62	0.51	0.52
No family in neighborhood	0.65	0.65	0.74	0.72
No friends in neighborhood	0.40	0.41	0.42	0.49
Chatted with neighbor in street or hallway at least once a week	0.52	0.55	0.63	0.56
Very likely to tell neighbor if saw neighbor's child getting into trouble	0.53	0.56	0.64	0.64
Streets near home very unsafe at night	0.48	0.49	0.57	0.54
Very dissatisfied with neighborhood	0.46	0.46	0.59	0.49
Primary or secondary reason for moving was drugs and gangs	0.77	0.78	0.83	0.81
Primary or secondary reason for moving was better schools	0.47	0.48	0.37	0.39
Very sure would be able to find an apartment in a different area of city	0.45	0.45	0.55	0.59
Household member had been victimized within six months	0.42	0.41	0.50	0.40
Boston	0.22	0.21	. . .	. . .
Baltimore	0.23	0.22	. . .	. . .
Chicago	0.16	0.16	. . .	. . .
Los Angeles	0.25	0.25	. . .	. . .
N (number of cases)	1,453	1,080	213	168

Source: Authors' calculations based on U.S. Department of Housing and Urban Development's Interim Survey data on the Moving to Opportunity program.
. . . Not applicable.
AFDC = Aid to Families with Dependent Children; TANF = Temporary Assistance for Needy Families.
a. Five cities include Boston, Baltimore, Chicago, Los Angeles, and New York.

Table A-2. Means of Variables Used to Match Noncompliers

Variable	Experimental noncomplier	Control likely noncomplier[a]
Age	42.0	40.6
Number of children	3.08	3.16
Full-time employment	0.61	0.63
Part-time employment	0.11	0.11
Job through formal search	0.17	0.26
Job through agency	0.17	0.16
Job through network	0.33	0.32
Dropout	0.29	0.32
Poverty rate in tract	0.65	0.63
High-school graduation rate in tract	0.40	0.38
College degree rate in tract	0.11	0.12
Employment rate in tract	0.37	0.39
Living in initial unit	0.17	0.16
Government assistance	0.37	0.37

Source: Authors' calculations based on qualitative interview data from the Moving to Opportunity program.
a. Selected based on matching of these characteristics, as described in the text. See below for variable descriptions.

Variables Used to Select Control Noncompliers

Age: Age of respondent.

Number of children: Number of children in household.

Full-time employment: 1 = respondent employed full-time; 0 = respondent not employed full-time.

Part-time employment: 1 = respondent employed part-time; 0 = respondent not employed part-time.

Job through formal search: 1 = respondent found current job through formal search (newspaper, Internet, Yellow Pages, direct application); 0 = respondent did not find current job through formal search or unemployed.

Job through agency: 1 = respondent found current job through agency (temporary employment agency or social services agency); 0 = respondent did not find current job through agency search or unemployed.

Job through network: 1 = respondent found current job through social network connection; 0 = respondent did not find current job through social network connection or unemployed.

Dropout: 1 = respondent did not graduate from high school; 0 = respondent graduated from high school.

Poverty rate in tract: Percentage of neighbors living below the poverty level at time of qualitative interview (2000 Census data).

High-school graduation rate in tract: Percentage in neighborhood with high school diploma or GED at time of qualitative interview (2000 Census data).

College degree rate in tract: Percentage in neighborhood with college degree at time of qualitative interview (2000 Census data).

Employment rate in tract: Employment rate among civilian population at time of qualitative interview (2000 Census data).

Living in initial unit: 1 = respondent living in reference unit at time of qualitative interview; 0 = respondent not living in reference unit at time of qualitative interview. Reference unit is placement unit if respondent moved through MTO. If respondent did not move through MTO, reference unit is baseline unit.

Government assistance: Average of **Medicaid** (1 = respondent receives Medicaid; 0 = respondent does not receive Medicaid), **HCV** (1 = respondent receives housing assistance; 0 = respondent does not receive housing assistance), **TANF** (1 = respondent receives TANF; 0 = respondent does not receive TANF), **Food stamps** (1 = respondent receives food stamps; 0 = respondent does not receive food stamps).

Comments

Jens Ludwig: There is widespread belief that a person's neighborhood of residence affects labor market outcomes, particularly for low-skilled minority workers living in central cities. This view stems from the results reported in a large body of theoretical and empirical research from across the social sciences. Yet the conclusion that neighborhoods matter for labor market outcomes seems to stand in sharp contrast to research on the Moving to Opportunity (MTO) randomized mobility experiment, which shows little impact on work or earnings measured four to seven years after random assignment.[1]

I consider ways of reconciling these conflicting strands of research as well as the implications for public policies designed to improve the labor market prospects of disadvantaged workers. I focus on three of the leading explanations that have been offered to explain why findings from MTO conflict with most people's reading of the existing literature on neighborhood effects: 1) the possibility that MTO did not generate large enough differences in neighborhood environments to affect outcomes; 2) whether estimates of neighborhood effects on the MTO population, which consists of the subset of public housing families who volunteered for the demonstration, generalize to other groups; and 3) the possibility that the effects of mobility on labor market outcomes become more pronounced over time.

This paper by Turney and her colleagues provides useful information on these candidate explanations in the form of detailed, qualitative accounts of MTO families' experiences in the Baltimore demonstration site. After discussing previous hypotheses to reconcile MTO with existing research in light of findings from this work and other studies, I consider the evidence on another explanation that seems to have received less discussion—the possibility of bias with the previous nonexperimental research.

---

1. Orr and others (2003); Kling, Liebman, and Katz (2007).

Did MTO Change Neighborhoods Enough?

It is natural to wonder whether MTO actually changed neighborhoods enough to plausibly affect labor market or other outcomes. After all, of those families assigned to the MTO experimental group, only a fraction moved through the MTO program (58 percent in the Baltimore demonstration site). Experimental-group families were only required to live in their new low-poverty neighborhoods for one year, at which point they were free to use their vouchers to relocate to higher-poverty areas, which many chose to do. In addition, some control-group families wound up moving to neighborhoods with lower poverty rates over time on their own or as a result of HUD demolitions of public housing projects.

Nevertheless, there are at least three reasons to believe that MTO generated important changes in the neighborhood environments of program participants, and therefore has something useful to say about the neighborhoods' role on labor market outcomes. First, across all five MTO cities, assignment to the experimental (rather than control) group reduced poverty rates by about 15 percent of the control group average in the tracts in which families were living four to seven years after random assignment (see table 1). In the Baltimore MTO site the experimental-control difference is more like 20 percent of the control mean for tract poverty, almost as large (17 percent) for tract employment rates, and more than twice as large (42 percent) as a share of the control mean for the presence of affluent (college-educated) adults in the neighborhood. These across-group differences pool together the experiences of families in the experimental group who did and did not move through MTO. The impact on those families who actually moved through the experimental MTO treatment in Baltimore will be about 1.7 times as large as the overall across-group differences.[2] The one exception to this general pattern of MTO-induced changes in neighborhood attributes is for racial integration, which was more modestly affected by the MTO experimental treatment.

A second reason to believe that MTO generated important changes in neighborhood environments is that MTO participants themselves perceive important differences in their neighborhood environments, as suggested by

---

2. Bloom (1984) demonstrates that if the treatment compliance rate is below 100 percent, so long as treatment assignment has no effect on those who are assigned to the treatment group and random assignment is in fact random, we can infer the effects of the treatment on those who are treated as the overall difference between the treatment and control group in some outcome (in this case postassignment neighborhood environments) divided by the treatment compliance rate (in this case, $1 / 0.58 = 1.72$).

the qualitative interviews described by this paper's authors. Families in the experimental group notice that a large fraction of their neighbors are employed (including some neighbors who are in higher-status, more-skilled office jobs) and these families think this has beneficial effects on the quality of community life in general. Other survey data from MTO reveal large experimental-control differences in overall reported satisfaction with neighborhoods measured four to seven years after random assignment, including pronounced changes in community safety and disorder.[3]

Finally, the possibility that MTO-induced neighborhood changes are large enough to change labor market outcomes is suggested by the fact that these neighborhood changes had some effect on other outcomes. Assignment to the MTO experimental rather than control group leads to detectable improvements in: adult mental health; some measures of physical health (reductions in obesity); and a wide variety of outcomes for female youth, such as risky behavior and mental health. There are even improvements in violent criminal behavior of male youth, at least in the short run.[4] One might wonder whether particularly large neighborhood changes are required to affect labor market outcomes, if work and earnings are somehow harder to influence than other behaviors or subject to some sort of tipping phenomenon. But a recent study finds little evidence for nonlinearities in the effects of neighborhood socioeconomic composition on labor market or other outcomes in MTO.[5]

How Do MTO Results Generalize to Other Populations?

MTO families were drawn from some of the country's worst public housing projects, located in some of the nation's most disadvantaged neighborhoods. This paper notes that many of the MTO adults were themselves brought up in public housing, and more generally have low levels of schooling and high rates of mental health problems. The qualitative interviews of Baltimore families highlight the implications of these factors for employment outcomes. So what can be learned about neighborhood effects more generally from studies of MTO?

Suppose that families need some minimum level of human capital to take advantage of the opportunities afforded by living in a lower-poverty neighborhood. The MTO findings in this case are still interesting in their own right

3. Orr and others (2003).

4. Orr and others (2003); Kling, Ludwig, and Katz (2005); Kling, Liebman, and Katz (2007).

5. Liebman, Katz, and Kling (2004).

because so many low-income families share similar human capital barriers to those facing the MTO program population. For example, in 1994 (the year MTO began), about 45 percent of poor American adults had less than a high-school education, and survey data around this time for a sample of less-educated women find that nearly two in five report poor mental health.[6] Moreover, since MTO families volunteered for the demonstration, it might be expected that the families who signed up are the ones who expect to benefit the most from moving. There is a plausible argument to be made that MTO provides upper-bound estimates for the effects of neighborhood mobility on similarly disadvantaged families in the population as a whole.

Will MTO Effects Become More Pronounced over Time?

The MTO interviews reported in this paper by Turney and her colleagues provide several reasons to believe that the program's effects on labor market outcomes could potentially increase over time. Adults in the Baltimore MTO experimental group are more likely than controls to work in the health sector, which MTO participants at least believe provides greater opportunities for upward mobility in the future. Some of the experimental families describe efforts to improve their educational credentials, a process that might take some time given these adults are likely to be limited to part-time study. In addition, many experimental families seem to not take full advantage of the social networks available in their new neighborhoods, in part because they are not yet comfortable interacting with their new neighbors. Put differently, this last problem may be one of demand rather than supply for helpful social interactions in these new neighborhoods, which in principle could change over time as MTO families become more comfortable in their lower-poverty communities.

Selection Bias

Implicit in any discussion of MTO is that the results may differ from previous studies because the latter are plagued by self-selection bias—that is, bias from hard-to-measure individual or family attributes that are associated with both neighborhood selection and labor market or other outcomes of interest. Yet in practice this possibility does not seem to be taken as seriously as it should by many analysts who currently believe that neighborhoods are extremely important for labor market outcomes.

---

6. For the first point, see Blank (1997, p. 17); for the second point, see Kaestner and Tarlov (2003).

One should be cautious about investing too much faith in most previous nonexperimental studies of neighborhood effects. Consider, for example, what happens when one analyzes the MTO data nonexperimentally, for example by relating variation in neighborhood attributes within, rather than across, randomly assigned MTO groups to variation in outcomes for MTO participants, controlling for a variety of individual and family baseline attributes. This type of standard nonexperimental method generates estimates that are not only of the wrong magnitude compared to experimental findings, they often are of the wrong sign.[7] These findings are important in part because the set of control variables available with the MTO data is relatively rich by the standards of this research literature.

Summary

This paper provides interesting descriptive information about how MTO changes the neighborhood environments and life experiences of program participants in Baltimore. These experiences seem relevant to understanding neighborhood effects on poor families more generally, since MTO induces substantial changes in neighborhood characteristics for those families who move and many low-income families in America have human capital barriers similar to those for the MTO population.

In about three years, when the final long-term results for MTO are available, we will know more about whether the difference in findings from MTO versus earlier studies is explained by differences in the residential duration of study samples in their current neighborhoods of residence. In the meantime there are reasons to suspect that differences in residential duration are unlikely to explain away the entire difference in results between MTO and previous studies, since residential mobility is a prevalent phenomenon among American families more generally, particularly among low-income minority families.[8]

Although the long-term MTO results have yet to be published, the findings available to date from the MTO demonstration still provide very useful information about the effects of different housing policy options on the labor market outcomes for disadvantaged families living in distressed public housing communities. Findings reported here and elsewhere suggest efforts to move public housing families into private-market housing through expanding voucher programs is very likely to improve the well-being and physical safety of these

7. Liebman, Katz, and Kling (2004); Ludwig and Kling (2006).
8. South and Crowder (1997); Briggs and Keys (2005).

families and may be worth supporting for that reason alone. However, expanding residential mobility for disadvantaged families alone is unlikely to generate detectable changes in work or earnings for many of these families, at least for a period of up to five years.

John Karl Scholz: Moving to Opportunity (MTO) is one of this generation's most important randomized social experiments. Like the negative income tax experiments of the 1970s, or major welfare reform evaluations of the 1990s (such as the Canadian Self-Sufficiency Project, Minnesota Family Investment Program, and Milwaukee's Project New Hope), the MTO demonstration examines factors that many believe fundamentally affect the lives of low-income Americans. But unlike most previous experiments (including those mentioned above), MTO does not focus on human capital acquisition and labor market incentives. Instead, it was designed to provide evidence on the ideas that:

—residence in a distressed community can limit an individual's economic prospects;

—inner-city, low-skilled minority workers are disadvantaged because job opportunities are disproportionately in suburban areas;

—housing market discrimination, commuting costs, and other barriers make it difficult to reach those suburban jobs.[1]

MTO provides evidence on these ideas by offering housing vouchers to randomly selected households in high-poverty public housing projects in five U.S. cities, and by comparing their experiences to a control set of households, also from high-poverty public housing projects in five U.S. cities.

MTO's results to date are unexpected and striking. Kling, Liebman, and Katz (2007), in a wide-ranging analysis of the experimental data, find the intervention succeeded in altering the neighborhoods in which treated households lived.[2] Namely, families that were offered vouchers lived in safer neighborhoods with lower poverty rates than families in the control group that were not offered vouchers. Despite the change in neighborhood quality, however, there is no significant evidence of beneficial treatment effects on earnings, welfare participation, or the amount of government assistance received after an average of five years following random assignment. This result leads Kling, Liebman, and Katz to conclude "housing mobility by itself does not appear to be an effective anti-poverty strategy—at least over a five-year period."

1. See Wilson (1987); Kain (1968).
2. This paper is available at www.nber.org/papers/w11577.

MTO had some measurable, experimental effects. Adult mental health improved for the experimental group relative to the control group across several specific measures, including distress, depression, anxiety, calmness, and sleep. The intervention did not have a statistically significant effect on overall physical health of adults, however. There are positive effects on mental health and risky behaviors for female youth and negative effects on mental health and risky behaviors for male youth. The findings on mental health and gender differences in some youth outcomes will fuel social science research in the years to come.

I view the results showing no beneficial effects of better neighborhoods on employment-related outcomes as being remarkable.[3] Hundreds of social science papers have been written examining the deleterious effects of bad neighborhoods on various outcomes, or examining harmful effects of spatial mismatch on employment outcomes. Kling, Liebman, and Katz (2007) cite a comprehensive survey, for example, that concludes the empirical evidence overwhelmingly supports the spatial mismatch hypothesis.[4] Given the surprising outcome of the MTO experiment, particularly given the extensive body of social science research that led me (and presumably many others) to expect different MTO outcomes, further work probing the MTO results would be valuable.

This paper by Turney and her coauthors is a nice step in that direction. The paper focuses on Baltimore, one of the five MTO cities (the others were Boston, Chicago, Los Angeles, and New York), and combines statistical evidence on the MTO sample, with completed, in-depth qualitative interviews of 104 Baltimore participants (fifty-one in the experimental group, fifty-three in the control group). This paper nicely illustrates the insights that qualitative research can provide in better understanding factors that may lie behind statistical, or quantitative, analysis. The authors also aspire to use the qualitative work to derive hypotheses that can be used to guide further qualitative work and guide the next rounds of survey work with the MTO population, scheduled for 2007.

The Baltimore MTO sample is overwhelmingly African American and female, which differs somewhat from the populations of other MTO cities. But the quantitative analyses of the Baltimore sample are similar to the results for the broader five-city MTO sample. Across nearly all measures of neighborhood

---

3. Kling, Liebman, and Katz (2007) are more understated, writing "it is somewhat surprising that the MTO intervention . . . had no discernable overall effects on unemployment."
4. See Ihlandfeldt and Sjoquist (1998).

quality, households in the treatment group were living in higher-quality neighborhoods than their control group counterparts, four to seven years after random assignment. Thus the MTO intervention successfully altered the feature of household environments that it was designed to affect. Nevertheless, across seven different outcomes, those assigned experimental group status do not have employment or earnings outcomes that are statistically different from their control group counterparts.[5]

When the quantitative evidence mentioned above is combined with the qualitative evidence, which is the heart of Turney and her coauthors' paper, it is useful to consider differences in the samples used for the two approaches. The authors show the quantitative results for Baltimore are consistent with the broader MTO results reported in Kling, Liebman, and Katz (2007). But it might also be interesting to confirm the quantitative results hold in the 124-household subsample selected for the qualitative study. With such a small sample, fewer of the appendix covariates can be used in estimating the regression-adjusted treatment effects. But when considering the qualitative evidence, I would like to know there are no statistically significant employment differences in the subsample used in the qualitative analysis.

More importantly, the regression work in the paper by Turney and her coauthors examines the "intent to treat." That is, the results measure differences between all treatments and controls. A substantial fraction (42 percent) of those given an offer of treatment chose not to accept the voucher to make a move to a low-poverty neighborhood. Yet these households are included in the intent-to-treat estimates. In contrast, much of the qualitative analyses focus on the "treatment on the treated," dropping treated households who refuse the MTO offer and a matched set of control group households.

It is not clear to me why, given the available data, the qualitative work focuses on the treatment-on-the-treated parameter. Doing so reduces already small samples. The authors drop eighteen treatment households who did not take up the MTO offer and a matched set of nineteen control group households.[6] The observable characteristics of the matched sample closely mirror the characteristics of the treatment sample that did not participate in the MTO pro-

5. Point estimates of treatment effects for the Baltimore subsample are larger than for the broader MTO sample. The treatment group have employment rates 5.7 percentage points higher, health insurance coverage is 7.9 percentage points more likely, and the number having a job more than one year is 8.5 percentage points higher than the corresponding rates for the control group, but none of these effects are statistically significant at the usual confidence levels.

6. Twenty of the 124 households in the sample for the qualitative analysis also did not complete their interviews.

gram. Because the characteristics of those who did not take up the MTO offer
were so carefully matched, the characteristics of the treated sample and the
remaining control group households, which is the sample used for the qualitative analysis, differ quite sharply on some important observable characteristics. For example, 47 percent of the control group sample are high-school
dropouts, but only 28 percent of the treated sample are (0 percent of the control group sample have a college degree, but 9 percent of the treated sample
have one). The control sample has one more person per household (4.5) on
average than the treated sample (3.4). These differences in observable characteristics raise a concern that the treatment and control group samples differ
in unobservable ways that may be relevant to the hypothesis-generating
spirit of the qualitative analysis.

It would be interesting to see two further extensions to the analysis. First,
I think it would make more sense to do the matching analysis to balance
the observable characteristics of the treated who did take the MTO offer and
control group households. Put differently, since the authors choose to explore
the treatment-on-the-treated parameter, their matching exercise could balance
the observable characteristics between the treated sample who did take the MTO
offer and control group households (rather than balancing the observable
characteristics between the treated sample who did not take the MTO offer
and control group households). Second, it would also be interesting to learn
whether the qualitative conclusions from the treatment-on-the-treated sample
differ in any important ways from the intent-to-treat samples. Given the general
nature of the results of the qualitative analysis, my suspicion is that it is not
necessary to restrict the sample to the treatment-on-the-treated subsample.

The qualitative results focus on three sets of factors—human capital short-
comings, social isolation, and spatial mismatch—that consistently are raised
in the in-depth interviews. Because I do not do qualitative research, it seems
that a fundamental challenge for the authors is to assess the relative importance of various themes or common factors that arise from the detailed interviews. The ethnographic work highlights many themes. Households have
low levels of human capital and find this inhibits labor market success. There
are treatment-control differences in the sectors in which people work, with
members of the treatment group being much more likely to work in the
health care sector. There are treatment-control differences in the nature of
unemployment, with unemployed members of the treatment group expecting to
have brief periods of unemployment, while unemployed control group members believe they will be out of the labor market for longer periods. Treatment
group households appear to be less well-integrated into the communities in

which they live, and face greater transportation challenges than control group households. The challenge for the authors (and for readers of the paper) is to get some idea of the relative importance of these different experiences.

The experimental design and results of MTO impose constraints on the qualitative analysis that often are not present in other qualitative studies. Specifically, one knows there are no aggregate treatment-control employment effects, at least in the intent-to-treat parameters. So if the qualitative sub-sample is representative of the entire Baltimore MTO sample, there are two possibilities. The first is that none of the treatment-control differences raised in the qualitative analysis are important in understanding employment. The second is that the differences are important, but coincidentally they are offset, so that the aggregate effect is zero. Offsetting effects are possible—treatment households have shorter periods of unemployment and better neighbors, both of which should improve employment outcomes. At the same time, they have more transportation difficulties and disrupted social networks that might make it more difficult to find jobs. The net effect (or the "complex story" to which the authors refer) might be that these effects indeed are important, but offset one another. I am skeptical of this, however, since (to my knowledge) there were no significant treatment-control differences in adult employment outcomes (broadly defined) across any of the five MTO sites. It strikes me as being unlikely that the treatment-control differences unearthed by the qualitative interviews were important in understanding employment outcomes and exactly offset each other in each of the five MTO locations.

There is abundant high-quality statistical evidence from a variety of experimental and nonexperimental analyses that human capital substantially affects employment outcomes. Evidence on the other factors is, in my view, more difficult to interpret. Common sense suggests that transportation difficulties or lack of access to informal networks that are important in securing jobs would inhibit employment prospects. But understanding the empirical effects of these barriers on employment is very difficult. Unobserved characteristics correlated with having access to unreliable transportation or having less-than-ideal job networks likely bias efforts to understand the effects of transportation difficulties, job networks, or the effects of neighborhoods on economic outcomes. The ability to account rigorously for such unobservables is what makes the MTO experiment so valuable. An example is highlighted in Turney and others' paper when they write, "living in high-poverty, economically depressed neighborhoods has a negative effect on one's health."[7] But the MTO intervention

7. Ross and Mirowsky (2001); Boardman and others (2001).

finds no statistically significant treatment-control differences in physical health, calling into question the assertion about neighborhoods and health. I suspect that failure to account appropriately for selection explains the link between neighborhoods and health in many nonexperimental settings, though other factors, of course, may come into play.

I have similar suspicions about the role of what the authors (and the literature) call "weak" and "strong" social networks in finding jobs. Would employment outcomes differ appreciably for workers if their social networks change, holding constant their skills, experience, mobility, and all other relevant characteristics? My guess is that human capital considerations dominate employment relationships and that there are enough sources of information about jobs through newspapers, posted ads, the Internet, radio, television, jobs centers, as well as through word of mouth, that social networks in fact are less important that one might infer from talking to people. The selection problems in studying this in a nonexperimental setting are formidable. Factors that result in people's having broad, rich social networks are presumably related to characteristics that are beneficial in the labor market. Hence it is possible that the emphasis placed on social networks in the qualitative study is misplaced.

I am puzzled by the first result highlighted in the final section of the paper, namely, that the authors "find important differences in the labor market attachment of those experimentals and controls who are currently unemployed." It is hard for me to believe that this difference is a treatment effect. If the MTO intervention caused greater labor market attachment of unemployed treatment group members (relative to controls), we would presumably see some significant employment-related treatment effects across sites (such as in annual earnings). But we do not see these differences. The authors are careful in the conclusions to say that they ". . . do not intend to make causal claims of any kind." But the beauty of a randomized social experiment is that one may be able to make well-grounded causal inferences from treatment-control differences. It seems, however, that the item highlighted first in the conclusions is unlikely to be a result of the MTO intervention. Hence it perhaps should get less emphasis from the authors.

A first-order question as one draws lessons from MTO is the degree to which the absence of beneficial employment effects is a result of the experiment's being implemented during a period of sustained economic growth, low unemployment, and a sharp change in the administration and rhetoric associated with Aid to Families with Dependent Children and Temporary Assistance for Needy Families (TANF). As the authors note, employment rates of control group households increased sharply in the MTO sample, which may reduce, to some extent, the likelihood of observing treatment-control differences. One might be able to learn more about this issue by examining whether there are cross-site differences in economic performance (and the work orientation of TANF programs) and then correlating differences in treatment effects with observed geographic differences.

In closing, the authors have produced a nicely written, well-reasoned paper. Employment issues facing low-skilled Americans are of first-order social, economic, and policy importance. This paper puts a spotlight on the role of neighborhoods and geography. Methodologically, it is very interesting to combine qualitative and quantitative approaches. The extensive interview work raises the possibility of learning more than what is revealed by regression coefficients from empirical models. The paper provides much to think about and I look forward to reading subsequent qualitative work with the MTO sample.

References

Becker, Gary S. 1975. *Human Capital: A Theoretical and Empirical Analysis, with Special Reference to Education.* Columbia University Press.

Blank, Rebecca M. 1997. *It Takes a Nation: A New Agenda for Fighting Poverty.* Princeton University Press.

Bloom, Howard. 1984. "Accounting for No-Shows in Experimental Evaluation Designs." *Evaluation Review* 8: 225–46.

Boardman, Jason D., and others. 2001. "Neighborhood Disadvantage, Stress, and Drug Use among Adults." *Journal of Health and Social Behavior* 42 (2): 151–65.

Briggs, Xavier de Souza, and Benjamin J. Keys. 2005. "Did Exposure to Poor Neighborhoods Change in the 1990s? Evidence from the Panel Study of Income Dynamics." Working Paper. Massachusetts Institute of Technology Department of Urban Planning.

Brooks-Gunn, Jeanne, Greg J. Duncan, and J. Lawrence Aber. 1997. *Neighborhood Poverty: Policy Implications in Studying Neighborhoods.* New York: Russell Sage Foundation.

Chapple, Karen. 2002. " 'I Name It and I Claim It—In the Name of Jesus, This Job Is Mine': Job Search, Networks, and Careers for Low-Income Women." *Economic Development Quarterly* 16 (4): 294–313.

Clampet-Lundquist, Susan. 2004. "Hope VI Relocation: Moving to New Neighborhoods and Building New Ties." *Housing Policy Debate* 15 (2): 415–47.

Danziger, Sandra K., Ariel Kalil, and Nathaniel J. Anderson. 2000. "Human Capital, Physical Health, and Mental Health of Welfare Recipients: Co-occurrence and Correlates." *Journal of Social Issues* 56 (4): 635–54.

Elliott, James R. 1999. "Social Isolation and Labor Market Insulation." *The Sociological Quarterly* 40 (2): 199–216.

———. 2000. "Class, Race, and Job Matching in Contemporary Urban Labor Markets." *Social Science Quarterly* 81 (4): 1036–52.

Fernandez, Roberto M., and Nancy Weinberg. 1997. "Sifting and Sorting: Personal Contacts and Hiring in a Retail Bank." *American Sociological Review* 62 (6): 883–902.

Granovetter, Mark S. 1973. "The Strength of Weak Ties." *American Journal of Sociology* 78 (6): 1360–80.

———. 1974. *Getting a Job: A Study of Contacts and Careers.* University of Chicago Press.

———. 1995. *Getting a Job: A Study of Contacts and Careers.* 2nd ed. University of Chicago Press.

Green, Gary P., Leann M. Tigges, and Irene Browne. 1995. "Social Resources, Job Search, and Poverty in Atlanta." *Research in Community Sociology* 5: 161–82.

Green, Gary P., Leann M. Tigges, and Daniel Diaz. 1999. "Racial and Ethnic Differences in Job Search Strategies in Atlanta, Boston, and Los Angeles." *Social Science Quarterly* 80 (2): 263–78.

Handel, Michael J. 2003. "Skills Mismatch in the Labor Market." *Annual Review of Sociology* 29: 135–65 (August).

Harmuth, Susan. 2002. "The Direct Care Workforce Crisis in Long-Term Care." *North Carolina Medical Journal* 63 (2): 87–94.

Holzer, Harry J. 1996. *What Employers Want: Job Prospects for Less-Educated Workers.* New York: Russell Sage Foundation.

Holzer, Harry J., and Sheldon Danziger. 1998. "Are Jobs Available for Disadvantaged Workers in Urban Areas?" Discussion Paper 1157-98. University of Wisconsin-Madison, Institute for Research on Poverty.

Ihlanfeldt, Keith R., and David L. Sjoquist. 1998. "The Spatial Mismatch Hypothesis: A Review of Recent Studies and Their Implications for Welfare Reform." *Housing Policy Debate* 9 (4): 849–92.

Kaestner, Robert, and Elizabeth Tarlov. 2003. "Changes in the Welfare Caseload and the Health of Low-Educated Mothers." Working Paper 10034. Cambridge, Mass.: National Bureau of Economic Research.

Kain, John F. 1968. "Housing Segregation, Negro Employment, and Metropolitan Decentralization." *Quarterly Journal of Economics* 82 (2): 175–97.

———. 1992. "The Spatial Mismatch Hypothesis: Three Decades Later." *Housing Policy Debate* 3 (2): 371–460.

Kasarda, John D. 1985. "Urban Change and Minority Opportunities." In *The New Urban Reality,* edited by Paul E. Peterson. Brookings.

Kleit, Rachel Garschick. 2001. "The Role of Neighborhood Social Networks in Scattered-Site Public Housing Residents' Search for Jobs." *Housing Policy Debate* 12 (3): 541–73.

———. 2002. "Job Search Strategies and Networks in Scattered-Site Public Housing." *Housing Studies* 17 (1): 83–100.

Kling, Jeffrey R., Jeffrey B. Liebman, and Lawrence F. Katz. 2007 (forthcoming). "Experimental Analysis of Neighborhood Effects." *Econometrica.*

Kling, Jeffrey R., Jens Ludwig, and Lawrence F. Katz. 2005. "Neighborhood Effects on Crime for Female and Male Youth: Evidence from a Randomized Housing Voucher Experiment." *Quarterly Journal of Economics* 120 (1): 87–130.

Liebman, Jeffrey B., Lawrence F. Katz, and Jeffrey R. Kling. 2004. "Beyond Treatment Effects: Estimating the Relationship between Neighborhood Poverty and Individual Outcomes in the MTO Experiment." Working Paper 493. Princeton University Industrial Relations Section.

Lin, Nan, and Mary Dumin. 1986. "Access to Occupations through Social Ties." *Social Networks* 8 (4): 365–85.

Lin, Nan, Walter M. Ensel, and John C. Vaughn. 1981. "Social Resources and Strength of Ties: Structural Factors in Occupational Status Attainment." *American Sociological Review* 46 (4): 393–405.

Ludwig, Jens, and Jeffrey R. Kling. 2006. "Is Crime Contagious?" Working Paper 510. Princeton University Industrial Relations Section.

Massey, Douglas S., and Nancy A. Denton. 1993. *American Apartheid: Segregation and the Making of the Underclass.* Harvard University Press.

Mendenhall, Ruby. 2005. *Black Women in Gautreaux's Housing Desegregation Program: The Role of Neighborhoods and Networks in Economic Independence.* Unpublished dissertation. Northwestern University.

Mendenhall, Ruby, Stefanie DeLuca, and Greg Duncan. "Neighborhood Resources, Racial Segregation, and Economic Mobility: Results from the Gautreaux Program." *Social Science Research.* Forthcoming.

Meyer, Bruce D., and Daniel T. Rosenbaum. 2000. "Making Single Mothers Work: Recent Tax and Welfare Policy and Its Effects." *National Tax Journal* 53 (4, part 2): 1027–61.

Mouw, Ted. 2002. "Are Black Workers Missing the Connection? The Effect of Spatial Distance and Employee Referrals on Interfirm Racial Segregation." *Demography* 39 (3): 507–28.

Orr, Larry, and others. 2003. *Moving to Opportunity Interim Impacts Evaluation.* U.S. Department of Housing and Urban Development.

Popkin, Susan, James E. Rosenbaum, and Patricia M. Meaden. 1993. "Labor Market Experiences of Low-Income Black Women in Middle-Class Suburbs: Evidence from a Survey of Gautreaux Program Participants." *Journal of Policy Analysis and Management* 12 (3): 556–73.

Reingold, David A. 1998. "Social Networks and the Employment Problem of the Urban Poor." *Urban Studies* 36 (11): 1907–32.

Ross, Catherine E., and John Mirowsky. 2001. "Neighborhood Disadvantage, Disorder, and Health." *Journal of Health and Social Behavior* 42 (3): 258–76.

South, Scott J., and Kyle D. Crowder. 1997. "Escaping Distressed Neighborhoods: Individual, Community, and Metropolitan Influences." *American Journal of Sociology* 102 (4): 1040–84.

Stoloff, Jennifer A., Jennifer L. Glanville, and Elisa Jayne Bienenstock. 1999. "Women's Participation in the Labor Force: The Role of Social Networks." *Social Networks* 21 (1): 91–108.

Tienda, Marta. 1991. "Poor People and Poor Places: Deciphering Neighborhood Effects on Poverty Outcomes." In *Macro-Micro Linkages in Sociology,* edited by Joan Huber. Newbury Park, California: Sage Publications.

Tigges, Leann M., Irene Browne, and Gary P. Green. 1998. "Social Isolation of the Urban Poor: Race, Class, and Neighborhood Effects on Social Resources." *Sociological Quarterly* 39 (1): 53–77.

Wilson, William Julius. 1987. *The Truly Disadvantaged: The Inner City, the Underclass, and Public Policy.* University of Chicago Press.

———. 1996. *When Work Disappears: The World of the New Urban Poor.* New York: Knopf.

RICHARD ARNOTT

Boston College

Effects of Property Taxation on Development Timing and Density: Policy Perspective

DIFFERENT FACETS OF THE property taxation policy debate move in and out of focus according to current policy concerns and academic interests. Recently, the property tax has been discussed as a factor contributing to suburban sprawl, exclusionary zoning, the current crisis of housing affordability in coastal U.S. metropolitan areas, and housing market volatility. In the context of local government, the thriving literature on capital tax competition treats property taxation implicitly. A generation ago, debate focused on the extent to which the property tax, in the presence of local zoning, is a benefits tax. This followed soon after another debate concerning the general equilibrium incidence of the tax, pitting the orthodox view that the tax is regressive against the revisionist view that the tax burden falls on the owners of land and capital.

This paper looks at yet another facet of the policy debate over property taxation that harkens back to an even older literature—the property tax's discouragement of density. According to the classic view, the property tax is an equal-rate, *ad valorem* tax on the land and capital services used in the production of structure services.[1] Land services are inelastically supplied, so

I would like to thank: Sheila Campbell, Eren Inci, Luigi Pascali, and Andrei Zlate for excellent research assistance; Robert Nail, assistant assessor for the City of Newton, Massachusetts, for information about current assessment practice; Petia Petrova for collaboration on work from which this paper draws (Arnott and Petrova, 2006); conference paper discussants Jan Brueckner and Robert Schwab as well as conference participants for useful comments; and conference organizers for urging me to provide clear intuition for the economic theory underlying the paper's arguments.

1. Ascribed to Marshall (1961).

189

that the property tax component that falls on land generates no distortion and is shifted back to landowners. Capital services, in contrast, are elastically supplied, so that the property tax component that falls on capital discourages capital, generates distortion, and is borne by the consumer. Property taxation therefore discourages density (capital intensity) while land taxation does not.

This classical theme is revisited here from the perspective of a relatively recent theoretical literature on property development that takes into account the durability and immobility of structures and examines property taxation effects using deterministic capital asset pricing theory. This literature examines the profit-maximization problem of an owner of vacant land who must decide when and at what density to develop the land.

This paper has two overriding objectives: 1) to urge those who suggest property tax reforms not to ignore how their proposals affect the efficiency of development timing and density, and 2) to provide a more sophisticated (yet still intuitive) framework for thinking about the proposed reforms' effects on the efficiency of property development and redevelopment.

Setting the Stage

Over the past thirty years, the literature on taxation's effects on the timing and density of development has greatly expanded.[2] The recent literature's distinguishing feature is its explicit treatment of the durability and immobility of structures. The basic model looks at a competitive landowner who owns undeveloped land. Once he or she develops the land at a certain density, it remains at that density forever. The landowner chooses development timing and density under perfect foresight. Taxation affects these margins of choice. This model has been extended to treat redevelopment (but without taxation), uncertainty, and the general equilibrium of a growing city.[3] This paper develops the partial equilibrium model without uncertainty and without redevelopment.[4]

2. Earlier contributions include Shoup (1970); Arnott and Lewis (1979); Skouras (1978); Bentick (1979); Mills (1981); Tideman (1982). More recent contributions include Turnbull (1988); Arnott (2005); Arnott and Petrova (2006).
   3. See Wheaton (1982); Capozza and Li (1994); Turnbull (1988), respectively.
   4. An earlier version of this paper extended the model to treat redevelopment. The extended model was excluded from this version since it generated more heat than light. The principal qualitative result was that property taxation discourages the density of redevelopments in essentially the same way that it discourages the density of initial development. Comments will be inserted indicating how results are modified by the treatment of redevelopment.

Model without Taxation

Consider an atomistic landowner who owns a unit area of vacant land and has perfect foresight concerning the future time path of structure rents. Once a structure is built on the land, it remains there as it is forever; the structure does not depreciate, nor is redevelopment possible. To simplify, it is assumed that the interest rate, construction technology, and price of capital remain constant over time, and that rents increase over time. The following notation is employed:

T: development time;
k: capital applied to the land;
$r(t)$: rent per unit floor area of structure at time t;
$q(k)$: the floor-area ratio as a function of capital applied to the land;
p: price per unit of capital;
i: interest rate.

$q(k)$ is termed the structure production function and exhibits positive but diminishing returns to capital. The landowner chooses development time and density so as to maximize the present value of rents minus the present value of construction costs:

$$(1) \qquad \max_{T,k} \int_T^\infty r(t)q(k)e^{-it}dt - pke^{-iT}.$$

The timing first-order condition is

$$(2) \qquad -r(T)q(k) + ipk = 0,$$

which states that it is profit-maximizing to develop the site when the benefit from postponing development one period equals the cost. The benefit from postponing development one period is the interest earned on the construction funds; the cost is the rent forgone. The density first-order condition is

$$(3) \qquad \int_T^\infty r(t)q'(k)e^{-it}dt - p = 0,$$

which states that capital intensity should be such that the marginal revenue from the last unit of capital discounted to development time equals its cost. A more intuitive way of stating the condition is that floors should be added to the structure until the top floor pays for itself (in discounted terms). To simplify, it is assumed that there is a unique solution to the landowner's problem, which occurs at the unique point of intersection of the two first-order conditions.

Figure 1. First-Order Conditions of the Landowner's Profit-Maximization Problem without Taxation

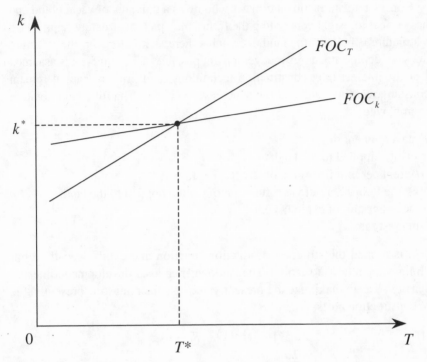

Source: Authors calc ulations.
k = capital-land ratio. T = development time. k^* = profit-maximizing capital-land ratio. T^* = profit-maximizing development time. FOC_k = first-order condition for k. FOC_T = first-order condition for T.

Figure 1 plots the two first-order conditions in T-k space. FOC_T is the timing first-order condition, and FOC_k the density first-order condition. The assumptions made imply that both first-order conditions are positively sloped,[5] and that the timing first-order condition is more steeply sloped than the density first-order condition (otherwise, profit is maximized with development infinitely far in the past or in the future). T^* and k^* denote the profit-maximizing T and k.

On the assumption that the site development does not affect distortion elsewhere in the economy, T^* and k^* are also the socially optimal development time and density. Before development, the social surplus from the site

5. An increase in k causes the time at which the timing first-order condition is satisfied to increase. Similarly, an increase in T causes the density at which the density first-order condition is satisfied to increase.

with optimal development, or the social value of the site, is the social benefit from its development minus the social cost of its development:

(4)
$$SS^* = \int_{T^*}^{\infty} r(t)q(k^*)e^{-it}dt - pk^*e^{-iT^*}.$$

With a competitive market for land development, the market value of land is bid up to the point where landowners make zero profit, and therefore equals social surplus.

Property taxation typically will cause one or both of the first-order conditions of the landlord's profit-maximization problem to shift, changing the profit-maximizing development time to $\hat{T}$ and density of development to $\hat{k}$. The corresponding social surplus generated by the site, $\hat{SS}$, is given in equation (4), but with $\hat{T}$ and $\hat{k}$ replacing T^* and k^*. Since social surplus is maximized with T^* and k^*, taxation will generally cause a loss in social surplus. The efficiency cost, or deadweight loss, of taxation is simply the loss in social surplus generated. Thus $DWL = SS^* - \hat{SS}$.

Figure 2 displays these results, showing the first-order conditions before (FOC^b) and after (FOC^a) taxation. It also plots iso-social-surplus contours, each of which gives the locus of (T,k) that generates a particular level of social surplus. (T^*,k^*) is at the top of the social surplus hill.

If application of a property tax system does not alter a landowner's choices of development time and density, it is said to be neutral and generates no distortion. If the property tax system alters the landowner's development decisions, it is distortionary and non-neutral.

Figure 2 ignores that the tax revenue collected from property taxation is spent on local government goods and services. Imposing a property tax when previously property was untaxed would then increase the property's attractiveness, causing rent to rise. Therefore it is appropriate to interpret the exercise being performed as one of differential incidence. Neutral property taxation is replaced by distortionary property taxation, holding fixed the revenue from taxation and level of local government goods and services. Thus what was referred to earlier as the situation without taxation should instead be interpreted as the situation with neutral taxation.

The discussion above also ignored land use controls, which may substantially affect the distortion created by taxation. At the extreme, one can imagine a situation where land use controls are so strict that they alone determine development timing and density, both before and after the change from a neutral to non-neutral tax regime. Since taxation then has no effect on development timing and density, it also has no effect on the efficiency of

Figure 2. Effects of Property Taxation on Development Time (*T*) and Capital Applied to the Land (*k*)

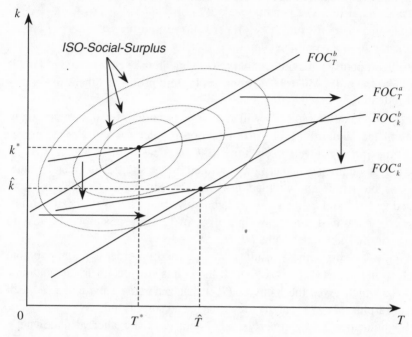

Source: Author's calculations.
k = capital-labor ratio. T = development time. * = profit-maximizing value before taxation. ^ = profit-maximizing value after taxation. FOC_k = first-order condition for k. FOC_T = first-order condition for T. a = after taxation. b = before taxation.

development. Land use controls are ignored through most of this paper, not because they are unimportant but because it is so difficult to ascertain where a particular system of land use controls would be on the continuum between being rigidly binding and completely accommodating. In a particular situation, one can observe what land use controls are in place, but not how responsive a zoning board is to a landowner's pressure to have the controls modified so he or she is allowed to develop at a more profitable time and density.

Other taxes (also ignored in the discussion above) are potentially significant for two reasons. First, they may interact with property taxation in important ways. Most obvious, it is the aftertax cost of property taxes paid that matters to the property owner, and this depends on their deductibility from income in computing local, state, and federal personal income tax liabilities. In addition, the treatment of interest income and the interest on personal debt under the personal income tax affects the individual's rate of discount. No doubt there are also complicated interactions between the corporate income tax and property tax payments made by corporations. Second, other taxes introduce distortions, and how property taxation affects the corresponding efficiency losses should be taken into account in computing the deadweight loss due to property taxation. Despite its potential importance, the interaction between property taxation and other aspects of the tax system has received little attention in the literature, and shall be ignored in this paper as well.

Property Tax Systems Typology

In the United States assessment offices administer local property tax. There are some 16,000 assessment offices in the country, each subject to relevant state and local regulations. In addition, each may follow its own assessment practices, employ its own land use classification system, decide which property classes are exempt from taxation, and set its own tax rates for the remaining property classes. Local property tax systems therefore show considerable variation. This paper's analysis abstracts from most of the variation details and works with a simple typology of property tax systems. It does not distinguish between property classes and therefore should not be interpreted as applying to a particular property class.[6]

Most U.S. property tax systems assess developed properties on the basis of their estimated market value, P, independent of what portion of that value is attributed to land or structures. Such property tax systems are here termed *conventional property tax systems*. To simplify, a conventional property tax system is treated as having two effective tax rates, one on predevelopment land value, τ_V, the other on postdevelopment property value, τ_P.

A few U.S. jurisdictions employ two-rate (or split-rate) property tax systems that tax postdevelopment land (or site) value and structure value at different rates. The sales of developed properties provide a basis for estimating the property value of developed properties. But because structures are durable and immobile, the market provides relatively little information concerning how to estimate the postdevelopment land value and structure value of developed properties. All U.S. jurisdictions that employ two-rate taxation assess

---

6. Property taxation may alter a landowner's choice of property class when deciding how to convert his or her vacant land. It may also give him or her incentives to modify the property in ways that permit its reclassification to a property type with a lower effective tax rate and to lobby for a reduction in the tax rate. All these behaviors, which affect the efficiency costs of property taxation, are ignored in this paper.

postdevelopment site value and structure value so their sum equals assessed property value. Therefore there are two general methods of imputation. The first directly imputes a site value and then imputes structure value as the residual (estimated property value minus imputed site value). The second imputes a structure value and then imputes site value as the residual (estimated property value minus imputed structure value.)[7]

Two classes of two-rate property tax systems are considered here. The first, *raw site value property tax systems,* imputes postdevelopment site value as raw site value, W, defined as what the site would be worth if there were no structure on it, even though in fact there is. Residual structure value, Z, is then calculated as $Z = P - W$. A raw site value tax property tax system has three tax rates, the first on predevelopment land value, second on imputed raw site value, τ_W, and third on residual structure value, τ_Z. The second class, termed *residual site value property tax systems,* imputes postdevelopment structure value as its (depreciated or replacement) construction cost, K, and then calculates postdevelopment residual site value as $S = P - K$. A residual site value tax system has three tax rates, on the value of: 1) predevelopment land; 2) imputed structure, τ_K; and 3) residual site, τ_S. Raw site value and residual site value property tax systems are ideal types. Since assessors employ information on both construction costs and land values when decomposing estimated property value into imputed site and imputed structure value, actual two-rate systems are a hybrid of the two ideal types.

Figure 3 illustrates the distinction between the two alternative imputation procedures in the absence of taxation. It plots various values against time. To simplify, it is assumed that rents grow at a constant exponential rate, η. For landowners to make the competitive rate of return, i, it is necessary that predevelopment land value, $V(t)$, grow exponentially at the rate i. After development, property value, $P(t)$, grows at the rate η;[8] rents provide a return equal to a proportion $i - \eta$ of property value, with the remainder of the required rate of return coming in the form of capital gains. The first panel of figure 3 presents the diagram for raw site valuation, along with residual structure valuation. Development occurs at time T^* at density k^*. Property value immediately after T^* equals land value immediately before T^* plus the costs of construction at density k^*. At development time, raw site value equals land value.

---

7. Actual assessment practice is some hybrid of these two general approaches (see discussion below).

8. Simple asset valuation theory gives that $P(t) = r(t)q(k) \div (i - \eta)$ so that $\dfrac{\dot{P}}{P} = \dfrac{\dot{r}}{r} = \eta$.

Figure 3. Decompositions of Postdevelopment Property Value: Raw Site and Residual Site

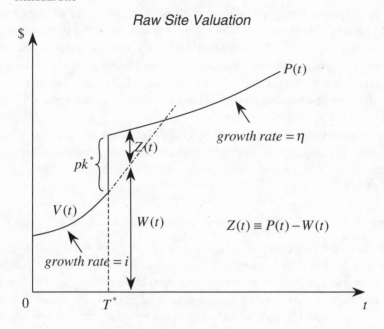

Raw Site Valuation

$$Z(t) \equiv P(t) - W(t)$$

growth rate $= \eta$

growth rate $= i$

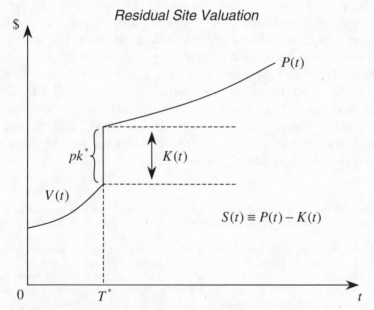

Residual Site Valuation

$$S(t) \equiv P(t) - K(t)$$

Source: Author's calculations.
t = time. p = price per unit of capital. k^* = profit-maximizing capital-land ratio. T^* = profit-maximizing development time. i = interest rate. η = growth rate of rents. $V(t)$ = predevelopment land value at time t. $P(t)$ = postdevelopment property value at time t. $W(t)$ = postdevelopment raw site value at time t. $Z(t)$ = postdevelopment residual structure value at time t. $K(t)$ = depreciated construction costs at time t. $S(t)$ = postdevelopmental residual site value at time t.

After development time, raw site value, $W(t)$, is calculated as what the land would be worth if there were no building on it. Since, under the stated assumptions, the land would then be developed right away, raw site value is what the land would be worth if it were vacant and developed immediately. The raw site value expression is complicated, but raw site value clearly increases over time and in due course exceeds property value.[9] Residual structure value is calculated as $Z(t) \equiv P(t) - W(t)$.

The second panel of figure 3 presents the diagram for residual site valuation. Under the assumption that the structure does not depreciate, imputed structure value is $K(t) = pk^*$, so that residual site value is $S(t) \equiv P(t) - K(t) = P(t) - pk^*$.[10]

Analysis

Whatever the property tax system employed, a profit-maximizing landowner will choose development time and density to maximize the present value of rents, less the present value of construction costs, less the present value of tax payments. With a competitive land market, the value of land before development equals this maximized present value. After development, the market value of a property equals the present value of rents less the present value of tax payments. Drawing on these principles, one can determine how the various property tax systems affect the timing and density first-order conditions, and from this one can determine the profit-maximizing development time and density as well as the deadweight loss generated by the tax system.

This section investigates only conventional property tax systems since they are the easiest to treat. Recall that a conventional property tax system is characterized by two tax rates: on predevelopment land value, τ_V, and on postdevelopment property value, τ_P. With conventional property taxation, the timing first-order condition becomes

9. Consider extending the model to include redevelopment. Since land is vacant between redevelopments, by definition raw site value equals the market value of land at redevelopment times.

10. Consider extending the model to treat redevelopment. Just before a redevelopment, residual site value equals property value minus the (depreciated) construction cost of the site's existing structure. However, the land's market value at that time exceeds property value by the cost of demolishing that structure. With profit-maximizing redevelopment, property value immediately after development equals the market value of land plus the cost of constructing the new structure on the site, so that residual site value immediately after development equals the market value of the land. Thus residual site value jumps up discontinuously at a redevelopment time.

(5) $$-r(T)q(k) + \tau_p P(T;k) + ipk - \tau_v V(T) = 0,$$

where

$P(T;k)$: the property value immediately after development, conditional on development at density k,
$V(T)$: the land value immediately before development.

This first-order condition is easily interpreted. The profit-maximizing time to develop at density k occurs when the gain from postponing development for one period equals the cost. At time T, the gain from postponing development is $ipk + \tau_p P(T;k)$. The first term is the interest earned on construction funds; the second term is the property tax payment that need not be paid as a result of postponing development. The cost of postponing development is $r(T)q(k) + \tau_v V(T)$. The first term is the rent forgone, the second is the tax payable on predevelopment land value. Thus the net benefit from postponing development is

$$ipk - r(T)q(k) + [\tau_p P(T;k) - \tau_v V(T)].$$

The term in square brackets is the addition to the net benefit from postponing development due to property taxation. It is positive if, as is typically the case, the property tax payable immediately after development exceeds that immediately before development. Under this condition, in terms of figure 2, conventional property taxation causes the timing first-order condition to shift to the right.

Equation (5) is intuitive, but provides an incomplete characterization of the profit-maximizing development time conditional on development density since it depends on the land value before development and property value after development, which are both affected by the tax system. Asset valuation functions for $P(T;k)$ and $V(T)$, which depend on the tax rates, can be derived, and insertion of these into equation (5) provides a characterization in terms of only exogenous parameters and functions.

The density first-order condition is

(6) $$\int_T^\infty r(t)q'(k)e^{-(i+\tau_p)(t-T)}dt - p = 0.$$

The conventional property tax system therefore affects development density by increasing the rate at which structure rents are discounted. Since this result is important, two alternative intuitions are presented. First, since the asset market for property is competitive, the property owner must make the competitive rate of return. This condition is written as

$$iP(t) = r(t)q(t) + \dot{P}(t) - \tau_p P(t).$$

The equation's left-hand side gives the required return from owning the property at time t. This equals the rent received plus the capital gain minus the tax liability. From this equation, it can be seen that i and τ_P enter as $i + \tau_P$. Thus the property owner is indifferent between a 7 percent interest rate or a 5 percent interest rate plus a 2 percent property tax rate. Second, one may ask what the value is today of an extra rent dollar received from the property a year from now. The extra rent dollar received will increase the value of the property today by, say, Δ, and result in an increase in tax liability of $\tau_P \Delta$. Since the property owner can sell the property immediately after it becomes known that an extra dollar will be received a year from now, Δ is the value today of the extra dollar in rent. If the property owner chooses to sell the title to this extra dollar and puts this amount in the bank, he will obtain $\Delta(1 + i)$ a year from now. If he or she chooses to retain the title to this extra dollar, the property owner will receive $1 - \tau_P \Delta$ a year from now. Under competitive asset pricing, he or she should be indifferent between the two courses of action. Thus $\Delta = 1/(1 + i + \tau_P)$. The first term in equation (6) therefore is the increase in property value from increasing the capital applied to the property at development time by one dollar, which is the marginal benefit of capital. The second term is the price of the extra capital unit, which is unaffected by taxation, and is the marginal cost of capital.

By the same line of reasoning, the tax on predevelopment land value causes the predevelopment discount rate to increase from i to $i + \tau_V$, and hence predevelopment land value to appreciate at the rate $i + \tau_V$.

Since imposition of conventional property taxation increases the rate at which rents are discounted, it causes the marginal benefit of capital to fall. The marginal cost of capital is unaffected by the tax. Thus holding fixed development time, conventional property taxation causes the profit-maximizing amount of capital to fall. In this sense, conventional property taxation discourages density.[11] In terms of figure 2, the tax system causes the density first-order condition to shift down.

---

11. When the model is extended to treat redevelopment, property taxation still increases the rate at which rents are discounted, and therefore still discourages density.

Thus the conventional property tax system causes the timing first-order condition to shift to the right and density first-order condition to shift down. How the combined shifts alter the profit-maximizing timing and density of development is ambiguous. Two possibilities, however, can be ruled out—earlier development at higher density and no change in development timing and density. By how much the two curves shift (and which shifts more) depends on the property tax rates, growth rate of rents, interest rate, and form of the structure production function.

More specific results can be obtained under particular assumptions. There are two reasonable assumptions that considerably simplify the algebra. First, the elasticity of substitution between land and capital in the production of structures, denoted by σ, is constant. Since there is still no consensus on even the approximate magnitude of this elasticity of substitution, the assumption that it is constant hardly can be falsified.[12] Second, rents grow at a constant rate. Under these assumptions, closed-form solutions can be obtained for profit-maximizing timing and density, as a function of the tax rates. How tax rates affect density is expressed most simply in elasticity terms:

(7) $$E(q, i + \tau_v) = -\sigma/(1 - \sigma) \text{ and } E(q, \tau_p) = 0,$$

where $E(a,b)$ denotes the elasticity of a with respect to b. The tax rate on postdevelopment property value has no effect on development density—it affects only the timing. The tax rate on predevelopment land value, however, does affect development density; in particular, the elasticity of the floor-area ratio with respect to the predevelopment discount rate, $i + \tau_v$, is $-\sigma/(1 - \sigma)$. If the construction technology is fixed-coefficients, implying $\sigma = 0$, property taxation has no effect on development density. If the elasticity of substitution is 0.5, which is at the low end of empirical estimates, the elasticity of the floor-area ratio with respect to the predevelopment discount rate is -1.0. If the elasticity of substitution is 0.75, which is at the high end of empirical estimates before Thorsnes (1997), the elasticity of the floor-area ratio with respect to the predevelopment discount rate is -3.0.

The optimal time of development can be written as

(8) $$T - T^* = \eta^{-1}\{\ln[(i + \tau_p - \eta)/(i - \eta)] - \ln f(\tau_v)\},$$

---

12. Thorsnes (1997) finds that this elasticity of substitution is insignificantly different from one. All prior estimates, however, find it to be significantly less than one. See McDonald (1981) for a survey of empirical estimates before that date.

Table 1. Numerical Example for the Simple Property Tax[a]

τ	k	q	T	V	R	D	MD
0.00	1.00	1.00	50.0	1.0	0.00	0.00	0.00
0.01	0.125	0.422	3.56	0.243	0.512	0.245	−4.99
0.02	0.037	0.216	−12.63	0.081	0.404	0.515	−1.51

Source: Arnott and Petrova (2006).

a. Production function is $q(k) = c_0(1 + c_1 k^\rho)^{1/\rho}$. Parameter values are $p = 2.2408$, $r(0) = 0.24731$, $c_0 = 3.375$, $c_1 = 0.5$, and $\rho = -0.3333$ (corresponding to an elasticity of substitution equal to 0.75).

τ = simple property tax rate. k = capital-land ratio. q = floor-area ratio. T = development time. V = land value at $t = 0$ (or land value at development time brought forward to $t = 0$ if T is negative). R = tax revenue discounted or brought forward to $t = 0$. D = deadweight loss discounted or brought forward to $t = 0$. MD = marginal deadweight loss.

where $f(\tau_V) = q'(k(\tau_V))/q'(k(0))$, with $f' > 0$.[13] Thus an increase in τ_P causes development to be postponed, while an increase in τ_V causes development to be brought forward.

Numerical Example

Instead of the explicit formula being presented for the deadweight loss, a numerical example is presented in table 1. The example considers what is termed the *simple property tax,* under which the tax rates on predevelopment land value and postdevelopment property value are the same, τ. This is what comes to mind when most people think of the property tax. It is assumed that the interest rate is 3 percent, the growth rate of rents is 2 percent, and the elasticity of substitution between land and capital in the production of structures is 0.75. The other parameters are chosen so that in the base case, with a zero tax rate, $k = q = 1.0$, development occurs fifty years into the future, and the value of land today ($t = 0$), denoted by V, equals 1.0.[14] R is the tax revenue raised, discounted, or brought forward (as the case may be) to today, D is the deadweight loss due to the tax discounted to today, and MD is the corresponding marginal deadweight loss, the increase in deadweight loss per extra dollar of revenue raised. In calculating R, it is necessary to make an assumption about when the tax rate on undeveloped land was first introduced. The figures are calculated on the assumption that the tax on undevel-

13. The function f gives the ratio of the marginal product of capital with a tax rate on predevelopment land value of τ_V to that with a zero tax rate. Since the floor-area ratio decreases with τ_V, the marginal product of capital is increasing in the tax rate.

14. There is a hurdle development rent at which development occurs. Thus at another location where rent is twice as high, development would occur $(\ln2)/\eta$ years earlier.

Figure 4. Effects of Simple Property Tax on Asset Values over Time

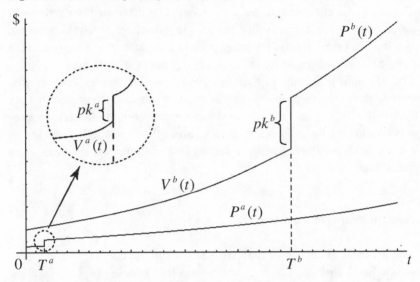

Source: Author's calculations.
t = time. p = price per unit of capital. k = profit-maximizing capital-land ratio. T = profit-maximizing development time. a = after taxation. b = before taxation. $V(t)$ = predevelopment land value at time t. $P(t)$ = postdevelopment property value at time t.

oped land was first introduced either today or at the time of development, if this is in the past.

The tax effects are shown another way in figure 4, which plots predevelopment land value, construction costs, and property value, both before (b) and after (a) the imposition of the tax. Note that the tax causes predevelopment land value to grow at the rate $i + \tau$, but does not alter the growth rate of postdevelopment property value.

One should view with skepticism a numerical example based on such a simple model. The model treats the taxation of a single site. If the tax were applied to a jurisdiction or an entire metropolitan area, results would be altered by general equilibrium effects. Most important, by altering the rate at which land is developed, the tax would alter the time path of rents. These qualifications notwithstanding, the numerical results provide the important insight that a simple property tax with a tax rate as low as 1 percent has substantial effects. Imposition of the property tax at this rate causes development to be brought forward by forty-six years and the floor-area ratio to be reduced to only 42 percent of its pretax level. The tax causes 51 percent of the social surplus associated with the property to be transferred from the landowner to the government, and 25 percent to be dissipated in deadweight loss. Even at this low taxation rate, the marginal deadweight loss is negative, indicating that taxation is on the wrong side of the Laffer curve—a rise in the tax rate causes deadweight loss to increase and revenue to decrease.

The example illustrates one of this paper's major themes, namely that even though the recent property tax policy literature tends to neglect the tax effects on the timing and density of development, property tax reform proposals should take the effects into account since the deadweight losses from distorting development timing and density—at even modest tax rates—can be substantial.

Neutral Property Taxation

The example given above indicates (at least in the context of the model developed and with the chosen parameters) that simple property taxation with a low property tax rate of 1 percent creates considerable distortion with respect to development timing and density. This suggests that it is important to employ a property tax system that is neutral or close to neutral with respect to development time and density. What property tax systems have this characteristic?

As demonstrated, no conventional property tax system (one tax rate for predevelopment land value and another for postdevelopment property value) is neutral. One set of neutral property tax systems are those that are *lump sum*—those for which the tax payable is independent of the landowner's actions. Any lump-sum tax achieves neutrality, but most lump-sum taxes would be deemed unfair on the basis of both ability-to-pay and benefit principles. A lump-sum tax that has widespread support is a land value tax, or a *raw site value tax.* This tax applies the same tax rate to predevelopment land value and postdevelopment raw site value. After development, the tax is based on what the land's market value would be were the site vacant, which is independent of the landowner's choice of density and type of use. Before development, the tax is based on the land's market value, which the landowner cannot influence. Since the tax rate on predevelopment land value is the same as that on postdevelopment raw site value, and since predevelopment land value right before development is the same as raw site value right after development, the tax does not distort development timing. This tax also scores respectably well in terms of the ability-to-pay and benefit principles, since land ownership is correlated to both ability to pay and the benefits received from public services.[15]

There are three major difficulties with the adoption of raw site value taxation in the United States. The first is that the tax, while scoring moderately well according to both ability-to-pay and benefit principles, may not score sufficiently well to be politically acceptable. Before the Industrial Revolution, most wealth was in land. Now, however, aggregate land value in the United States constitutes a considerably smaller fraction of total wealth.[16] Furthermore, the benefits from the government goods and services financed by property taxation are only loosely tied to land.

The second major difficulty is that while it might be desirable to impose a raw site value tax if there were currently no system of property taxation in place, a jurisdiction would encounter considerable opposition if it were to replace the current property tax system with raw site value taxation. Eliminating structures from the property tax base while holding the revenue yield constant would entail substantial property tax liability redistribution. Landowners holding undeveloped land or land that had been developed at low density

15. The virtues of land taxation have long been recognized. Over the last 125 years, the advocacy of land taxation has been closely associated with George (1879), which advocated land taxation as the single tax. The continuing appeal of land taxation is illustrated by the impressive list of signatories—including four Nobel Prize winners in economics—to an open letter to Chairman Mikhail Gorbachev in 1990–91, urging him to adopt land taxation in Russia (www.taxreform.com.au/essays/russian.htm).

Land taxation is neutral, whether the tax base is land rent or land value. This paper considers land value taxation, since data on land value are more generally available than data on land rent. However, as noted below, the neutral residual site value tax system is equivalent to (in the sense of generating the same time path of revenue) a tax on site rent at a constant rate over time, where site rent before development equals zero and after development equals structure rent minus the opportunity cost of capital. A tax on site rent at a constant rate over time is analogous to a tax on pure profits at a constant rate over time, and therefore neutral.

16. The U.S. Flow of Funds Accounts list the net worth of households and nonprofit organizations to be $40.7 trillion in 2001 (table B.100). The World Bank estimates the U.S. value of natural capital (which includes subsoil assets, timber resources, nontimber forest resources, protected areas, cropland, and pastureland) to be $14,752 per capita in 2000, and population to be 282,224,000, for a total value of $4.16 trillion (World Bank, 2006, appendix 2). It also estimates the value of produced capital and urban land in the United States to be $79,851 per capita in 2000, for a total value of $22.54 trillion. The document assumes that the value of urban land equals 24 percent of the value of produced capital, which implies a value of urban land of $4.36 trillion. Davis and Heathcote (2004, fig. 12), based on Flow of Funds Accounts data, give an estimate of the nominal value of the quality-adjusted stock of residential land in the United States in 2000 as approximately $2.8 trillion, which is broadly consistent with the World Bank's estimate. Thus it appears that the value of land in 2001 was slightly in excess of 20 percent of total wealth.

could face significantly higher property tax bills than under conventional property taxation. These property tax liability increases would be capitalized into land and property values, resulting in possibly substantial capital losses for owners of vacant land and low-density properties.

The third major difficulty is raw site valuation. Until recently, raw site value estimation would have been unacceptably noisy. In the last few years, however, considerable progress has been made in the estimation of land value surfaces.[17] This progress is due to more readily accessible and detailed data on vacant land parcels that have been sold and on teardowns,[18] as well as the development of improved estimation techniques. Thus soon it may be administratively practical for cutting-edge assessment offices to implement raw site valuation. However, because of their sophistication, it will likely be a long time before these valuation techniques are widely adopted.

Raw site value tax systems constitute the set of neutral raw site value property tax systems.

What about residual site value property tax systems? A series of papers published a quarter-century ago demonstrated that a property tax system that taxes the market value of land before development and its residual site value after development at the same rate is non-neutral, discouraging development (but not distorting the timing first-order condition).[19] This important result is not straightforward. One explanation, cast in the context of the model presented earlier, starts with the situation where no property tax is applied (or where the tax is lump sum). The landlord will add floors to the structure up to the point where the top floor breaks even—the discounted rents from the top floor just cover its marginal construction costs. This implies that at development time, the top floor does not contribute to the property's residual site value. After development time, however, the discounted rents from the top floor increase, while the top floor's imputed structure value remains constant or falls, so that the top floor does add to the property's residual site value. Now introduce residual site value taxation. The top floor that broke even in the absence of taxation now loses money, since it adds to the building's tax liability. Another explanation

17. For example, McMillen (1996); Plassmann and Tideman (2003).
18. A teardown is a developed property that is purchased with the intention of tearing down the existing structure and redeveloping the site. If a site is redeveloped soon after the developed property is purchased, the property was presumably purchased for its land. Thus the sales price of a teardown should give an accurate valuation of the land on which it is sited. See Dye and McMillen (2006) for a recent study of Chicago-area teardowns.
19. Skouras (1978); Bentick (1979); Mills (1981).

draws on the result that the tax on residual site value increases the postdevelopment discount rate. Before taxation, the discounted *site rent* (gross rent less the opportunity cost of capital, and therefore akin to profit, which is alternatively termed net rent) from the top floor equals zero. The site rent increases over time, being negative in the early years after development and positive thereafter. Since residual site value taxation increases the postdevelopment discount rate, in the valuation of discounted site rents it causes more weight to be put on the early years of negative site rent and less on the later years of positive site rent. Thus again, a top floor that breaks even in the absence of taxation loses money under residual site value taxation.

How can this distortion be corrected? One crude intuition is that a residual site value property tax system provides three instruments—tax rates on predevelopment land value, postdevelopment imputed structure value, and postdevelopment residual site value—which should be sufficient to achieve the three policy objectives of neutrality with respect to development time, neutrality with respect to development density, and extraction of a given proportion of the site's social surplus via taxation. A more precise intuition can be given in terms of figure 2. Residual site value taxation distorts the development density condition, causing FOC_k to shift down, but leaves unaltered the development timing condition, and hence FOC_T. The discouragement of density can be offset by subsidizing structure value. But subsidizing structure value reduces the marginal benefit from postponing development, causing the development timing condition to shift to the left. This distortion in turn can be offset by applying a lower tax rate to predevelopment land value than to postdevelopment residual site value. In earlier work, I proved that there is a neutral residual site value tax system that extracts a specified proportion of the site's social surplus via taxation.[20] In the special case where structure rents grow at a constant rate after development, I showed that neutral residual site value property taxation entails exempting predevelopment land value from taxation, taxing residual site value, and subsidizing structure value, with the ratio of the subsidy rate on structure value to the tax rate on residual site value being $\eta \div (i + \tau_s - \eta)$. Furthermore, this tax system generates the same revenue stream as a constant-rate tax on site rent, which is analogous to a time-invariant tax on pure profits—and therefore neutral. Hence in this special case, this residual site value property taxation is equivalent to a neutral land rent tax (see footnote 15).

20. Arnott (2005).

Would a neutral residual site value property tax system be practical? For buildings whose construction costs are known, structure value could be imputed as depreciated construction costs, with an empirically estimated depreciation schedule. For buildings whose construction costs are not known, structure value could be imputed as the cost of constructing a comparable, new structure commanding approximately the same rents, using construction cost handbooks. Determining the appropriate subsidy rate to apply to a particular structure would present difficulties, since it requires knowledge not only of the interest rate, but also of the growth rate of future rents. The growth rate of future rents of course is not known, but market expectations concerning the future growth rate of rents at a location can be inferred from the ratio of property value to construction costs of nearby, newly developed sites.[21] Another difficulty is that either the structure value subsidy rate would have to vary over properties, reflecting differences in properties' expected rental growth rates, or else a uniform subsidy rate would have to be applied to properties with different expected rental growth rates, resulting in deviation from neutrality. Yet another difficulty would be application of residual site value taxation to distressed neighborhoods, where some property values could be lower than the corresponding imputed structure values, resulting in negative tax liabilities. In addition, as with a switch from conventional property taxation to raw site value taxation, the redistribution of property tax liability across property types would generate considerable opposition from those land and property owners with higher tax bills.[22]

While the sudden replacement of a current property tax system with a neutral raw site value or a neutral residual site value taxation system would be politically impractical, gradual transition from the current property tax system toward a neutral property tax system merits serious consideration. Whenever a tax system is distorted, in principle it is possible to adjust the tax

21. Arnott (2005).

22. A somewhat more subtle redistribution would occur across properties according to development time. To see this, consider the replacement of a raw site value tax with the neutral residual site value property tax system that, aggregated over properties that differ in development time, generates the same discounted revenue from today forward. Since both tax systems are neutral, the switch would not alter the timing and density of properties' development. The switch, however, would alter the timing of tax revenue collected. Before the switch, revenue collected would be from both vacant land and developed properties, while after the switch all the revenue collected would be from developed properties. Thus properties that had already been or would soon be developed would find their discounted tax liabilities increased, while properties that would not be developed for a long time would find their discounted tax liabilities reduced.

system marginally such that everyone benefits. This is referred to as *Pareto-improving taxation.* If existing property tax systems are close to being as distorted as suggested by the numerical examples based on this paper's simple model, it should be possible to adjust the tax rates in such a way that, holding government revenue constant, almost all major classes of property owners benefit from reform.

Now, to debunk a popular fallacy. In property taxation discussions, one encounters the argument that while land taxation is the ideal, it would not generate enough revenue to finance the provision of an adequate level of local public services; to raise enough revenue, structure taxation (while regrettably distortionary) must be employed as well. But if the tax rates are set sufficiently high, neutral property taxation can extract the entire social surplus from land without distortion. No non-neutral property tax system can generate more revenue than this, and indeed non-neutral property tax systems dissipate surplus by introducing distortion.

Taxation of Undeveloped Land

Use value is an assessment based on the current use of land or property.[23] When agricultural land is assessed according to its use value, conceptually the assessed value of the land is what the land would be worth if it were held in agricultural use forever, in contrast to its market value. In 1956 Maryland became the first state to apply use value assessment to agricultural land. Use value assessment for agricultural land is now applied in the majority of states, and some form of preferential treatment for agricultural land is employed in all states.[24] How agricultural use is defined, and how agricultural use value is assessed, varies widely across and within states.[25] In some states, only a nominal agricultural activity on the land is required for agricultural use classification, while in others the definition is more stringent. The property tax treatment of land that is withdrawn from agricultural use for urban development varies widely across and within states. Some states apply rollback provisions that retroactively tax the land as nonagricultural,

23. The discussion of the history and practice of use value assessment in the United States applied to agriculture draws heavily on Youngman (2005).

24. Some states have extended use value assessment to forests and open space.

25. There is no national database on property tax policies and administrative practices. An incomplete picture of current policies and practices is provided in International Association of Assessing Officers (2002).

undeveloped land for a certain number of years before its withdrawal from agricultural use. Massachusetts, for example, uses a five-year rollback provision, and many other states have no rollback provision.

Standard rationales for assessing agricultural land according to its current use are to preserve the family farm, protect agricultural land, and prevent urban sprawl. Since this paper's model assumes an economy that is undistorted, it cannot address these presumed market failures.

There is, however, another rationale for this policy, based on (second-best) efficiency with respect to development timing and density, that has not previously been discussed in the literature. As discussed earlier, the conventional property tax has two tax rates, one on predevelopment land value, the other on postdevelopment property value. It was demonstrated that all conventional property tax systems are non-neutral. It seems likely that for a long time to come the vast majority of U.S. jurisdictions will continue to tax developed properties based on their assessed market value, rather than switching to raw site value taxation or two-rate property taxation, for example. What, then, is the (second-best) efficient tax rate to apply to undeveloped land?

A simple property tax system is a conventional tax system in which the tax rate on predevelopment land value is the same as that on postdevelopment property value. Thus a simple property tax is at one extreme in providing no preferential treatment to land before development. Table 1 presented a numerical example of simple property taxation's effects on timing and density. With the functional forms and parameters assumed, simple property taxation results in considerably earlier development at considerably lower density.

Look now at the other extreme case, where the tax rate on predevelopment land value is zero, so that land before development is exempt from taxation. Because of the very favorable treatment under property taxation currently accorded predevelopment land in most states, for want of a better term I refer to this as a *modern property tax system.*

The results for modern property taxation are especially simple when the structure rent growth rate is constant, which will be assumed. In terms of figure 2, modern property tax systems cause the timing first-order condition to shift to the right, and the density first-order condition to shift down, such that development occurs at the same density as in the absence of taxation, but later. This implies the discounted revenue obtained from taxation, as well as the deadweight loss it induces, is independent of the structure production function form, which considerably simplifies the algebra and calculations.

Table 2. Numerical Example for the Modern Property Tax[a]

τ	k	q	T	V	R	D	MD
0.00	1.00	1.00	50.0	1.00	0.00	0.00	0.00
0.01	1.00	1.00	84.7	0.354	0.530	0.116	1.0
0.02	1.00	1.00	104.9	0.192	0.577	0.23	∞
0.03	1.00	1.00	119.3	0.125	0.563	0.312	−3.0

Source: Arnott and Petrova (2006).

a. Parameter values are $p = 2.2408$, $r(0) = 0.24731$, $c_0 = 3.375$, $c_1 = 0.5$, and $\rho = -0.3333$ (corresponding to an elasticity of substitution equal to 0.75).

τ = modern property tax rate. k = capital-land ratio. q = floor-area ratio. T = development time. V = land value at $t = 0$. R = tax revenue discounted to $t = 0$. D = deadweight loss discounted to $t = 0$. MD = marginal deadweight loss.

Where b denotes before tax, and a after tax, it can be shown that

(9)
$$R = V^b \left(\frac{i\tau}{\eta(i - \eta)} \right) \left(\frac{i - \eta}{i + \tau - \eta} \right)^{\frac{i}{\eta}},$$

and

(10)
$$V^a = V^b \left(\frac{i - \eta}{i + \tau - \eta} \right)^{\frac{i}{\eta}},$$

from which the deadweight loss from taxation can be calculated easily. It follows directly from equations (9) and (10) that with modern property taxation, the revenue-maximizing tax rate on postdevelopment property value is η, and the marginal deadweight loss with property tax rate τ is $\tau/(\eta - \tau)$. The former result is so simple that there should be a simple explanation, but it has proved elusive. Tax revenue is maximized at that rate for which the elasticity of the tax base (with respect to the tax rate) equals -1.0. There are two reasons that the tax base shrinks as the tax rate is increased: property value falls as the tax is capitalized, and development is postponed.

Table 2 provides a numerical example. The parameters are the same as those employed in the numerical example of table 1 (the base case is the same, with $T = 50$, $k = q = 1.0$, and $V = 1.0$). As with the simple property tax, the modern property tax's effects are substantial. With the chosen parameters, a 2 percent tax rate, for example, causes land value today to fall to only 19 percent of pretax value, generates a deadweight loss of 23 percent of pretax value, and causes development to be postponed by fifty-five years. Since a 2 percent tax rate maximizes the discounted revenue collected from the tax, the marginal deadweight loss is infinite, indicating that taxation is at the top of the Laffer curve.

Table 3. Effective Property Tax Rates, Percentage of True Market Value, Selection of Cities with High Property Tax Rate, 2005

City	Homestead[a]	Apartment[b]	Commercial[c]	Industrial[d]
Detroit, Mich.	3.23	4.10	3.84	3.27
Buffalo, N.Y.	2.55	4.19	3.67	2.20
Milwaukee, Wisc.	2.47	2.51	2.51	1.38
Houston, Texas	2.33	2.68	2.79	3.07
Chicago, Ill.	1.50	2.49	3.26	1.96

Source: Minnesota Taxpayers Association (2006).

a. Rate for a median-valued home in the city.

b. Rate for $600,000 valued property with $30,000 in fixtures.

c. Rate for $1 million valued property with $200,000 in fixtures.

d. Rate for a $1 million valued property with $500,000 of machinery and equipment, $400,000 in inventories, and $100,000 in fixtures.

Table 3 shows a selection of effective property tax rates for different classes of property in different U.S. cities. The selection is not random and is intended to show how high effective property tax rates are in some major cities, especially for property classes other than single-family, detached housing.

In both examples, the revenue-maximizing tax rate was low, less than 1 percent in the case of simple property taxation and 2 percent in the current example. How can this be reconciled with the much higher property tax rates in some states for some property classes, as shown in table 3? One possibility is that the model is unrealistic in some important respects that, if taken into account, would result in higher revenue-maximizing tax rates. But while the model is highly simplified, it is not obvious what particular realistic complication, such as a time-varying interest rate or uncertainty, would lead to systematically higher revenue-maximizing tax rates. A second possibility is that the examples' parameters are unrealistic. But the revenue-maximizing tax rate under the modern property tax equals the growth rate of (real) rents, and the assumed growth rate is on the high side; if a more representative growth rate were chosen, the revenue-maximizing tax rate would be lower than 2 percent. A third possibility is that the observed high tax rates were not anticipated at the time of development. This is plausible. The model assumes that the tax rates are constant over time. But since structures are immobile, there is a time-inconsistency problem. After development a jurisdiction has an incentive to raise the property tax rate since the structure cannot move to avoid the tax. It is hard to believe, however, that local developers would be fooled for long by this opportunistic behavior.[26]

26. I have not seen time series of effective property tax rates for particular cities. It is reasonable to conjecture, however, that in central cities and inner suburbs they arose by historical accident. The post–World War II suburbanization resulted in these cities' property tax bases shrinking, to which the local governments responded by raising tax rates.

Figure 5. Efficiency of Undeveloped Land under Conventional Property Taxation

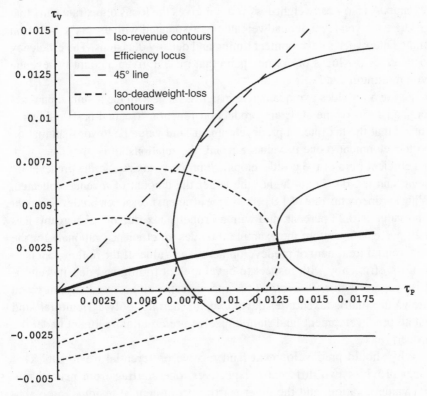

Source: Author's calculations.
τ_V = tax rate on predevelopment land value. τ_P = tax rate on postdevelopment property value.

The fourth possibility is that high observed property tax rates are indeed on the wrong side of the Laffer curve. One recent study estimates that Houston and New York City are at the top of their property tax revenue hills, and that Philadelphia is on the efficient side of the hill but close to the top.[27]

Is either the simple or modern property tax system the most efficient in its treatment of predevelopment land, or is some intermediate, conventional property tax system that gives preferential treatment to predevelopment land but does not exempt it from taxation? Figure 5 plots iso-revenue contours and iso-deadweight-loss contours in τ_P-τ_V space, assuming the parameter values that were employed in the example of table 1. An iso-revenue curve

27. Haughwout and others (2004, fig. 1).

gives the locus of tax rate pairs that generate a given level of discounted tax revenue. An iso-deadweight-loss contour gives the locus of tax rate pairs that generate a given level of deadweight loss, associated with the tax's distortion of the landowner's development timing and density decisions. The efficiency locus gives the locus of tax rate pairs that raise a given amount of revenue with minimum deadweight loss.

Figure 5 provides two qualitative insights. First, with the assumed parameters and form of the structure production function, (second-best) efficiency entails that the tax rate on predevelopment land value be lower than that on postdevelopment property value. Second, the relationship is nonlinear, with the efficient ratio of the postdevelopment property tax rate to the predevelopment land tax rate being higher the larger the amount of revenue collected. With a property tax rate of 1.0 percent, the efficient tax rate on predevelopment land value is 0.23 percent, and with a property tax rate of 1.5 percent, it is 0.29 percent. Therefore the example provides an efficiency rationale for the preferential treatment of predevelopment land value. If the policy goal is to achieve efficiency with respect to development timing and density, and if it is property value (in contrast to separate rates on assessed·structure and site value) that is taxed after development, then not only agricultural land but all predevelopment land should receive preferential treatment under the property tax.

Why should predevelopment land receive preferential treatment? This paper provides two different perspectives, one starting from neutral raw site value taxation, and the other starting from neutral residual site value taxation. First, start with the neutral raw site value tax system, and then replace the postdevelopment taxation of raw site value with the postdevelopment taxation of property value, all at the same rate, so that a simple property tax system is obtained. The switch distorts both the timing and density first-order conditions. The increased postdevelopment tax liability encourages the postponement of development, while the taxation of postdevelopment property value raises the postdevelopment discount rate, discouraging density. The combined effect leaves density unchanged. If distortion associated with the density first-order condition is high, which will tend to be the case with a high elasticity of substitution in structure production, it is efficient to lower the tax rate on predevelopment land value, even though this will lead to greater distortion with respect to the timing first-order condition. Second, start with neutral residual site value taxation (which, recall, entails exempting predevelopment land value, subsidizing assessed structure value, and taxing postdevelopment residual site value), and then switch from subsidizing assessed structure value to taxing it at the same rate as residual site value. This has no effect on the density first-order condition but introduces distortion with respect to the timing first-order condition. If potential distortion with respect to the density first-order condition is high, it is then efficient to tax predevelopment land value at only a low rate.

This argument provides a rationale for the preferential treatment of pre-development land value in terms of second-best efficiency with respect to development timing and density. The proponents of the preferential treatment of agricultural land provide a different set of rationales: preserving agricultural land, protecting the family farm, and curbing suburban sprawl. While this paper's model provides no insight into these rationales (they derive from presumed market failures that the model assumes away), a few comments based on first principles are in order. If agricultural land indeed generates positive externalities, then on efficiency grounds it merits subsidization, and subsidization via the property tax system is sensible. However, one may challenge the rationale on distributional grounds since the scenic benefits of agricultural land accrue primarily to relatively wealthy suburbanites, and since the protection of agricultural land leads to higher urban land values and rents, which helps owners of land and property but hurts renters. If an exurban family farmer can borrow against his farmland's capital gains in perfect capital markets to pay his or her property tax bills, there is no market failure. If the farmer cannot, the appropriate way to address the market failure is to provide him or her with a loan to pay property tax bills. This is achieved by taxing agricultural land at a preferential rate but with full rollback, so that when the family farmer sells his land for urban development he effectively repays the loan. It is hard to see how curbing sprawl provides a valid justification for subsidizing undeveloped land. If the presumed market failure associated with sprawl is that development is too scattered, then property tax policy is not the appropriate tool. What is needed are land use controls that discourage scattered development. If the presumed market failure is instead the negative visual externalities of ugly strip development, then the appropriate remedy is aesthetic or architectural zoning. In addition, if the presumed market failure is that development occurs at insufficient density, then minimum lot size zoning should be replaced by maximum lot size zoning. Whatever the validity of their rationales, the proponents of use value assessment of agricultural land are correct in their reasoning that the policy slows down the transition of agricultural land to urban use.

Two-Rate Property Taxation

Under two-rate (or split-rate) property taxation, after a property is developed separate tax rates are applied to assessed structure value and assessed land or site value. Two-rate property taxation has been widely employed around the world,[28] but it has not been used widely in the United States.[29] Fourteen smaller cities in Pennsylvania, as well as a larger city, Scranton, currently use two-rate taxation.[30] Pittsburgh employed two-rate taxation from 1913 until its reversion to conventional property taxation in 2001.[31] Kaui, Hawaii, has two-rate property taxation, as do Connelsville and Washington, Maryland. Enabling legislation has been passed permitting many other jurisdictions to implement two-rate property taxation, including other counties of Hawaii, some school districts in Pittsburgh, the state of Maryland, and the cities of Fairfax and Roanoke, Virginia.[32]

The attraction of two-rate property taxation is understandable. Since raw site value taxation is neutral, two-rate taxation provides a simple way of transitioning from current distortionary property taxation to a neutral tax system. Unfortunately, implementation of two-rate property taxation in the United States has encountered two major obstacles.[33] The first is that deviation from an existing property tax system to another system that raises the same amount of revenue causes redistribution of property tax liabilities, which via capitalization results in capital gains and losses. The losers—those whose property tax bills increase and whose property values fall—object vociferously to the property tax system change. The second is that a switch from a conventional property tax system to a two-rate tax system, even if the tax rates on assessed structure value and assessed land value are set at the same level, entails a qualitative change in the method of assessment. Under

28. See Youngman and Malme (1994), and Bird and Slack (2004).

29. In many states, a property owner's assessment notice decomposes the assessed value of his property into land value and structure value. This decomposition is typically done according to a formula that has little scientific or empirical basis. And, since the tax is based on the assessed market value of the property, the decomposition employed does not affect the property owner's tax liability.

30. For a list of cities, see Hartzok (1997).

31. From 1913 to the 1979–80 period, the tax rate on buildings was twice that on land. In the 1979–80 period, the tax rate on land was raised to more than five times that on structures. Pittsburgh's experience has been explored in a widely cited study by Oates and Schwab (1997).

32. See Cohen and Coughlin (2005), and Reeb (1998).

33. One may also argue that property taxation scores better than land taxation according to both ability-to-pay and benefit principles.

conventional property taxation, a developed property's tax liability is based on its assessed market property value. Since assessment offices have vast experience in the market value assessment of developed properties, in most jurisdictions current procedures are well established, reasonably sophisticated, and acceptably accurate. Under two-rate taxation, it is necessary to adopt new valuation procedures to decompose assessed market property value into assessed structure value and assessed land value. When these new valuation procedures are first employed, many valuations are likely to be inaccurate.[34] Furthermore, the adoption of inappropriate valuation procedures can seriously undermine the potential benefits from two-rate taxation.

There are two important points to be added to the two-rate property taxation discussion—one that strengthens the case for this type of taxation, the other that weakens it. The first point is that in principle it is possible to modify most tax systems so all major stakeholders benefit. By making the tax system more efficient social surplus is increased, and by adjusting the tax rates this social surplus increase can essentially be redistributed so all taxpayers benefit, holding government revenue constant. Modifications to a tax system that achieves this goal constitute a Pareto-improving tax reform. The more distortionary the existing tax system, the broader the set of reforms that would be Pareto-improving. The simple model used here suggests that at the rates applied in many U.S. jurisdictions (particularly to property classes other than single-family residential), property taxation indeed may generate very substantial distortion with respect to development timing and density. The second point is that while a revenue-neutral movement from simple property taxation to two-rate property taxation that correctly assesses raw site value unambiguously improves efficiency, a movement from a conventional property tax system to a two-rate property tax system that assesses postdevelopment land value as residual site value or in some other way may worsen inefficiency.

Pareto-Improving Property Tax Reform

Imagine a situation where a simple property tax is applied to an undeveloped property at the rate τ that is on the wrong side of the Laffer curve (in the example presented in table 1, the rate at the top of the Laffer curve is 0.85 percent). Now lower the tax rate by a small amount. Doing so benefits both the government and landowner. Because taxation is on the wrong side of the Laffer curve, by definition lowering the tax rate increases government

---

34. See Reeb (1998) for the history of Amsterdam, New York, and its unhappy attempt to switch from conventional property taxation to two-rate property taxation.

revenue. But also landowners are better off from the lower tax rate. In table 1, if the simple property tax rate is lowered from 2 to 1 percent, land value increases from 0.08 to 0.24, and discounted tax revenue increases from 0.40 to 0.51. Simple property taxation on the wrong side of the Laffer curve is the first and most obvious situation where Pareto-improving tax reform is possible, and is achieved simply by lowering the tax rate.

Now imagine a situation where a simple property tax is applied to an undeveloped property at the rate τ that is right at the top of the Laffer curve, but move to a two-rate raw site value tax system in which the raw site value tax rate is held at τ (so that $\tau_w = \tau$) but the tax rate on residual structure value is lowered slightly (so that $\tau_z < \tau$). Owners of land and property unambiguously benefit because the tax rate on residual structure value is reduced. Also, the government collects more in discounted revenue. Remember that raw site value is what the land would be worth if there were no structure on the site, even though in fact there is, and this is increased by lowering the tax rate on residual structure value. Thus the discounted revenue from the raw site value tax increases. The discounted revenue from the residual structure value tax may decrease, but if it does, it can be demonstrated that this revenue decrease is smaller than the revenue increase from the raw site value tax.[35] Now continue reducing the tax rate on residual structure value while holding fixed the tax rate on raw site value. Land and property owners unambiguously continue to benefit, and government revenue continues to increase for a while, until it reaches a maximum. The essential point is that for a range of tax rates below the revenue-maximizing simple property tax rate, reducing the tax rate on residual structure value while holding constant the tax rate on raw site value not only makes land and property owners better off, but also increases government revenue. Government revenue, of course, cannot increase without some land or property owners' tax bills increasing. But all land and property owners whose tax bill increases make capital gains exceeding their increase in discounted tax liability.

The same argument does not apply to properties that have already been developed, at least in the context of the basic model where redevelopment does not occur. Once a property has been developed, the social surplus it

---

35. Imagine plotting iso-revenue curves in τ_z-τ_w space. Each iso-revenue curve must intersect the τ_w axis, since any amount of discounted tax revenue, from zero up to the entire social surplus, can be obtained from a tax on raw site value alone. Thus the top of the Laffer curve for simple property taxation occurs at a point of tangency of an iso-revenue curve and the 45-degree line. It follows from the geometry that a small reduction in τ_z from this point, holding fixed τ_w, unambiguously increases tax revenue.

generates is fixed. Any increase in property value therefore is associated with an equal reduction in government revenue.

In an actual city, some sites are undeveloped, others just developed, and yet others ripe for redevelopment. For any particular city, there is a range of simple property tax rates for which a switch to a two-rate raw site value tax system (holding the tax rate on raw site value at the level previously applied under simple property taxation but lowering the tax rate on residual structure value) would increase government revenue and benefit most, if not all, owners of land and property.

In practice, it would be difficult for a particular city to forecast whether a switch to two-rate raw site value taxation, accompanied by a reduction in the tax rate on residual structure value, indeed would increase property tax revenue. Also, initially the decomposition of property value into assessed raw site value and assessed residual structure value no doubt would be noisy. But since no landowner or property owner would experience an increase in the effective tax rate applied to his or her property, and since all landowners and property owners would benefit by the switch, there is basis for optimism that the political cost of assessment errors would be low.

Postdevelopment Site Value Assessment

If postdevelopment site value is assessed as raw site value, a revenue-neutral move from simple property taxation to two-rate taxation unambiguously improves efficiency. If, however, postdevelopment site value is assessed as residual site value, a revenue-neutral move from simple property taxation to two-rate taxation may increase distortion.

Table 4 illustrates the latter result, which gives the revenue-maximizing two-rate residual site value property tax rates for different values of the elasticity of substitution between land and capital in the production of structures, with the interest rate (and so on) used in the earlier examples, and with the parameters of the structure production function chosen so that $T = 50$, and $k = q = 1$ in the base case. Observe that with an elasticity of substitution of 0.75, which accords with empirical estimates, the optimal tax rate on imputed structure value is higher than that on residual site value. The broad intuition for the result is as follows. Recall that the neutral residual site value tax system entails the exemption of predevelopment land value from taxation, the taxation of residual site value, and the subsidization of imputed structure value. Moving from this neutral residual site value tax system to simple property taxation entails two distortions. First, the tax rate on predevelopment land

Table 4. Two-Rate Residual Site Value Property Value Taxation, Revenue-Maximizing Tax Rates

σ	τ_L	τ_K	R	k	q	T
0.25	0.0251	0.0039	0.862	0.658	0.817	45.39
0.50	0.0150	0.0099	0.728	0.399	0.666	38.69
0.75	0.0092	0.0229	0.540	0.188	0.513	28.04

Source: Author's calculations.

σ = elasticity of substitution between land and capital in the production of floor area. τ_L = common tax rate on predevelopment land value and postdevelopment residual site value. τ_K = tax rate on postdevelopment imputed structure value. R = tax revenue discounted to $t = 0$. k = capital-land ratio. q = floor-area ratio. T = development time.

value is set equal to that on residual site value. Second, imputed structure value is taxed rather than subsidized. If distortion on the first margin is more significant than that on the second, it may be second-best efficient to lower the tax rate on residual site value relative to that on imputed structure value. Thus whether lowering the ratio of the tax rate on postdevelopment assessed structure value to that on site value improves efficiency depends critically on how postdevelopment property value is decomposed into assessed structure value and assessed site value.

Assessment practice lies between the two extremes of raw and residual site valuation. On one hand, assessors realize that the ideal is to assess postdevelopment land value as raw site value. On the other, assessment practice entails making the best use of all available information. In the absence of land value data, assessors impute structure value according to depreciated construction cost or replacement cost, and then calculate land value as the residual—they employ residual site valuation. When there are some land value data, but not for closely comparable properties, assessors use their best judgment, which presumably entails site valuation that is between raw site valuation and residual site valuation. Thus when there are few vacant land sales (or teardown sales) for comparable sites, site valuation is typically closer to residual site valuation, and when there are many, it is closer to raw site valuation. As a result, one expects that site valuation tends toward raw site valuation in locales where there is considerable development or redevelopment and toward residual site valuation where there is little development or redevelopment. Therefore it is reasonable to argue that site valuation tends toward raw site valuation close to development or redevelopment times, and toward residual site valuation in between development times. Now, the timing decision is based on valuation close to development or redevelopment time, while the density decision is based on anticipated taxation over the structure's lifetime. Consequently, in practice a move toward two-rate property taxation is likely to reduce distortion on the timing margin, but may increase it on the density margin.

Two-rate property taxation is not on the policy agenda of many U.S. jurisdictions. But at the current rate of technological improvement in land valuation, it may not be too long before the raw site valuation of developed land becomes acceptably accurate. When that occurs, modest movement toward two-rate property taxation through lowering the tax rate on residual structure value may be politically popular, especially in those jurisdictions with relatively high property tax rates for which the distortion associated with the current system is substantial. The reduction in the efficiency loss due to property taxation may be so large that lowering the tax rate on residual structure value would not only benefit landowners and all major classes of property owners, but would also generate at least as much revenue.

Conclusion

While property taxation's distortionary effects on development timing and density are generally acknowledged, they have received little attention in recent property taxation policy debates. The model presented in this paper is tailor made to examine these distortions. It considers a landowner who must decide when and at what density to develop his or her site. In the absence of taxation, the landowner makes the efficient decisions, but property taxation, in general, distorts these decisions and generates a deadweight loss. Property tax systems are characterized by a trio of tax rates: 1) on predevelopment land value, 2) on imputed postdevelopment structure value, 3) on imputed postdevelopment land value. The sum of imputed postdevelopment structure value and imputed postdevelopment land value are constrained to equal postdevelopment property value. Simple property taxation entails these three rates being equal. Conventional property taxation taxes property value after development, which entails that the same rate is applied to imputed postdevelopment structure value and land value, but may tax predevelopment land value at a lower rate. The land value tax advocated by Vickrey (1970) and others entails equal tax rates being applied to land before and after development, and structures being exempt from taxation, with land value after development defined as what the land would be worth were there no building on the site, even though in fact there is, and so on. Varying the three tax rates therefore permits the analysis of a wide variety of stylized property tax systems.

This paper demonstrated that, for realistic parameter values and tax rates, conventional property tax systems generate substantial deadweight loss with respect to the timing and density of development. Two neutral property tax systems were identified and some of the difficulties in moving from current property tax systems to less distortionary ones were discussed. Two-rate taxation is potentially Pareto improving, but can be undermined by inappropriate assessment of postdevelopment land value. Also, the preferential treatment of agricultural land may be justified on second-best efficiency grounds.

This paper's straightforward analysis of some intrinsically difficult policy issues was due to simplifying assumptions. It remains to be seen whether the basic conclusions hold up when realistic complications—such as land use controls, uncertainty, and general equilibrium effects—are introduced. Nevertheless, after reading this work, one should be persuaded of two things: first, the distortionary effects of property taxation on development timing and density are likely to be sufficiently substantial that they merit serious attention in any property tax reform proposal; and second, the paper's simple model provides a useful vehicle for thinking about the effects of alternative property tax systems on development efficiency.

Comments

Robert M. Schwab: Arnott's current paper and related recent research are very valuable contributions to the property tax literature. Together, they are excellent examples of the way economic theory can inform policy debates. I am certain that this line of research will have a profound effect on the way people think about the property tax.

This paper sets out a model where a landowner needs to make two decisions: when and how intensely to develop land. Equations (2) and (3) in the paper characterize the solution to this problem in the absence of any taxes. Equation (2) shows that the landowner should wait to develop until forgone rents just equal the cost of capital. Equation (3) shows that the optimal density requires the present value of the increase in rents from the last unit of capital to just equal the cost of purchasing that unit of capital. That is, along both the timing and density dimensions, optimality requires the landowner to balance costs and benefits at the margin. The paper then looks at how various forms of property taxation alter the landowner's timing and density decisions and investigates the necessary ingredients of a neutral tax system. The paper also examines two interesting policy questions: the taxation of undeveloped land and two-rate taxation.

At several points in the paper, Arnott argues that there are not many examples of two-rate taxes (or the most extreme case, a pure land tax) because of the difficulty of assessing land and structures separately. He suggests that some recent advances in assessment techniques may offer solutions to these assessment problems. For example, he points to Dye and McMillen's (2005) work on teardowns as an important step forward. I argue that the assessment problem is not really the key reason we see so few deviations from the traditional property tax where land and structures are taxed at the same rate. In particular, I argue that the two-rate tax and land tax will remain unpopular (even if the assessment problems were solved) for at least two reasons: they raise troubling equity concerns and

223

are inconsistent with the prevailing view of property rights in the United States.

Land taxation has a long intellectual history. Henry George's 1879 *Progress and Poverty* is certainly an important contribution to that history. In that book, George argued that one should tax away the returns from land. Such a tax, George said, would penalize speculation and thus encourage people to develop their land. George further argued that the land tax would be just; returns to land are an "unearned increment."[1] That is, those returns are the result of public policies and the public should enjoy the benefits of those policies.

While George was very popular and influential at one time (he nearly won the New York mayoral election in 1886), it is difficult to see any current examples of his influence in the United States. Two U.S. towns—Fairhope, Alabama, and Arden, Delaware—were founded on Georgist principles. A number of small towns in Pennsylvania have a long history of two-rate taxes. But Pittsburgh is clearly the most prominent example in the United States of a graded tax. Pittsburgh instituted a two-rate tax in 1913. The tax on land was raised several times. By 1980 the tax rate on land in Pittsburgh was roughly six times as high as the tax on structures. But Pittsburgh unceremoniously abolished the two-rate tax in 2001. This was clearly a blow to Georgism; as one observer put it, "How could the shining light be doused so easily?"[2]

What can one make of all of this? It is difficult to argue that it is impossible to implement a two-rate tax. After all, a graded tax survived in Pittsburgh for nearly a century. Admittedly, the assessment of land values is undoubtedly far from perfect. But as Arnott explains in this paper, it is important to recall that from an economic perspective assessment practices do not need to be perfect. The neutrality result requires only that tax liability be independent of the way land is actually used. Random taxation, from this perspective, would work just as well as accurate assessment of the value of land in its highest and best use (though clearly, assessment errors raise a wide range of daunting legal, political, and ethical issues).

If administrative feasibility is not the key stumbling block to a land tax, then (to borrow the title of Hughes, 2005) why so little Georgism in America? As I suggested at the outset, I believe there is a good case to be made

---

1. George (1879).
2. Hughes (2005, p. 8). Graded taxes are much more common outside the United States. All Danish cities rely on a two-rate tax, and two-rate taxes are common in Australia and South Korea.

that the key issues here are equity concerns and the prevailing view of property rights in the United States.

Two-rate taxes involve both vertical and horizontal equity issues. The vertical equity issue arises for at least two reasons. First, there is reason to believe that a two-rate tax will shift the burden of the property tax from commercial property owners to homeowners. There is not much empirical evidence on this issue, but it is difficult to dismiss the concern that lowering the tax on downtown skyscrapers (while admittedly raising the tax on the land on which the skyscrapers sit) would not be a benefit to commercial property owners. Second, a two-rate tax might shift the burden of the property tax from high-income homeowners to low-income homeowners. Here again, there is not a great deal of empirical evidence on this issue (though England and Zhao (2005) suggests that this concern might not be well founded).

A simple example makes the horizontal equity concerns clear. Suppose A owns a home with structures valued at $200,000 and land at $100,000; B owns a home with structures valued at $100,000 and land at $200,000. Under the traditional property tax, A and B face the same property tax bill. That is consistent with many people's notion of equity; A and B are equal in the sense that they both own homes worth $300,000 and they should be treated equally. Under a two-rate tax, however, B would pay more than A (assuming that land would be taxed more heavily than structures). There are some obvious possible rebuttals to this argument. For example, the traditional property tax ignores many types of wealth (for example, stocks and bonds). Why should a person be concerned that a two-rate tax treats one particular type of wealth (structures) more favorably than a second type of wealth (land)? But in the end, it is very difficult to quickly dismiss this notion that the appropriate base of a property tax is the total value of property. This is, after all, the way property has always been taxed nearly everywhere in the United States. In many ways, this is the same sort of issue that surrounds the shift from an income tax to a consumption tax. Whatever the relative merits of the two types of taxes, it would be difficult to convince many people that taxing savers and spendthrifts (who have the same income) differently is consistent with a sensible definition of equity.

It is important to recall the land tax's intellectual roots. As I noted above, the Georgists favored the taxation of land on the grounds than landowners were not entitled to the returns from their land. Land is valuable, from this perspective, because of public policies and the decisions of other people. Certainly there is something attractive about this idea. Homes in good school districts, for example, are more valuable than homes in poor districts. Downtown land would be of little value if local governments failed to invest in police protection, public utilities, streets, roads, and public transportation.

While this argument may have seemed compelling to Henry George and his followers, it seems out of step with the prevailing views in the United States today. This is, after all, the time when the property rights movement continues to gather momentum. The strength of the property rights movement became clear once again in the uproar over the U.S. Supreme Court's 2005 decision in *Kelo* v. *City of New London,* which upheld a city's right to use eminent domain to condemn privately owned property so that it could be used as part of a comprehensive redevelopment plan. At the heart of the property rights movement is our common law and cultural heritage that ". . . affirms that individuals have rights in their property and property in their rights."[3] While the property rights movement often involves regulatory issues such as land use laws, I suspect that very much the same issues will always make it very difficult for George's intellectual descendants to ever make much headway in their efforts to institute a land tax on a broad scale.

Jan K. Brueckner: Richard Arnott's paper provides an exhaustive discussion of what is wrong with the property tax and what can be done to modify the tax in a desirable direction. It has long been understood that by taxing both land and the capital embodied in structures, the property tax reduces land-use intensity by depressing the level of capital improvements. Literature initiated around 1980, however, identified another distortion that arises in a dynamic context: alteration of development timing. The added complexity of a dynamic model means that the direction of the distortions to capital (k) and the development date (T) are ambiguous in general. However, under plausible assumptions, the property tax turns out once again to depress the level of capital improvements, and an example provided by Arnott shows the tax as speeding up development (with T falling).

These distortions can be eliminated by shifting to a land tax, which Arnott calls a *raw site value tax.* For undeveloped land, the tax would be levied on the land's market value, while for developed land, the tax would be levied on the imputed value of the land, computed as if there were no structure on it. Recognizing that implementation of a raw site value tax is impractical, mainly because of the difficulty of properly imputing land values, Arnott asks whether some less-drastic modification of the current property tax could generate the same efficient outcome.

3. Eagle (2001, p. 1).

In prior work (which he briefly summarizes in the present paper), Arnott (2005) showed that such a tax regime is feasible. The required regime is a variant of a residual site value tax, and it works as follows. Undeveloped land is taxed at the rate τ_V, which is applied to the land's market value. Following development, residual site value, denoted S, is computed as the value of the developed site, P, minus the cost of the capital in place on the site, pk, where p is capital's unit price (in practice, capital's depreciated value could be used). A second tax rate τ_S is then applied to residual site value, $S = P - pk$. Finally, a third tax rate τ_K is applied to the value of the capital on the site, pk. This regime is more practical than the raw site value tax given that the only new information it requires is construction cost, pk, which is more readily estimated than land value (and is directly observable for new construction).

Arnott shows that the efficient outcome realized under a land tax can be generated under a residual site value tax provided that the tax rates are set appropriately. First, the tax rate on undeveloped land should be set at zero, so that $\tau_V = 0$. Second, the capital tax rate τ_K should be negative, so that the tax becomes a subsidy. The tax on residual site value can then be set to raise the desired amount of revenue. The subsidy to capital is designed to offset the tendency of a residual site value regime to depress capital improvements when all the tax rates are equal ($\tau_V = \tau_S = \tau_K$). The zero tax on undeveloped land is designed to offset the tendency for too-early development under an equal-rate residual site value regime.

As shown by Arnott, this regime's practicality is enhanced once it is recognized that the regime is equivalent to one where a property tax is levied on the value of the developed site, after an appropriate deduction of capital costs, and where vacant land is untaxed. In other words, the property tax rate is applied to $P - dpk$, where d is an appropriate deductibility rate, rather than to P itself, while τ_V is set at zero.

The magnitude of d is a crucial question, but before considering this issue it is helpful to ask what deductibility rate for capital costs would be appropriate in a static model to offset the distortions of the property tax. In such a model, let r denote rent per unit of housing floor space and $q(k)$ denote floor space per acre of land as a function of capital per acre. Then, in the absence of taxation, the developer's profit per acre gross of land cost is $rq(k) - \rho k$, and the first-order condition for choice of k is $rq'(k) - \rho = 0$.

In this setting, the property tax can be viewed equivalently as a tax on rental income or as a tax on the inputs of capital and land. Taking the former approach and letting τ denote the tax rate, profit is then $(1 - \tau)rq(k) - \rho k$, and the first-order condition for choice of k under property taxation becomes

$(1 - \tau)rq'(k) - \rho = 0$. Since the term multiplying $q'(k)$ is smaller than before, it follows that the chosen k is also smaller, so that the property tax depresses capital improvements.

This distortion can be remedied by allowing the developer to deduct the appropriate share of capital costs. Letting this share be denoted d, profit is then given by

$$rq(k) - \rho k - \tau(rq(k) - d\rho k).$$

If $d = 1$, so that the developer can deduct the entire capital cost, this profit expression reduces to $(1 - \tau)(rq(k) - \rho k)$. The profit-maximizing k is then the same as in the absence of taxation, eliminating the distortion from the tax.

In contrast to this full-deductibility rule, the appropriate rate of capital deductibility under Arnott's proposed regime equals

$$d = 1 + \eta/(i + \tau + \eta),$$

where η is the rate of increase of rents and i is the interest rate. The key observation is that this deductibility rate exceeds one, so that the developer must be allowed to deduct *more* than the cost of the capital used in the structure, unlike in the static model, where the rate is unity. Moreover, the deductibility rate depends on the property tax rate itself, as well as on the interest rate and rate of increase in rents, facts that would complicate implementation of the system.

In the interests of practicality, it is interesting to appraise the error involved in using the static d value of 1 under Arnott's regime. To this end, suppose that the interest rate is $i = 0.05$, the rate of increase of rents is $\eta = 0.03$, and the property tax rate is $\tau = 0.015$, all realistic values. Then, $d = 1.32$, a value not far above 1. If rents increase at a smaller rate of $\eta = 0.02$, then $d = 1.24$. On the other hand, if τ must rise to a value like 0.025 to offset the loss of tax revenue from structures and vacant land, then $d = 1.29$ (assuming $\eta = 0.03$). In each case, the d required to ensure efficiency under Arnott's regime is not far above 1. This conclusion suggests that much of the efficiency gains from such a system might be realized by using the static rule, where $d = 1$ and a developer deducts an amount equal to capital costs.

Thus a system that involves relatively simple departures from the current property tax regime would appear to yield substantial efficiency gains. Under this system, vacant land would not be taxed, and property owners would be allowed to deduct capital costs from property value before computing their tax liability.

References

Arnott, Richard. 2005. "Neutral Property Taxation." *Journal of Public Economic Theory* 7 (1): 27–50.

Arnott, Richard, and Frank Lewis. 1979. "The Transition of Land to Urban Use." *Journal of Political Economy* 87 (1): 161–9.

Arnott, Richard, and Petia Petrova. 2006. "The Property Tax as a Tax on Value: Deadweight Loss." *International Tax and Public Finance* 12: 241–66.

Bentick, Brian L. 1979. "The Impact of Taxation and Valuation Practices on Timing and Efficiency of Land Use." *Journal of Political Economy* 87 (4): 858–68.

Bird, Richard, and Enid Slack, eds. 2004. *International Handbook of Land and Property Taxation.* Cheltenham, U.K.: Edward Elgar.

Capozza, Dennis, and Yuming Li. 1994. "The Intensity and Timing of Investment: The Case of Land." *American Economic Review* 84 (4): 889–904.

Cohen, Jeffrey P., and Cletus C. Coughlin. 2005. "An Introduction to Two-Rate Taxation of Land and Buildings." *Federal Reserve Bank of St. Louis Review* 87 (3): 359–74.

Davis, Morris A., and Jonathan Heathcote. 2004. "The Price and Quantity of Residential Land in the United States." Working Paper 2004-37. Finance and Economics Discussion Series (FEDS). Washington: Board of Governors of the Federal Reserve System.

Dye, Richard F., and Daniel P. McMillen. 2006. "Teardowns and Land Values in the Chicago Metropolitan Area." *Journal of Urban Economics* (forthcoming).

Eagle, Steven J. 2001. "The Birth of Property Rights Movements." Policy Analysis 404. Washington: Cato Institute.

England, Richard W., and Min Qiang Zhao. 2005. "Assessing the Distributive Impact of a Revenue-Neutral Shift from a Uniform Property Tax to a Two-Rate Property Tax with a Uniform Credit." *National Tax Journal* 58: 247–60.

Federal Reserve Statistical Release. 2006. *Flow of Funds Accounts of the United States: Historical Data 1995–2005.* Washington.

George, Henry. 1879. *Progress and Poverty.* Republished, Preface to Centenary edition. New York: Robert Schalkenbach Foundation, 1979.

Hartzok, Alanna. 1997. "Pennsylvania's Success with Local Property Tax Reform: The Split Rate Tax." *American Journal of Economics and Sociology* 56 (2): 205–13.

Haughwout, A., and others. 2004. "Local Revenue Hills: Evidence from Four U.S. Cities." *Review of Economics and Statistics* 86 (2): 570–85.

Hughes, Mark Alan. 2005. "Why So Little Georgism in America? Using the Pennsylvania Cases to Understand the Slow, Uneven, Progress of Land Value Taxation." Unpublished paper. Cambridge, Mass.: Lincoln Institute of Land Policy.

International Association of Assessing Officers. 2000. *Property Tax Policies and Administrative Practices in Canada and the United States.* Chicago.

Marshall, Alfred. 1961. *Principles of Economics.* 9th ed. Appendix D. London: Macmillan.

McDonald, John. 1981. "Capital-Land Substitution in Urban Housing: A Survey of Empirical Estimates." *Journal of Urban Economics* 9: 190–221.

McMillen, Daniel P. 1996. "One Hundred Fifty Years of Land Values in Chicago: A Nonparametric Approach." *Journal of Urban Economics* 40 (1): 100–24.

Mills, David E. 1981. "The Non-Neutrality of Land Value Taxation." *National Tax Journal* (34): 125–9.

Minnesota Taxpayers Association. 2006. "Fifty-State Property Tax Comparison Study." Saint Paul, Minn.

Oates, William E., and Robert M. Schwab. 1997. "The Impact of Urban Land Taxation: The Pittsburgh Experience." *National Tax Journal* 50: 1–21.

Plassmann, Florenz, and T. Nicolaus Tideman. 2003. "A Framework for Assessing the Value of Downtown Land." Working Paper 0306. State University of New York at Binghamton.

Reeb, Donald J. 1998. "The Adoption and Repeal of Two-Rate Property Taxation in Amsterdam, New York." Working Paper 98DR1. Cambridge, Mass.: Lincoln Institute of Land Policy.

Shoup, Donald. 1970. "The Optimal Timing of Urban Land Development." *Papers of the Regional Science Association* 25: 33–34.

Skouras, Athanassios. 1978. "The Non-Neutrality of Land Taxation." *Public Finance* (30): 113–34.

Thorsnes, Paul. 1997. "Consistent Estimates of the Elasticity of Substitution between Land and Non-Land Inputs in the Production of Housing." *Journal of Urban Economics* 42 (1): 98–108.

Tideman, Nicolaus. 1982. "A Tax on Land Is Neutral." *National Tax Journal* 35: 109–11.

Turnbull, Geoffrey K. 1988. "The Effects of Local Taxes and Public Services on Residential Development Patterns." *Journal of Regional Science* 28 (4): 541–62.

Vickrey, William S. 1970. "Defining Land Value for Taxation Purposes." In *The Assessment of Land Value,* edited by Daniel M. Holland. University of Wisconsin Press.

Wheaton, William C. 1982. "Urban Spatial Development with Durable but Replaceable Capital." *Journal of Urban Economics* 12 (1): 53–67.

World Bank. 2006. *Where Is the Wealth of Nations? Measuring Capital for the 21st Century.* Washington.

Youngman, Joan M. 2005. "Taxing and Untaxing Land: Current Use Assessment of Farmland." *State Tax Notes* 37 (10): 727–37.

Youngman, Joan M., and Jane H. Malme. 1994. *An International Study of Taxes on Land and Buildings.* Deventer, the Netherlands: Kluwer Law and Tax Publishers.

EDWIN S. MILLS
Northwestern University

Sprawl and Jurisdictional Fragmentation

THE SUBJECT OF sprawl as it relates to jurisdictional fragmentation begs for analysis in the tradition of industrial organization. There are obvious advantages to the comparison between general purpose local governments in a metropolitan area and firms in an industry. At least some dangers are equally apparent.

Sprawl means excessive suburbanization. Excessive means more than can be utility enhancing.[1] Of course, how much suburbanization is utility enhancing depends on context. Suburbanization, nearly universal during the last fifty or sixty years, has been evident in the United States for more than a century. Among the best-studied causes of suburbanization are rising incomes and falling commuting costs. Beyond doubt, both of these factors have been important, but neither relates directly to local government actions. Suburbanization has been both inevitable and mostly utility enhancing, but it can also be excessive.

My measure of sprawl is conceptually simple. Zoning, as it applies to housing, lowers the density-distance function, increasing the radius of the urban area for a fixed population. Thus on average, workers must commute farther to and from work than if there were no controls. Residents may be willing to commute farther as the price of controlled lower density, but no worker is willing to commute farther with controls than he or she would need to commute by moving far enough out to obtain the same density without controls. If the average commuting distance increases more than would be needed to achieve the same density without controls, controls impair welfare.

The author is indebted to Dennis Epple and other participants in the Brookings-Wharton conference for comments on an earlier draft.
    1. A measure of sprawl in the context of urban location theory is in Mills (2005b).

My measure of sprawl, which is in the context of fixed and centralized locations of jobs, is dramatically contrary to fact. There are many studies of employment suburbanization, but none that I am aware of places employment and population suburbanization in a model that carefully analyzes their interaction. I would welcome a study of this topic. Employment and population suburbanization not only influence each other, but are also likely to be influenced by other similar variables. Transportation improvements seem to be obvious candidates, but jurisdictional fragmentation may be another.

Fragment of Institutional Background

In the U.S. context, a government is an organization directed by elected officials. At the federal and state levels, there is no ambiguity. At the local level, there are general and special purpose governments. Counties and municipalities are general purpose. Special purpose governments have more limited duties, and school districts are the prime example. There are many other examples, most of which are appointive (that is, agencies of local governments) in some states and elective in other states. The Chicago metropolitan area, which has more local governments than most large metropolitan areas, includes six or seven counties, several dozen municipalities, and hundreds of elective special districts (school districts, water districts, forest preserves, and so on). Chicago is reputed to have more local governments than any other U.S. metropolitan area. Why Chicago has so many local governments is the topic for another paper. Here I am concerned only with municipalities.

Local governments have no national constitutional status in the United States. They are incorporated by state governments and have powers that states assign them. Although the U.S. federal government has no formal authority over local governments, the national government influences local governments in many ways, by providing both money and regulations (especially in the areas of education, transportation, health care, and the environment.)

States tell municipalities what taxes they can levy and how they can spend their money. Although municipalities are constitutionally impotent, larger ones (especially central cities) are politically powerful. States grant municipalities almost exclusive power over land use allocation and regulation, partly pursuant to 1960s national legislation that urges land use controls to be in the context of a comprehensive plan for the development of the municipality. Clearly, this is not the case in Chicago. The most intrusive state action is the establishment of so-called *growth boundaries* around metropolitan areas, but they are almost entirely restricted to U.S. Pacific Coast states. Whatever their goals, municipal land use controls are constrained in various ways.

The most important federal control is the U.S. Constitution's Fifth Amendment, which requires compensation for taking for a public use. The Fifth Amendment was substantially weakened by a 2005 U.S. Supreme Court decision that gives local governments authority to take private land and sell it to private developers.[2] Physical seizure is an extreme form of taking. Property rights can be, and frequently are, almost destroyed by sufficiently strong local government restrictions on land use, but courts are extremely loath to enter that morass. Serious uncompensated partial seizures result from federal and state laws that are ostensibly intended to protect the environment and endangered species. Those laws are extremely blunt instruments, but are unlikely to cause serious harm in metropolitan areas.

An important issue here, as in industrial organization studies, is the definition of the industry. The logical issue in both cases is the magnitude of cross-elasticities of demand, although they are rarely estimated in practice. Presumably, a metropolitan complex is intended to include land where cross-elasticities of demand for land are relatively high. The national government has used close to ten terms to define an urban complex since the term *metropolitan place* was first used in 1940. If population densities declined monotonically from a well-defined urban center, the definitional problem would be relatively simple. Additional urban land is created and absorbed as an urban complex grows and suburbanizes. Physical impediments, transportation systems, and other factors cause metropolitan subareas to develop in places even though rural land exists closer to the city's center. The situation is exacerbated by laws that subsidize perpetual retention of land in farms even though they are well within metropolitan complexes. Despite these complications, new firms or municipalities are certainly added to the urban complex as time passes. The extent to which entry of new municipalities is free or restricted depends on state governments. In Illinois, residences that are not in an incorporated municipality are under county government. The state appears quite willing to create new incorporated municipalities when residents become plentiful enough that they lobby for incorporation. Thus entry of new municipalities appears to be relatively easy there. The current situation regarding creation of new municipalities is comparable to the nineteenth century, when each new industrial corporation required an act of the state legislature.

2. *Kelo* v. *New London,* 04-108 268 Conn. 1, 843 A. 2d 500, affirmed.

As in industrial organization studies, an issue is how municipalities are allowed (or forced) to relate to each other. An extreme case is when states order (or permit) the partial or complete merger of several local governments, occasionally forming a unified metropolitan government. Such entities are common in countries that have unitary national governments, but are rare in the United States or other federal systems. Here the predominant relationship among municipalities in a metropolitan complex is competition, sometimes fierce but usually muted.

A flurry of interest arose some years ago when a few municipalities were convicted under the Sherman Act of collusion (in deciding how emerging urban settlements would be allocated between two nearby municipalities). The issue became moot when courts ruled that state government could (I believe quite properly) exempt municipalities from federal antitrust statutes.

Within relatively mild federal and state restraints, municipalities impose myriad constraints on how land can be used in metropolitan areas. Typically, separate but similar constraints are imposed on businesses and housing. In the *Chicago Zoning Ordinance* (2004), it would be easy to count twenty or more different controls imposed on residences that directly limit densities. The ordinance's complexity makes the oracle of Apollo seem crystal clear. The constraints on suburbs are worse. The Chicago ordinance is preceded by fourteen indisputably desirable purposes. Nowhere in' this more than one-inch-thick volume (counting pages is nearly impossible because of multiple numbering) does the ordinance say how any provision relates to any purpose, or which purposes justify government controls.

Municipalities' Objective Functions

The notion that high land values are an important goal of municipalities, if not the sole goal, is an assumption in many publications, but mostly not a tested proposition. That statement applies to my analysis as well as to others' work.

Local governments, of course, provide many services. Prominent are education, criminal justice, transportation facilities, water supply, sanitation, and waste removal. Such services are provided because residents want them and, in most cases, want local governments to provide them. Most controversial are services that are mainly redistributional. Most such services are at least partly financed by federal and state governments. Uncompensated federal mandates are the most controversial of all.[3] Common sense and many studies indicate

---

3. See Inman (2005).

that efficient local government services not only serve residents' wishes but also contribute to high land values. Schools, followed by transportation, have been best studied.

In the city and suburbs of Chicago, which I believe to be typical in this respect, residential land use controls are intended to maintain or reduce residential population densities, or residential capital-land ratios, below competitive levels, at least in high-income neighborhoods. They also have the possibly incidental, but demonstrable, effects of raising dwelling prices far beyond levels elsewhere in the metropolitan area and decreasing the numbers of moderate income and minority residents who can live in the high income areas.[4]

Chicago is divided into seventy-seven contiguous community areas of about 50,000 residents each. The highest income and housing value community area is Lincoln Park, one of six community areas that stretch north along Lake Michigan, from River North to the Evanston, Illinois, border. Together with the Loop, Chicago's historic downtown center, they house most of the city's high-income residents. Total and minority populations have decreased substantially in these community areas since about the mid-1970s, when the Housing Acts of the mid-1960s acquired enough bite to make private discrimination a dangerous game. Downzoning has been rampant in these community areas for thirty to forty years. In similar areas south of the Loop that have large minority populations, downzoning has been almost nonexistent. Homeowners' associations have been powerful in the community areas north of the Loop and have lobbied city council members intensively. Things are worse in high-income suburbs along the north shore and west of the city, especially in Lake and Dupage counties. Stringent land use controls on population densities limit housing supply below competitive levels and contribute to high house values, especially in desirable neighborhoods. I believe it is a sound theory that land use controls are employed to support house values, especially in high-income and desirable areas of U.S. cities and suburbs.

Having been a proximate observer of Chicago city politics during the twelve years I lived in Lincoln Park, I claim that the following is typical. A developer proposes to build a high-rise condominium building on or near the lakefront, and the proposal is consistent with current zoning provisions. The local homeowners' association phones a few stalwarts and requests a meeting with the local city council member. At the meeting, the association indicates its strong opposition to the development. Arguments are undocumented,

4. See Mills (2005a).

ritualistic, and largely false or defective, but the city council member can count votes, and he or she uses council courtesy to pass a downzoning amendment to the zoning code. The developer withdraws the proposal and sells the property at a loss. Recently, developers have ceased even to make proposals in some areas. No new high-rise has been built on or near the lake between River North and Evanston for twenty years.

Competitive housing densities may not generate utility-maximizing outcomes for residents. Residents may value neighborhood densities that are lower than competitive values. That would justify local government density limits. My analysis in previous work indicates that Chicago density controls are much more stringent than can be utility enhancing.[5]

Fragmentation and Sprawl

Monopoly controls of metropolitan land uses are, of course, endemic in nondemocratic countries. Controls are likely in democratic countries that have unitary forms of national governments and the national government dictates detailed land uses. South Korea, until recent years, was a good example. No land could be converted from rural to urban uses without national government permission, and the national government specified in detail what land could be converted, when, and for what purposes. Northern European countries (Denmark, Finland, France, Germany, the Netherlands, Norway, and Sweden) appear to be similar. In all such examples, development in metropolitan areas has been compact and at high densities, apparently higher than unregulated competitive development would have produced. China under Mao Zedong had an additional extremely strong antiurban bias, namely that ration books were valid only in the community in which the holder was born. India also had a strong antiurban bias, but little was done to interfere with rural-to-urban migration except, in some places, to have housing quality controls that made criminals of poor residents. Japan limited densities in Tokyo (via building heights) to protect views of the Royal Palace and to minimize potential earthquake damage.

The United Kingdom is anomalous. It has a strong unitary government, but London has been permitted to develop at extremely low densities and the metropolitan area spreads over much of southern England, creating a city that is more spread out than Los Angeles.

If unitary governments impose monopoly controls on metropolitan land use densities that restrict development to greater than competitive densities, then

---

5. Mills (2005b, 2005c).

such controls are welfare decreasing if residents prefer densities that are no greater than competitive densities.

Monopolies make money by restricting supply, so Northern European dictates of high-density metropolitan areas should be no surprise. My belief is that popular U.S. enthusiasm for low densities mostly reflects preferences for high-quality schools, safe streets, and so on. Those characteristics are hardly correlated with stringent density controls and the causation runs from high-income to desirable neighborhood characteristics. In the United States, high incomes are strongly correlated with strict density controls, but the correlation does not represent direct causation.

Another important issue is that residents of low-density neighborhoods, especially in suburbs, often claim that they prefer their low-density environments to crowded or congested inner cities. But density controls demonstrably increase commuting distances by segregating work and residential locations. Probably at least as important, density controls imply suburban densities that are too low to enable the assembly of enough commuters to support fixed-rail transit systems. Thus 80 to 90 percent of workers commute by car, even in large U.S. metropolitan areas. Fixed-rail systems are probably not optimum in any but the largest U.S. metropolitan areas. Benefit-cost studies cast doubt on the optimality of all post-World War II fixed-rail systems (for example, those found in Atlanta, Baltimore, Los Angeles, San Francisco, and Washington). On the other hand, metropolitan road travel is underpriced by about a factor of two in U.S. metropolitan areas. Before the run-up in fuel prices in mid-2005, gasoline should have been taxed to produce a price of about $4 a gallon instead of $2 a gallon. This calculation is simply to reimburse governments for the opportunity costs of metropolitan roads, not to price congestion. Congestion would largely disappear in a few years if gasoline were appropriately priced, as people would move closer to work (largely by swapping dwellings), eliminate frivolous trips, and take other steps to reduce car usage.[6]

---

6. Transportation economists such as Small advocate metering and charging for road use by location and time of day (see Parry and Small, 2005). Metering is more subtle and obviously superior to a fuel tax except for transaction costs. A fuel tax is as cheap as any tax to collect and cannot be evaded. Transactions costs of metering systems include the costs of needed electronic systems in roads and vehicles, and the cost of diversions, multioccupancy of cars, and the costs of decisionmaking imposed on drivers, some of which may need to be made in real time. In Chicago, congestion could be eliminated by a fuel tax if it motivated small reductions in superfluous driving and about 15 percent of commuters to swap dwellings to be closer to work. The likelihood of substantial house swapping is suggested by similar rush hour travel in both directions on both radial and circumferential highways. Almost no new housing or employment relocation would be required.

Thus my guess is that unitary northern European governments make urban life tolerable by restricting metropolitan areas to excessively small sizes through limitations on land use conversion from rural to urban uses and by compelling high-density development in the metropolitan areas. High gasoline prices force commuters to rely heavily on public transit (trolleys, buses, some subways). Probably, the biggest cost is the limitation thus imposed on scale and agglomeration economies.[7]

Things are somewhat different in the United States. The three West Coast states—Washington, Oregon, and California—are similar to northern European countries in that they restrict metropolitan sizes by urban growth boundaries as well as by imposing a panoply of land use regulations within their metropolitan areas.[8] The predictable result is the highest housing prices in the United States, probably close to Northern European levels. As in Northern Europe, development boundaries are imposed by state governments in the United States that can dictate to municipal governments.[9]

In other U.S. states, conditions appear more nearly to approximate those that would be expected in a federal system. Entry of new municipalities in a metropolitan area is relatively easy and municipalities appear to compete for (especially high-income) residents.

Of course, municipalities have myriad land use controls on residential (and commercial) development within their borders. Certainly in Chicago (and elsewhere), local governments employ controls to restrict densities in high-income neighborhoods below competitive levels much more than in low- and moderate-income neighborhoods.[10] The easy explanation is that such controls cater to residents' wishes for low-density neighborhoods.[11] However, it seems unlikely that the desire for less than competitive residential densities is peculiar to high-income residents. More important, every study I have seen concludes that density restrictions are much greater, and housing prices are much higher, than could be justified by residents' desires for low densities.[12] In earlier work, I estimate that Chicago density controls cause about three miles (out of a radius of about twenty-five miles) of greater land use than can possibly be

---

7. See Inman (2005).
8. See Quigley and Rosenthal (2005); Glaeser, Gyourko, and Saks (2005b).
9. This conclusion is conjectural, but based on data and analysis in Mills (1998).
10. For other examples, see Glaeser, Gyourko, and Saks (2005a, 2005b).
11. See Brueckner (1995).
12. In recent years, statewide controls have spread to Florida, Maryland, and, apparently, New Jersey. Press reports suggest predictable housing price escalation, but careful studies appear not yet to have been carried out. See Mills (2005c); references in Mills (2005b).

justified by residents' desires for low-density neighborhoods, a waste of 3 percent of worker earnings and 400 square miles of land.[13]

Density controls result in excessive house price inflation. The benefit goes to landlords in rental units and to residents of owner-occupied units. I have argued previously, as have other economists, that the benefits of abnormal house prices inflation are mostly illusory, but I doubt that one in a thousand upper-middle-class owner-occupiers understands the doubtful nature of such benefits.[14]

If excessive density controls cause welfare-reducing sprawl, as I have argued, and the benefits of resulting capital gains are mostly illusory, why do local governments control densities so ruthlessly? State and local governments are democracies in this country and appear to respond to strongly felt wishes of the electorate.

Density controls have one other benefit that is certainly peculiar to upper-middle-class residents—they segregate the lower- and middle-class residents, especially minorities.[15] In Chicago, density controls have become increasingly stringent in upper-middle-class lakefront neighborhoods starting about the early 1970s. I believe it is more than coincidental that the growing stringency coincides with the time when the open housing acts of the mid-1960s acquired enough bite to place private racial discrimination in danger of both civil and criminal prosecution.

Thus my conclusion is that the purpose of stringent residential density controls in Chicago and similar metropolitan areas is mainly to segregate moderate income (and especially minority) residents from dwellings in upper-middle-class neighborhoods. The result is excessive housing costs, commuting costs, and sprawl. Low- and moderate-income as well as minority populations are highly correlated. The fact that some predominantly black suburbs, such as Prince George's County, Maryland, near Washington, also have strict density controls suggests that income segregation is an important part of the discrimination syndrome. As I suggested above, the motive to maximize land values pervades local government actions.

---

13. Mills (2005c).

14. Mills (2005c). High housing prices increase the opportunity costs of ownership about proportionately, and increase the cost of a dwelling to which one moves, eating up the capital gain on the dwelling from which one moves. One can sell one's million-dollar house in Southern California and move to Phoenix, where houses are cheaper, but it would be equally profitable to do that if house prices were lower, unless California prices increased relative to those in Phoenix, which is doubtful.

15. I have documented this effect on Chicago's north lakefront in Mills (2005a).

Dennis Epple, in a series of pathbreaking papers, has shown that in a set of independent municipalities with linear tax-subsidy functions whose two parameters are determined by median voters (but no land use controls), competitive equilibrium locations of mobile residents almost completely segregate residents by income, other relevant characteristics, or both.[16] Contrary to assertions of many authors, low-income residents are not tempted to reside in inexpensive housing in high-income municipalities in order to obtain the same services as high-income residents while paying low taxes on their modest dwellings.[17]

In a new emphasis on local public goods, a recent study presents a model in which zoning is needed to provide stratification by income of residents among communities in order to provide Tiebout matching of supply and demand for public goods.[18] Most assumptions in the new model are similar to those in Epple and Platt's (1998) model, to which the new paper does not refer. In the new model, as in the earlier one, local government services are financed by a proportionate housing tax. However, in the new model, local government services are a pure public good of which all residents of a given community receive the same amount. This egalitarian assumption about the distribution of local public services provides an incentive for freeloading in which low-income residents locate in high-income communities to receive their preferred local public good quantity. Zoning is needed to prevent this outcome. In the zoning model, it is estimated that the poorest 77 percent of households are worse off than if zoning were prohibited in the same model, but the upper 23 percent are better off. It appears that neither the solution in the 1998 model nor the 2004 model can be shown to be Pareto efficient.

The classical urban model is dramatically contrary to fact. In contemporary metropolitan areas, most jobs are located in suburbs, rather than in the central city. In Chicago, about two-thirds of the total jobs are dispersed throughout the city's entire metropolitan area. Some of these jobs have been driven to suburbs by excessive land use controls on commercial properties and by suburbanization of their employees and customers. Job suburbanization would upset the income segregation pattern in the classical model as well as both models described above if job suburbanization were predominantly of relatively low-income workers. But according to much data and a large spatial mismatch literature, job suburbanization has been biased toward highly paid jobs.

16. See Epple and Platt (1998).
17. See Quigley and Rosenthal (2005, p. 77).
18. Calabrese, Epple, and Romano (2007).

The application of land use controls to promote segregation within a jurisdiction such as Chicago (discussed above) is easier to understand within the Epple framework. Legally, whatever its shape, the same local tax subsidy is faced by all residents of the city. In practice, whether cause or effect, local government services are certainly of higher quality in Lincoln Park than in low-income neighborhoods in Chicago.[19]

Although of questionable legality, the provision of higher quality local government services and the segregation of low-income and minority residents by controls that restrict housing supply and escalate dwelling prices, discussed above, are plausible suspects as to the motivation for stringent land use controls in high income neighborhoods within a large jurisdiction.[20]

What is the dynamic of collecting a substantial group of high-income residents in a neighborhood? In Chicago the answer is easy. The north lakefront is the highest amenity part of the city, and was predominantly a high-income area well before land use controls were of much importance. The south lakefront is a similarly high-amenity area, but Richard J. Daley, mayor of Chicago from 1955 to 1976, put large amounts of low-income public housing there. I am not sure about the dynamics in other cities. Brooklyn Heights is certainly a high-amenity area of Brooklyn, New York, as are waterfront neighborhoods in some other areas of that city. Knob Hill qualifies in San Francisco, as do Pacific Palisades and Beverly Hills in Los Angeles, and Beacon Hill in Boston. In some cases, parks, such as Fairmont in Philadelphia, qualify.

It is certainly possible that similar motivations wholly or partly account for excessive density controls in suburbs. First, my suburban friends have never heard of Dennis Epple or his analysis. The results in both models were a surprise to me and must be to other scholars who have read and contemplated the papers. As with many fine papers, they are counterintuitive. Second, suburbanites may feel, possibly correctly, that density controls produce capital gains on their dwellings in any case, and reinforce a nice effect in protecting them from proximity to low-income and minority residents. Third, they know that they prefer low-density neighborhoods and have little appreciation for the analysis that suggests sprawl effects and social waste.

---

19. Three times during my twelve-year Lincoln Park residence, burglar or smoke alarms were set off in my house by accident. On all three occasions, police or fire personnel were at the door within three minutes. It was tempting to acquire a larger sample of response times by intentionally setting off the alarms, but local rumor was that service providers quickly tired of excessive calls. In addition, the city had a set of progressive fines for false alarms. And, of course, I was too conscientious to permit my experiment to be financed by taxpayers. Newspaper reports suggest that twenty- to thirty-minute response times to 911 calls are typical in Chicago.

20. Calabrese, Epple, and Romano (2007).

Conclusion

My conclusions from this discursive paper are as follows. European and East Asian countries appear to have not only excessive density controls but also excessively strong restrictions on conversion of land from rural to urban uses. One reason is politically powerful farm groups (especially in France and Japan) that resist market operation related to rural land. Another reason is probably a misguided (in my view) preference for a system of large numbers of small urban areas instead of a system that permits a few more large urban areas. In the United States local governments have strong powers to control land uses, and there is relatively free entry of new local governments at metropolitan fringes. The result is sprawl caused by excessive density controls, especially to keep low-income and minority residents out of upper-middle-income communities.

I do not know whether the European or U.S. system produces greater land use and value distortions. However, if anyone would listen, I would advocate moves toward a free market land allocation system in every country in which I have had experience.

There are by now at least a baker's dozen of careful U.S. studies of effects of zoning on house prices. All that I have seen conclude that the effects are to raise house prices, increase suburbanization beyond optimum levels, or both.[21] All careful studies conclude that the deleterious results are substantial. Why?

In a perfect Tiebout/Epple world the result cannot happen in the absence of zoning. Tiebout (1956) pioneered the modern analysis of local government expenditures. His paper has led to a vast literature, most recently Epple and Platt (1998). The basic tenet of the literature is that, under appropriate assumptions, residents segregate themselves among local government jurisdictions so that local government goods and services approximate the way that private markets would allocate the goods and services. With free entry of metropolitan areas or with competition among a substantial set of jurisdictions, any jurisdiction that introduced controls resulting in house prices above competitive equilibrium would lose population to competing jurisdictions. Many scholars (and residents) believe that residents' preferences justify densities below competitive levels. My analysis in earlier papers indicates that zoning dictates densities substantially below those that could enhance utilities for residents with preferences for densities below competitive levels.[22]

21. See Mills (2005b, 2005c) and references therein.
22. Mills (2005b, 2005c).

The only hypothesis that I can credit is that one purpose of low-density zoning is to use democratic local governments to keep down the number of low- and middle-income residents, especially minorities, in competitive jurisdictions. My belief is that residents have turned over to local governments the job of class and race discrimination as private discrimination has become legally dangerous because of national legislation. Nevertheless, intuition suggests that relatively easy entry of new municipalities in a metropolitan area must provide some limitation of excessive density controls.

Comments

Dennis Epple: This is an ambitious and exceedingly valuable paper, which makes several significant contributions. Mills provides readers with an overview of density controls in the United States and several other countries. This overview highlights the roles of local and federal governments in land use regulations. He offers a critical assessment of the effects of growth controls in various U.S. regions, and he discusses the objectives that motivate adoption of growth and density controls. Mills also comments on the current state of growth and density control research, and suggests issues for future study. Mills makes several important observations and raises key questions about research linking sprawl and fragmentation. In sum, he says there is a need for:

—models that capture employment and population suburbanization and their interaction;

—better understanding of factors governing entry (or lack of entry) of new municipalities;

—better understanding of how municipalities interact with each other (that is, extent and forms of competition among municipalities).

Mills also indicates the need for further research to answer questions such as what is the relative importance of various potential motives in determining popularity of density controls. Is the answer property-value maximization; improving education quality, safety, other local services; low congestion; or keeping out low-income and minority households? Another question he raises is why are land use controls so popular if housing prices are sufficient to induce population stratification. In his paper, Mills discusses the downzoning in a wealthy Chicago area resulting from residents' objections to buildings that would increase density. In reading this discussion, it occurred to me that data that my colleagues and I have assembled might provide some further evidence to supplement Mills's presentation.[1] In particular, I investigated lot size

---

1. Allegheny County maintains a website with data for the universe of taxable properties in the county. See Epple, Gordon, and Sieg (2006).

Figure 1. 25th, 50th, and 75th Percentiles of Lot Size

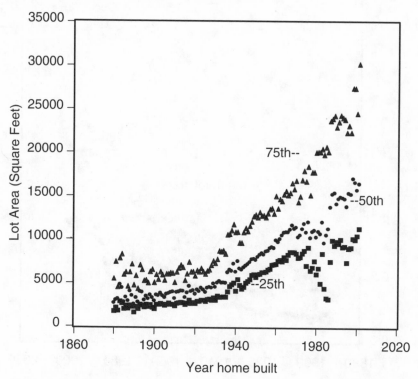

heterogeneity and trends in lot sizes among municipalities in the Pittsburgh, Pennsylvania, metropolitan area. A brief summary of this evidence follows.

The data presented here are for approximately 370,000 residential properties in Allegheny County, Pennsylvania, which includes Pittsburgh and the surrounding area. The county, which has a population of approximately 1.3 million, includes 130 municipalities (four cities, forty-two townships, and eighty-four boroughs). A virtue of this data set is that properties are included, whether rental or owner-occupied. Figure 1 shows percentiles of lot size for houses constructed over the past 120 years in the county, and figure 2 shows that lot sizes throughout this period are skewed, with the mean being well above the median for the entire period. Figure 3 shows predicted lot sizes from a regression of ln (lot size) on a fourth-order polynomial in age, a second-order polynomial in travel time, and an interaction of travel time and age.[2] It is evident

---

2. All terms in this regression are highly significant. Graphs of fitted values from other polynomial specifications yielded graphs qualitatively similar to that in figure 3.

Figure 2. Mean and Median Lot Sizes

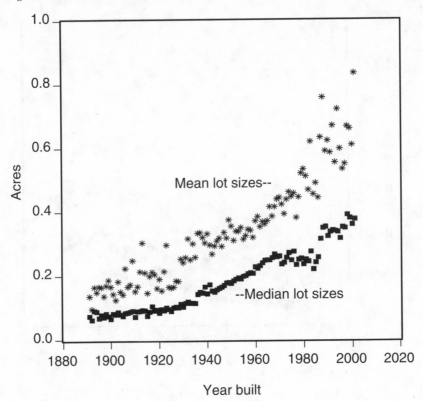

from this figure that lot sizes increase with distance (travel time), and lot sizes have trended up over time at each distance.

It is also interesting to investigate the extent to which lot sizes vary within and across municipalities. Table 1 provides decompositions of variance. Consider, for illustration, the two results shown in bold in the table's top panel. When houses of all ages are considered, and properties within the city of Pittsburgh are included, the variance of the logarithm of lot areas within municipalities equals the variance across municipalities. The variance within municipalities is 63 percent when only houses built since 1995 are considered. When observations for the city of Pittsburgh are excluded, the corresponding within-municipality percentages of variance are higher. When the decompositions are done without using logarithms, the within-municipality percentages are

Figure 3. Predicted Lot Size for Travel Times to Downtown of 10, 20, and 30 Minutes

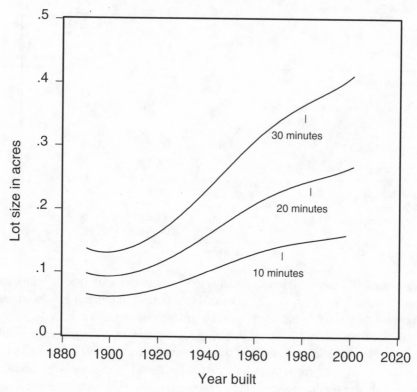

greater still. The table's second panel presents the corresponding decompositions for house values. Comparison across both panels reveals that the within-municipality percentage of variance is higher for lot sizes than for house values.

In summary, the figures tell us that lot sizes have trended upward over time, are highly skewed, and tend to be higher at greater distances from the central business district. The results in the table are, perhaps, somewhat surprising. If communities zone to enforce a minimum lot size, then one would expect bunching of lot sizes within a community at that minimum size. This in turn leads to the expectation that the decomposition of variance of lot sizes would reveal that most of the variance in lot sizes is across communities rather than within communities. This conjecture is not

Table 1. Decomposition of Lot Size and House Value Variance, Allegheny County
Percent unless otherwise noted

| | | All houses | | Houses built 1995–2001 | |
		Without Pittsburgh	*With Pittsburgh*	*Without Pittsburgh*	*With Pittsburgh*
Lot size variance					
Within	Ln(lot area)	55	**50**	74	**63**
municipalities	Lot area	92	91	86	85
Across	Ln(lot area)	45	50	26	37
municipalities	Lot area	8	9	14	15
No. of houses		265,509	357,496	5,956	6,363
House value variance					
Within	Ln(value)	38	50	47	49
municipalities	Value	50	59	52	54
Across	Ln(value)	62	50	53	51
municipalities	value	50	41	48	46
No. of houses		265,509	357,496	5,882	6,362

Source: Epple, Gordon, and Sieg (2006) and author's calculations.

supported.[3] Of course, it is still possible that minimum lot size zoning plays an important role in determining land use. For example, minimum lot sizes may increase over time within municipalities, giving rise to the within-community variance observed in the data. Pursuing this further in this comment would take me too far afield. However, I think there may be a payoff to more extensive study of the evidence on lot size for Pittsburgh and other metropolitan areas. Also, in his discussion of the Chicago example, Mills emphasizes restrictions limiting construction of multifamily buildings. While the descriptive summary provided above does not address multiunit housing, Mills's emphasis on this type of density control strikes me as being well placed, suggesting investigation of data with respect to location of multiunit dwellings.

In his paper, Mills is kind enough to make reference to my work with Glenn Platt developing a model in which households stratify by preferences

---

3. This finding of heterogeneity in lot sizes and house values within communities is very much in accord with the findings of the comprehensive study by Pack and Pack (1977) of heterogeneity within Pennsylvania communities with respect to income and other socioeconomic characteristics. Ioannides and Hardman (2004) also show that there is substantial income heterogeneity within even small neighborhoods in U.S. metropolitan areas. Nechyba (1997) and Epple and Platt (1998) develop multicommunity models with equilibrium characterized by intracommunity heterogeneity in incomes and housing consumption. Epple and Sieg (1999), Bayer, McMillan, and Rueben (2004), and Ferreyra (forthcoming) implement strategies for estimating equilibrium models with intracommunity heterogeneity.

and income across jurisdictions.[4] The stratification predictions follow from single-crossing conditions on household utility functions.[5] In his paper, Mills asks, quite naturally, why density controls are so popular if stratification is induced by differentials in housing prices. I offer some thoughts on this issue.

For expositional convenience, I use the term *zoning* as a generic term to capture the panoply of density and building controls used by communities. I believe the answer to Mills's question is as follows. First, I believe that housing price differentials indeed are sufficient to induce stratification. In inducing stratification, housing prices play two roles with respect to households. One role is the familiar one that price plays in influencing the demand for any commodity. The other role is rationing access to communities. This second role for housing distorts housing prices, creating potentially large inefficiencies in housing allocation. Were they permitted to do so, I believe communities would rely primarily on head taxes rather than property taxes to finance provision of public goods. Head taxes would then play the primary role in rationing access to communities, permitting housing prices to perform their usual role in demand. Absent the ability to impose head taxes, communities may then opt to try to use zoning ordinances to accomplish some of the same objectives.

In Calabrese, Epple, and Romano (2007), my colleagues and I study a multi-community setting in which households vote on zoning as well as community tax and expenditure policy.[6] Households are owner-occupants and anticipate potential capital gains or losses when voting.[7] We find that if zoning is permitted, communities opt for relatively stringent zoning requirements. In a parallel computational analysis, we find that relative to the equilibrium without zoning, zoning reduces housing price distortions, leading to an increase in allocative efficiency. However, the distributional effects are very much in accord with the perspective that Mills offers. The benefits flow largely to higher-income households; poor households are made worse off.

An important feature of our analysis to date is that all residents are subjected to the zoning ordinance. There is no scope for initial residents to impose a

---

4. Epple and Platt (1998).

5. Epple and Sieg (1999) present evidence that the single-crossing conditions are satisfied.

6. We build on Hamilton (1975), the work in Mills and Oates (1975), Mills (1979), and Fernandez and Rogerson (1997).

7. Mills refers to this paper as reflecting a change of view on my part relative to my earlier work. I see the paper as adding a further dimension to the analysis of multicommunity equilibrium rather than a change of view.

stringent zoning requirement on future residents while exempting themselves. Of course, as Mills emphasizes, community residents often do attempt to restrict the use of undeveloped land in ways that they would not choose to restrict the use of their own property. An important task for future work is to develop a dynamic framework that permits analysis of the evolution of zoning over time. Such a framework would permit an investigation of the potential inefficiencies that may arise if residents have broad latitude to set terms for future arrivals that they do not impose on themselves.

In closing, I would like simply to reiterate that Mills has provided an informative and valuable perspective on density controls. I enjoyed reading the paper and recommend it highly.

Jacob L. Vigdor: Mills's paper provides a wealth of insightful observations, based not only on the author's thorough knowledge of the existing literature on the subjects, but on his firsthand experience as a long-time resident of the Chicago area. In the end, however, the paper comes to exactly the wrong conclusion—that competition among governments is the key to eliminating excessive density controls, and hence the key to reducing sprawl. Mills presents a dense thicket of interconnected arguments, and my efforts to distill them will invariably entail some oversimplification. With this caveat stated, the central thesis of Mills's article comprises three points: (1) sprawl is a bad thing, by definition; (2) sprawl is caused, at least in part, by the use of inefficient zoning restrictions that force density below the level that the free market would provide. These zoning restrictions are popular because they lead to price appreciation (on which homeowners may place too much value) and because they allow affluent residents to exclude poorer households from their neighborhood; (3) in areas where local governments have the power to set zoning policy (that is, outside Europe), competition among jurisdictions will limit this type of zoning.

The first idea, by construction, is beyond dispute. The second has intuitive appeal, but upon closer inspection, there is at least as much evidence against it as in favor of it. If zoning causes sprawl, then Houston should be a compact city. The importance of zoning as a cause of sprawl pales in comparison to the central factors: population growth and changes in transportation technology. The third is also appealing, as it makes reference to the first fundamental welfare theorem of economics: that competition, in the absence of market failures, roots out inefficiency. Once again, however, further analysis reveals this to be an imperfect application for that theorem.

Sprawl Is a Bad Thing

The de-densification of modern cities has been driven primarily by changes in technology, most clearly the substitution of the private automobile for fundamentally slower modes of transportation. Where there is inefficiency in this reaction to technological change, it results primarily from the existence of negative externalities: traffic congestion, pollution, and the valuation of undeveloped land by individuals who do not themselves own it. As Mills alludes to in the article, there are clear policy interventions that address these externalities directly. Congestion can be alleviated by the use of peak-pricing on roadways. Pollution can be addressed by implementing Pigovian taxes on fuel, which internalize the externality by forcing consumers to bear the costs that they would otherwise indirectly impose on others. The public good aspects of undeveloped land are being realized by a growing number of citizens in a number of metropolitan areas who have authorized their local governments to purchase land for preservation, or have formed private coalitions to achieve the same goal.

If the externalities generated by sprawl cannot be internalized using these policies, a reasonable alternative would be to directly impose restrictions on the density of development—requiring development at or above a certain density, or forbidding development from occurring in certain areas. As Mills notes, policies of this nature are common in continental Europe and certain parts of the United States. If mandating higher density reduces sprawl, then mandating lower density—the effect of zoning regulations derided in Mills's paper—must increase sprawl, right?

Zoning Regulations Increase Sprawl

At first glance, it seems obvious that forcing lower-density development in certain parts of a metropolitan area must lead to greater development on the urban fringe. The strength of this cause-effect association is greatly challenged, however, by the existence of Houston, Texas, a city with no zoning laws whatsoever. The incorporated city is among the nation's geographically largest, at nearly 600 square miles. Suburban development stretches the metropolitan area's footprint well beyond this boundary. Harris County, Texas, the county overlaying Houston, has roughly one-third the population density of Cook County, Illinois, which overlays Chicago. Clearly, Houston's relative sprawl is explained by the fact that it developed in the era of the personal automobile. The importance of zoning relative to changes in transportation technology must be slight.

Beyond this simple counterexample, there are other points of contention with Mills's core argument. It is true that the neighborhoods along the lake-front north of downtown Chicago have seen little development in recent years. It is hard to imagine, though, that any of the scuttled high-rise buildings would have targeted a poor clientele. It therefore is difficult to believe that residents' opposition to these towers was motivated by a desire to exclude low-income residents from the neighborhood. Even in cases where zoning serves to exclude the poor from certain neighborhoods, the elimination of such zoning might actually increase sprawl. Mills links the advent of exclusionary zoning to the threat of neighborhood integration that followed the passage of fair housing laws in the 1960s. Had it not been for zoning regulations, rich urban residents may have responded to this threat of integration in the more traditional way— by fleeing to the suburbs. The zoning laws Mills decries in Chicago may have prevented the city from becoming like Detroit, a hollow core of intense poverty surrounded by more affluent suburbs.

Mills dismisses the other traditionally advanced rationale for zoning to reduce density, the desire to encourage price appreciation by preserving the scarcity of units in their desirable location. He argues that such a desire is folly, as the increase in residents' wealth is exactly offset by an increase in the purchase price of any replacement units. This argument presumes that rates of price appreciation are equal in all places at all times. The folly of this pre-sumption is demonstrated by many of my own neighbors, who have decamped from locations in the northeastern and western United States to the North Carolina piedmont, where the price elasticity of housing supply, for the fore-seeable future at least, is much greater than in the areas from which they came.

Free Entry Is the Cure for Inefficient Zoning

Most of Mills's paper describes the link between zoning and sprawl. The role of jurisdictional fragmentation in the argument is most clearly seen in the paper's very last sentence. There is a clear economic logic followed here: zoning restrictions inefficiently reduce density; free entry and market com-petition root out productive inefficiency. Hence competition among zoning authorities, measured by jurisdictional fragmentation, must increase density and therefore reduce sprawl.

Although intuitively appealing, the market metaphor fails in this instance for two reasons. First, the inefficiency created by zoning is an externality—the costs, in the form of additional sprawl, fall largely if not entirely upon individuals who cannot be directly compensated for their inconvenience. In the presence of externalities, markets alone cannot be relied upon to root out inefficiency. Zoning authorities are not behaving inefficiently because they are not giving people what they want. Quite the contrary, they are doing so, and imposing costs on nonresidents in the process. Second, the parties engaging in this inefficient activity—local governments—do not face the same competitive pressures as would a private sector firm.[1] Local governments that make inefficient decisions are not competed out of existence—they continue to exist.

The more convincing argument in this case points to the opposite conclusion. Sprawl is inefficient because of externalities. Fragmented planning authorities have very weak incentives to internalize these externalities. Why should planners in Aurora, Illinois, care if development in their jurisdiction creates congestion problems for residents of nearby Naperville, Illinois? A consolidated planning authority serving both jurisdictions has a much greater incentive to internalize these externalities.

Figure 4 presents basic evidence pointing toward the conclusion that governmental consolidation, rather than fragmentation, promotes density. Using data for 208 metropolitan areas, it plots a measure of density against a measure of governmental fragmentation. The density measure is equal to the weighted average of density in each census tract in the area with weights equal to tract population. It represents the degree of neighborhood density experienced by the average resident, more accurately describing density in areas such as the West Coast, where metropolitan areas often combine compact settlements with vast uninhabited areas. The fragmentation measure is equal to the number of municipal and township governments per 100,000 residents, using data from the 1962 Census of Governments. Lagged government data address the concern that sprawl may have led to the creation of additional governments.

The scatter plot in figure 4 shows a clear negative relationship: metropolitan areas divided into small governments serving relatively small numbers of people are less dense, not more. This simple analysis certainly should not be construed as proving any sort of causal relationship between the variables, but this finding clearly lends more support to the hypothesis that fragmentation creates, rather than ameliorates, sprawl.

---

1. Epple and Zelenitz (1981).

Figure 4. Number of Municipalities per 100,000 Residents and Density, 1962

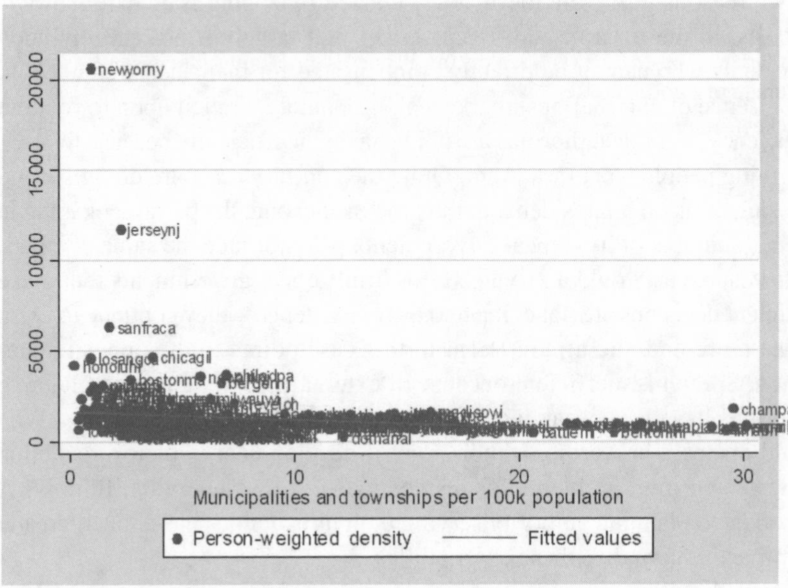

Source: U.S. Department of Commerce, Bureau of the Census (1962).

Conclusion

There are many reasons to dislike the practice of zoning to limit density. It exacerbates housing affordability problems. It raises serious concerns of equity, as the poor are excluded from areas offering superior local public goods and amenities. But those who worry about the impact of sprawl on the health and well-being of the American population should not point to zoning as the culprit. Sprawl is problematic because it creates externalities in the form of traffic congestion, pollution, and the elimination of valued open space. The coordination of local government planning authority, not fragmentation, is the best weapon against these externalities.

References

Bayer, P., McMillan, R., and Rueben, K. 2004. "An Equilibrium Model of Sorting in an Urban Housing Market." Working Paper 10865. Cambridge, Mass.: National Bureau of Economic Research.

Brueckner, Jan K. 1995. "Strategic Control of Growth in a System of Cities." *Journal of Public Economics* 57 (3): 393–416.

———. 2005. "Urban Sprawl: Diagnosis and Remedies." *International Regional Science Review* 23 (2): 160–71.

Calabrese, Stephen, Dennis Epple, and Richard Romano. 2007 (forthcoming). "On the Political Economy of Zoning," *Journal of Public Economics.*

City of Chicago. 2004. Chicago Zoning Ordinance. Index Publishing Corp.

Epple, Dennis, Brett Gordon, and Holger Sieg. 2006. "A Flexible Approach to Estimating Production Functions When Output Prices Are Unobserved." Working Paper. Carnegie Mellon University (March).

Epple, Dennis, and Glenn J. Platt. 1998. "Equilibrium and Local Distribution in an Urban Economy When Households Differ in Both Preferences and Incomes." *Journal of Urban Economics* 43 (1): 23–51.

Epple, Dennis, and Holger Sieg. 1999. "Estimating Equilibrium Models of Local Jurisdictions." *Journal of Political Economy* 107 (4): 645–81.

Epple, Dennis, and Allan Zelenitz. 1981. "The Implications of Competition among Jurisdictions: Does Tiebout Need Politics?" *Journal of Political Economy* 89: 1197–217.

Fernandez, Raquel, and Richard Rogerson. 1997. "Keeping People Out: Income Distribution, Zoning, and the Quality of Public Education." *International Economic Review* 38 (1): 23–42.

Ferreyra, Maria Marta. Forthcoming. "Estimating the Effects of Private School Vouchers in Multidistrict Economies." *American Economic Review.*

Glaeser, Edward L., Joseph Gyourko, and Raven E. Saks. 2005a. "Urban Growth and Housing Supply." Working Paper 11097. Cambridge, Mass.: National Bureau of Economic Research (January).

———. 2005b. "Why Have Housing Prices Gone Up?" Working Paper 11129. Cambridge, Mass.: National Bureau of Economic Research (February).

Hamilton, Bruce. 1975. "Zoning and Property Taxation in a System of Local Governments." *Urban Studies* 12: 205–11.

Hardman, A., and Ioannides, Y. 2004. "Neighbors' Income Distribution: Economic Segregation and Mixing in U.S. Urban Neighborhoods." *Journal of Housing Economics* 13: 368–82.

Inman, Robert P. 2005. "Financing Cities." Working Paper 11203. Cambridge, Mass.: National Bureau of Economic Research (March).

Mills, Edwin S. 1979. "Economic Analysis of Urban Land Use Controls." In *Current Issues in Urban Economics,* edited by Peter Mieszkowski and Mahlon Straszheim, pp. 511–41. Johns Hopkins University Press.

————. 1998. "Excess Commuting in U.S. Metropolitan Areas." In *Network Infrastructure and the Urban Environment,* edited by Lars Lundquist, Lars-Gwan Mattsson, and Tschangho John Kim, pp. 72–83. Berlin: Springer-Verlag.

————. 2005a. "Report on Effects of Chicago Land Use Controls." Mimeo.

————. 2005b. "Why Do We Have Urban Density Controls?" *Real Estate Economics* 3 (3): 571–85.

————. 2005c. "Urban Invasion of the Countryside." Draft prepared for symposium on Frontiers in Resource and Rural Economics.

Mills, Edwin S., and Wallace E. Oates, eds. 1975. *Fiscal Zoning and Land Use Controls: The Economic Issue.* Heath-Lexington Books.

Nechyba, Thomas J. 1997. "Existence of Equilibrium and Stratification in Local and Hierarchical Tiebout Economies with Property Taxes and Voting." *Economic Theory* 10 (2): 277–304.

Pack, Howard, and Janet Rothenberg Pack. 1977. "Metropolitan Fragmentation and Suburban Heterogeneity." *Urban Studies* (14): 191–201.

Parry, Ian W. H., and Kenneth A. Small. 2005. "Does Britain or the United States Have the Right Gasoline Tax?" *American Economic Review* 95 (4): 1276–89.

Quigley, John M., and Larry A. Rosenthal. 2005. "The Effects of Land Use Regulation on the Price of Housing: What Do We Know? What Can We Learn?" *CityScape* 8 (1): 69–110.

Tiebout, Charles M. 1956. "A Pure Theory of Local Public Expenditures." *Journal of Political Economy* 64 (5): 416–24.

U.S. Department of Commerce, Bureau of the Census. 1962. *Census of Governments.* Government Printing Office.